Liberated Texts

Liberated Texts
Collected Reviews: Volume One


Edited by Louis Allday and Mahmoud Najib


Ebb

Ebb Books
Unit 241
266 Banbury Road
Oxford, OX2 7DL

© 2022 Ebb Books

All articles are licensed under a Creative Commons Attribution-NonCommercial-ShareAlike 4.0 International license.

ISBN: 9781739985226

*British Library Cataloguing-in-Publication Data*
A catalogue record for this book is available from the British library.

Typeset in Garamond
liberatedtexts.com
ebb-magazine.com

## Contents

| | |
|---|---:|
| *Contributors* | 6 |
| *Liberated Texts*: The Power of Books as Propaganda<br>Louis Allday | 11 |
| Fascisation as an Expression of Imperialist Decay:<br>Rajani Palme Dutt's *Fascism and Social Revolution*<br>Alfie Hancox | 18 |
| Imperialism and the Deep State: Peter Dale Scott's<br>*The Road to 9/11—Wealth, Empire, and the Future of America*<br>Patrick Higgins | 29 |
| Mutiny in Vietnam: Richard Boyle's *Flower of the Dragon: The Breakdown of the U.S. Army in Vietnam*<br>Marlon Ettinger | 51 |
| Penetrating Curtains of Deceit: I.F. Stone's *The Hidden History of the Korean War*<br>Tim Beal and Gregory Elich | 72 |
| Socialist Construction in Korea: Suzy Kim's *Everyday Life in the North Korean Revolution, 1945-1950*<br>Ju-Hyun Park | 88 |
| Revolution as Historic Necessity: Edgar Snow's *Red Star Over China*<br>Lewis Hodder | 101 |
| The Cause of Anti-colonialism and Liberation is One: Fayez Sayegh's *Zionist Colonialism in Palestine*<br>Louis Allday | 114 |

| | |
|---|---|
| A History of the Anonymous Masses: Rosemary Sayigh's *Palestinians: From Peasants to Revolutionaries*<br>Steven Salaita | 131 |
| Liberation, Wonder, and the "Magic of the World": Basel al-Araj's *I Have Found My Answers*<br>Hazem Jamjoum | 142 |
| Ireland's Struggle for Self-determination: Robbie McVeigh and Bill Rolston's *Ireland, Colonialism and the Unfinished Revolution*<br>Chris Beausang | 162 |
| The Capitalist Roots of Anti-Indigenous Racism in Canada: Howard Adams' *Prison of Grass*<br>Owen Schalk | 182 |
| Independence with Blood: The Decolonial Vision of the Malayan Conscious Youth Movement's *Political Testament*<br>Fadiah Nadwa Fikri | 195 |
| Walter Rodney's Lost Book: *One Hundred Years of Development in Africa*<br>Leo Zeilig | 208 |
| African Socialism in Retrospect: Karim Hirji's *The Travails of a Tanzanian Teacher*<br>Zeyad el-Nabolsy | 223 |
| Critiquing Human Rights Like It Matters: Issa Shivji's *The Concept of Human Rights in Africa*<br>Paul O'Connell | 235 |
| Insurgent Theory in Times of Crisis: Dani Wadada Nabudere's *The Political Economy of Imperialism*<br>Corinna Mullin | 246 |

| | |
|---|---|
| Reflections on Workers' Organization: Makhan Singh's *History of Kenya's Trade Union Movement to 1952*<br>Noosim Naimasiah | 266 |
| Entrenching Inequality: The European Dependency School's *Underdeveloped Europe*<br>Sam Parry | 276 |
| A Pedagogy of the Collective—From the Soviet Union to Latin America: *Makarenko, His Life and Work*<br>Alex Turrall | 288 |
| Reading Ivan Illich's *Deschooling Society* in the Neoliberal University<br>Justin Podur | 302 |
| A Pedagogy of Nature: Vasily Sukhomlinsky's *My Heart I Give to Children*<br>Alex Turrall | 320 |
| *Index* | 342 |

## *Contributors*

Louis Allday, a writer and historian, is the founding editor of *Liberated Texts*.

Alfie Hancox is an Editor at *Ebb Magazine* and is currently undertaking a PhD at the University of Birmingham on the British Black Power movement. His writing on Marxism and anti-imperialism can also be found in *Discover Society, Liberated Texts*, and *Cosmonaut Magazine*.

Patrick Higgins is a writer and historian living in Houston, Texas.

Marlon Ettinger lives in New York. You can follow him on Twitter @MarlonEttinger.

Tim Beal is a retired New Zealand academic who has written extensively on Asia with a special focus on the Korean Peninsula. His recent work includes the entry on Korea for *The Palgrave Encyclopedia of Imperialism and Anti-Imperialism* (Springer, 2019), *US Imperialism, the Korean Peninsula and Trumpian Disruption* (International Critical Thought, 2020), and *In Line of Fire: The Korean Peninsula in U.S.-China Strategy* (Monthly Review, 2021).

Gregory Elich is a Korea Policy Institute associate and on the Jasenovac Research Institute's board of directors. He is also a member of the Solidarity Committee for Democracy and Peace in Korea. His website is https://gregoryelich.org. Follow him on Twitter at @GregoryElich.

Ju-Hyun Park is a writer and an organizer with Nodutdol.

Lewis Hodder is an Editor at Ebb Magazine, whose writing engages with topics ranging from the Frankfurt School to British communist parties.

Steven Salaita's latest book is *Inter/Nationalism: Decolonizing Native America and Palestine*. His personal website can be found at http://stevesalaita.com.

Hazem Jamjoum is a doctoral candidate in the modern history of the Middle East at New York University.

Chris Beausang was born, and continues to live, in Dublin. His novel *Tunnel of Toads* is forthcoming from Marrowbone Books.

Owen Schalk is a writer from Winnipeg, Manitoba. He has written for *Monthly Review, Protean Magazine, Alborada*, and more. Additionally, his work regularly appears in *Canadian Dimension*.

Fadiah Nadwa Fikri is a Ph.D. candidate at the Department of Southeast Asian Studies, National University of Singapore, studying resistance to British colonialism in Malaya. Her research interests include decolonisation, transnational solidarity, and Third World feminisms.

Leo Zeilig is an editor on the *Review of African Political Economy*. He has written widely on African history and politics, and his study on Walter Rodney, *A Revolutionary for Our Time* (2022) is published by Haymarket Books. He is also a novelist and his latest novel, *The World Turned Upside Down* was released in 2021.

Zeyad el Nabolsy is a Ph.D. student in Africana Studies at Cornell University. He works on African philosophy of culture, African Marxism, the history and philosophy of science in the context of modern African intellectual history, and history and sociology of philosophy in the context of global intellectual history.

Paul O'Connell teaches law at SOAS, University of London and is a founding member of The Beehive in Manchester and the Political Education Project.

Corinna Mullin is an anti-imperialist, adjunct professor in the political science, economics, and global studies departments at John Jay and Brooklyn College (CUNY) & The New School.

Noosim Naimasiah is a panafricanist, an activist and an editor at Vita Books, a Nairobi-based publishing house.

Samuel Parry is a Ph.D. candidate in Political Economy at Cardiff University, where he studies the links between culture, geography and the economy through a Marxist lens to explain the peripherality of some European nations, namely his home of Wales. His work is researching the viability of using dependency and world-systems theory to explain the core-periphery paradigm and the tensions between minority and majority nationalisms that exist in Europe.

Alex Turrall is an independent researcher and primary school teacher.

Justin Podur is a Professor and Author based in Toronto.

## *Liberated Texts*: The Power of Books as Propaganda
Louis Allday

> Brecht said, "hungry man reach for the book." Why? Because to get rid of hunger, you have to get rid of the system that produces hunger, and to get rid of that system you must understand it and you can only do that by reaching for the book.
>
> Prabhat Patnaik

In November 1965, the Deputy Director of the CIA was sent an in-house book review by the curator of the Agency's Historical Intelligence Collection. Its subject was Kwame Nkrumah's seminal work, *Neo-Colonialism: The Last Stage of Imperialism*, first published in London earlier that year. The review, released into the public domain in 1999, largely focussed on "The Mechanisms of Neo-Colonialism", the chapter in Nkrumah's book that was said to have most "caught the eye of the press" and was "of greatest interest to the CIA".

Within the book, Nkrumah analyses in detail the techniques through which modern imperialist powers achieved the objectives they had previously accomplished through overt colonialism and identifies the United States as the worst offender in this regard. In doing so, Nkrumah named names and drew attention to the neo-colonial role of, among others, the CIA, US Peace Corps, USIA and USAID. The tenor of the review is largely neutral, but the author's concern with both the book's contents and Nkrumah as a figure more broadly are not hard to discern beneath its superficially objective tone. It concludes by reporting that copies of the book had been sent to a number of CIA departments including the African Division of the Deputy Directorate for Plans (DDP), the Agency's clandestine service and covert action arm, for study and "whatever action these components consider advisable".[1]

Only three months later, in February 1966, Nkrumah was deposed as President of Ghana in a coup that was engineered by the Agency.[2] The late June Milne, Nkrumah's editor, literary executor and long-time confidante, believed that because *Neo-Colonialism* had demonstrated the workings of international finance capital in Africa in such detail, the exposure its publication constituted was "just too much… the last straw" and led directly to the decision to depose Nkrumah in a coup.[3]

---

1   "Memorandum for Deputy Director of Central Intelligence—Book review: *Neo-Colonialism: The Last Stage of Imperialism* by Kwame Nkrumah", 8 November 1965.

2   Charles Quist-Adade, "How Did a Fateful CIA Coup—Executed 55 Years Ago this February 24—Doom Much of Sub-Saharan Africa?", *Covert Action Magazine*, 2021.

3   Doreatha Drummond Mbala, *Kwame Nkrumah: The June Milne Interview* (2019), 67.

Milne's speculation is well-founded, not only because of the undeniably explosive content of Nkrumah's book, but because senior figures within the CIA were already well aware of the dangers that such material posed to US interests. In the words of its Covert Operations Director in 1961:

> Books differ from all other propaganda media, primarily because one single book can significantly change the reader's attitude and action to an extent unmatched by the impact of any other single medium… this is, of course, not true of all books at all times and with all readers—but it is true significantly often enough to make books the most important weapon of strategic (long-range) propaganda.[4]

As such, the Agency acted accordingly and developed an extraordinary level of control and influence within the publishing industry globally. Details of the extent of this reach were revealed to the public in 1975 by the Church Committee, a US Senate investigation into the activities of a number of US intelligence agencies, including the CIA. The most well-known revelations of this committee include details of the now infamous CIA-run programmes MKULTRA, COINTELPRO, Family Jewels and Operation Mockingbird. Less well known are the details it contains on the Agency's clandestine control over book publishing and distribution which, as per the committee's findings, enabled it to:

---

4   "Foreign and Military Intelligence, Book 1: Final Report of the Select Committee to Study Governmental Operations with Respect to Intelligence Activities" (1975), 193.

(a) Get books published or distributed abroad without revealing any US influence, by covertly subsidizing foreign publications or booksellers.

(b) Get books published which should not be "contaminated" by any overt tie-in with the US government, especially if the position of the author is "delicate."

(c) Get books published for operational reasons, regardless of commercial viability.

(d) Initiate and subsidise indigenous national or international organizations for book publishing or distributing purposes.

(e) Stimulate the writing of politically significant books by unknown foreign authors-either by directly subsidizing the author, if covert contact is feasible, or indirectly, through literary agents or publishers.[5]

Utilising this immense influence, before the end of 1967, well over 1,000 books had been produced, subsidised or sponsored by the Agency. Of these works, 25 percent were written in English, with the remainder in a number of different languages published around the world. Sometimes these books were published by organisations backed by the CIA without the author's knowledge, while others involved direct collaboration between the Agency and the writer.

Frequently, books were published in order to bolster the US imperialist narrative about enemy states, for example, the Agency produced a number of works about China that were intended specifically to combat the

---

5   Ibid., 193.

"sympathetic view of the emerging China as presented by Edgar Snow".[6] As the committee's official report stated, an American who read one of those books, purportedly authored by a Chinese defector, "would not know that his thoughts and opinions about China are possibly being shaped by an agency of the United States Government".[7] The Agency's concern extended to book reviews which it utilised to refute the attacks of critics and promote works that it had sponsored. On at least one occasion, a book produced by the CIA was then reviewed in the *New York Times* by another writer also contracted by the Agency.[8]

In the time that has passed since the revelations of the Church Committee, technological developments have transformed the way in which people consume information globally. The internet has become a new battle ground of propaganda and has been subject to comparable levels of infiltration and manipulation by the CIA and other intelligence agencies. The idea that books remain the most important weapon of strategic propaganda, as determined by the CIA in 1961, would now be contested by many.

However, the terrain of contemporary publishing implies that US intelligence agencies have not ceased to be concerned with the power and influence of books as objects of propaganda. Take one example, since the

---

6. Ibid., 198. See also Lewis Hodder, "Revolution as Historic Necessity: Edgar Snow's *Red Star Over China*" contained in this volume.

7   Ibid., 199.

8   Ibid., 198.

US' proxy war against Syria[9] began a decade ago, a raft of books supporting the imperialist narrative have been published, many of them by ostensibly radical and leftist publishers. In many cases, these books are then endorsed and reviewed by an affiliated network of magazines, podcasts and other media, while works that go against the hegemonic narrative are reviewed negatively or simply ignored.

It is with this historical context and lamentable present reality in mind that *Liberated Texts* was established in March 2021. It aims to provide a platform for reviews of works of ongoing relevance that have been forgotten, underappreciated, suppressed or misinterpreted in the cultural mainstream since their release. Of course, not all of the works reviewed will have been subject to overt suppression or silencing by imperialist intelligence agencies—the reasons why books that go against prevailing ideas usually do not receive the attention and readership they deserve are countless—but all remain relevant and deserve a wider readership. The same is true of works that do not get translated into English for political reasons, such as the late Domenico Losurdo's study of Stalin, which his English language publishers, *Verso Books*, have refused to translate and publish in spite of repeated requests for them to do so.[10]

The life stories of prominent revolutionaries and thinkers are littered with references to how reading

---

9   Patrick Higgins, "The Enemy at Home: US Imperialism in Syria", *Viewpoint Magazine*, 2018.

10   Domenico Losurdo, *Stalin. Storia e critica di una leggenda nera* (Carocci, 2008).

individual books or authors changed the trajectory of their life, and notwithstanding the dramatic shift in the educational and media landscape that has taken place in the decades since the publication of *Neo-Colonialism*, books remain powerful tools that have the ability to fundamentally transform one's worldview.

*Liberated Texts* seeks to provide a home for all those people who still believe that to be the case and want to write about books they feel passionate about and believe—whether they were published 100 years ago or in recent years—remain pertinent to issues of the present moment and deserve to be read and discussed more widely.

# Fascisation as an Expression of Imperialist Decay: Rajani Palme Dutt's *Fascism and Social Revolution*

Alfie Hancox

> Imperialism and fascism march hand in hand; they are blood brothers.[1]

These are the words of Jawaharlal Nehru, the first Prime Minister of independent India and a longstanding political colleague of Rajani Palme Dutt (1896-1974), the leading theoretician in the Communist Party of Great Britain. In his day Dutt was one of the most influential communists in the English-speaking world, primarily known for his analysis of colonial underdevelopment, but his magnum opus was his full-length study of the rise of fascism.[2]

Intended as a sequel to Lenin's *Imperialism*, Dutt's

---

1   Quoted in Michele L. Louro, *Comrades Against Imperialism: Nehru, India, and Interwar Internationalism* (Cambridge University Press, 2018), 238.

2   John Callaghan, *Rajani Palme Dutt: A Study in British Stalinism* (Lawrence and Wishart, 1993), 7.

*Fascism and Social Revolution* (1934) is remarkable for its global perspective, locating the conditions of fascist ascendancy in the "intensified conflict of the imperialist powers".[3] The imperial dimension of fascism, and its continuities with liberal colonialism, have only recently begun to receive serious scholarly attention. Yet Dutt is absent from the most notable published collection of interwar Marxist writings on fascism, and he does not even get a mention in Trotskyist historian David Renton's newly revised classic *Fascism: History and Theory*.[4] Dutt's fealty to Stalin and the Communist International (Comintern) has largely consigned his works to obscurity, but charges by his detractors on the left that he was just an opportunistic "shyster lawyer" overlook his deep-seated commitment to anti-imperialist causes.[5]

*Empire, "the British form of fascism"*

While conventional accounts stress the exceptional character of fascism, owing to national and cultural peculiarities, when contextualised within the long history of European colonialism, the horrors of the 1930s-40s

---

3   R. P. Dutt, *Fascism and Social Revolution* (Revised 2nd ed., Martin Lawrence Ltd., 1935), 63.

4   David Beetham ed., *Marxists in the Face of Fascism: Writings by Marxists on Fascism from the Inter-War Period* (Haymarket Books, 2019); David Renton, *Fascism: History and Theory* (Pluto Press, 2020). In the original edition, Dutt is only discussed in a dismissive footnote as exemplifying the Comintern's "class-blind analysis". Renton, *Fascism: Theory and Practice* (Pluto Press, 1999), 134.

5   Duncan Hallas, "The Shyster Lawyer", *Socialist Review*, No.167, September 1993.

appear less of an aberration. As the son of a Bengali immigrant residing in the metropolitan heart of darkness, Dutt viewed the great social turmoil of the interwar years through an anti-colonial lens—the "alien eye" as he called it—and as early as 1923 he argued that "the Empire is the British form of Fascism".[6] He elaborated on this conviction in the book, which highlights how in the poems of Rudyard Kipling and the Boer War agitation of the *Daily Mail*, "the spirit of Fascism is already present in embryonic forms." Dutt exposed the hypocrisy of the "democratic" imperialists, noting that "bourgeois critics of Fascism in Western Europe and America express their shocked indignation as if Fascist Germany and Fascist Italy were the first and only countries to go in for jingoism, wholesale war-incitement and war-preparation, and as if England, France and the United States were innocent angels of peace".[7] In the British Empire, the 1930s was a decade that witnessed the suppression of anti-colonial labour rebellions in the Caribbean, and the crushing of the Indian independence movement.

Having experienced imperial racism first-hand in England, Dutt identified that fascism's "national-chauvinist ideology, the anti-Semitism and the racial theories are all borrowed, without a single new feature, from the stock in trade of the old Conservative and reactionary parties".[8] He pointed out that Britain's

---

[6] John Callaghan, "The Heart of Darkness: Rajani Palme Dutt and the British Empire—A Profile", *Contemporary Record*, 5:2 (1991), 257-75.

[7] Dutt, *Fascism and Social Revolution*, 182; 213.

[8] Ibid., 183; Callaghan, *Rajani Palme Dutt*, 10.

home-grown fascists led by Oswald Mosley took their inspiration from not only Mussolini's Black Shirts but also the perpetrators of the Amritsar massacre in India, and the paramilitary Black-and-Tans in Ireland. The American ruling class was "equally adapted to Fascism", having "had plenty of experience in their own domain in the suppression of the twelve million Negroes within the United States and of the heavily exploited immigrant populations". Dutt singled out the Scottsboro trial, Red-baiting, Haymarket hangings and Ku Klux Klan lynchings as examples of "the plentiful basis for Fascism in American bourgeois traditions".[9] The Nazi race laws indeed drew directly on the precedents of Jim Crow, as well as the genocide of Native Americans.

A parallel analysis was advanced by the Trinidad-born communist George Padmore (a regular contributor to Dutt's *Labour Monthly*), who wrote after Mussolini's invasion of Ethiopia in 1935 that slaughtered 275,000 Africans, that "the Colonies are the breeding ground for the type of fascist mentality which is being let loose in Europe today".[10] This interpretation was most famously advanced in Aimé Césaire's 1950 *Discourse on Colonialism*, which argued that Hitler's real crime in the eyes of "civilised" Europeans was "that he applied to Europe

---

9  Dutt, *Fascism and Social Revolution*, 238-41. The centrality of imperial politics to British fascism has only recently been acknowledged by historians. See Liam J. Liburd, "Beyond the Pale: Whiteness, Masculinity and Empire in the British Union of Fascists, 1932-1940", *Fascism: Journal of Comparative Fascist Studies,* 7: 2 (2018), 275-96.

10  George Padmore, *How Britain Rules Africa* (Negro Universities Press, 1969), 4.

colonialist procedures which until then had been reserved exclusively for the Arabs of Algeria, the 'coolies' of India, and the 'n****s' of Africa". Years earlier, Dutt had already suggested that Nazism was the rogue child of conventional European imperialism: "If Hitler applied the match to the gunpowder, it was the British and French ruling class that laid the trail of gunpowder and placed the match in his hand".[11] Hitler referred to his hoped-for German *Lebensraum* in Russia as "our India", and the Nazis learned from previous colonial atrocities such as the Herero and Nama genocide in Namibia.[12]

*Colonial Rivalry and Hungry Imperialists*

The book also cuts through Britain's patriotic mythos of WW2 as a straightforwardly anti-fascist war fought in the name of democracy. At the time Dutt was writing, it was "the widespread hope of imperialist circles, especially in Britain, to use a re-armed Fascist Germany, in unity with Japan, for war on the Soviet Union".[13] So long as the Nazis faced eastwards they were financed by the British ruling class, which backed Hitler's rearmament programme in the Anglo-German naval agreement. Former Liberal Prime Minister David Lloyd George described Hitler as a bulwark against Bolshevism, while Churchill declared that if he were Italian he would "wholeheartedly" support Mussolini's counterrevolution.

---

11    Quoted in Neil Redfern, *Class or Nation? Communists, Imperialism and Two World Wars* (Tauris Academic Studies, 2005), 101.

12    Renton, *Fascism: History and Theory*, 16.

13    Dutt, *Fascism and Social Revolution*, 217.

Unlike the more influential Marxist theorists of fascism including Georgi Dimitrov and Leon Trotsky, Dutt situated its rise in the crucible of inter-imperialist rivalry for colonial markets in the context of a global economic crisis like that which preceded WW1. The arrival of fascism, Dutt argued, can "only be correctly understood in relation to its general social role as the expression of the extreme stage of imperialism in break-up". The divergent national trajectories were principally accounted for by the fact that while Britain and France were "sated" colonial powers "gorged with world-plunder," Germany, Italy and Japan were "hungry" imperialists "intent on an aggressive policy of expansion".[14] A similar conclusion was drawn by the German left-social democrat Richard Löwenthal, who identified the essence of fascism in "an imperialism of paupers and bankrupts".[15] Mussolini himself described Italy as a "proletarian nation" in Europe unjustly denied its share of colonial possessions.[16]

In a misfortune of history, Dutt's farsighted anti-imperialist analysis was marginalised only months after the book was published—when the Soviet Union turned towards courting alliances with the "democratic" Allied powers—and downplayed its previous anti-colonial commitments. Dutt resorted to ideological contortions to justify the Comintern's volte-face, but the notion he was merely "Stalin's mouthpiece" in Britain is simplistic.

---

14  Ibid., 213-16.

15  Richard Löwenthal, "The Fascist State and Monopoly Capitalism" (1935), in Beetham ed., 339.

16  Renton, *Fascism: History and Theory*, 13.

For instance, during the "People's War" phase after the German invasion of Russia he argued—in contradiction to the Soviets' conciliatory approach—that support for Britain's anti-fascist war effort should be "combined with continued struggle against Churchill and British imperialism".[17]

Dutt's insights have sustained relevance in our present era of far-right resurgence and renewed antagonisms between the "core" capitalist powers with a principle difference being that today, there are only hungry imperialists. While contemporary incarnations of fascism require special attention, the danger of exceptionalism remains: as Joshua Briond reminds us in his article titled "Hitler Is Not Dead" (a nod to Césaire), the mass incarceration and deportation of migrants, anti-black police brutality and imperialist wars in West Asia "occurred long before Trump and will continue to escalate long after Trump".[18]

*From Social Imperialism to "Social Fascism"*

Dutt also analysed the internal "fascisation" of bourgeois democracy. Following Lenin's framework of "the law of unequal capitalist development", he noted that social contradictions were sharpest in the "poorer" imperialist countries, where the ruling classes were no longer able to purchase social peace, and thus had to

---

17  Callaghan, *Rajani Palme Dutt*, 198.

18  Joshua Briond, "Hitler is Not Dead: On Bourgeois Electoralism, Liberalism as the Left Wing of Fascism, and the Politics of Exceptionalizing Donald Trump", *Hampton Think Tank*, November 2020.

rely on increasingly authoritarian measures to keep workers at heel.[19] Dutt was off the mark in arguing that the entire capitalist world was entering a state of "pre-fascism", but his apocalyptic tone can be excused given the circumstances—few living through the calamity of the thirties could have anticipated capitalism's post-war recovery.

The book presents the most systematic defence of the controversial "social fascism" thesis, showing how social democratic parties helped pave the way for fascism through implementing emergency powers, refusing anti-fascist alliances with communists, and forestalling proletarian revolution. The social fascist position was promoted by the Comintern during its Third Period (1928-34) when it designated reformist politicians as class enemies. Dutt glossed over the undoubted sectarian excesses of this policy, but those who write it off as "ultra-left idiocy"[20] too readily forget the line was solidified only after a series of fatal betrayals by governing social democrats, climaxing in the 1929 shooting of May Day demonstrators in Berlin.[21]

Whereas Trotskyist accounts tend to overstress the middle-class base of fascism, Dutt correctly saw that it was able to mobilise and deceive swathes of the "demoralised working class" disaffected from social democracy. This dynamic enabled fascism to become a truly mass movement with the capacity for self-radicalisation,

---

19  Dutt, *Fascism and Social Revolution*, 216.

20  Jim Higgins, "R.P. Dutt: Stalin's British Mouthpiece", *International Socialism*, 75, February 1975.

21  Ibid., 116.

distinguishing it from previous "dictatorships from the right".[22] The purported "twinned" character of fascism and social reformism was more sophisticated than is often implied: the argument was not, as Renton suggests, "that social democracy was just another kind of fascism".[23] Both are in the last instance "instruments of the rule of monopoly capital", both attempt to place "the state above classes", but their methods differ. Where fascism "shatters the class organisations of the workers from without", social democracy "undermines [them] from within". For Dutt, what was novel in the fascist dictatorship was that rather than incorporating the existing labour movement into the imperialist state, it aimed at "the violent *destruction of the workers' independent organisations*".[24]

More originally, the book argues that fascism was specifically indebted to a western socialism that had betrayed class internationalism, and "left the masses an easy prey" to far-right demagogy.[25] Dutt recognised that European social democracy itself had "been built on the foundation of colonial slavery; as was strikingly

---

22   Ibid., 82; 76. To his credit, Renton also acknowledges this dynamic: "Even if the petty bourgeoisie played a disproportionate role in fascist parties, it was such a small minority in society that it could not be the source of every single fascist… Part of the horror of fascism was that it recruited people who could easily have been won over by Socialist parties". *Fascism: History and Theory*, 153.

23   Renton, *Fascism: History and Theory*, 79.

24   Original emphasis. Dutt, *Fascism and Social Revolution*, 115; 203.

25   Ibid., 162.

demonstrated when the Labour Government, the champion of 'democracy', brought in a reign of terror to maintain despotism in India and jailed sixty thousand for the crime of asking for democratic rights". The fascist conception of imperial "self-sufficiency" was a familiar one among the reformist left in the 1930s. Dutt noted that when the Labour MP and future fascist Oswald Mosley advanced his programme for national economic growth based on "socialistic imperialism", prominent left-Labour politicians, including Aneurin Bevan (the later architect of the National Health Service), "rallied to his support and assisted his campaign."[26]

Like many communists, Dutt had been radicalised when the reformist parties of the Second International succumbed to the jingoist frenzy and backed their respective governments in the imperialist First World War. He observed that the ultra-nationalist rhetoric of "war-socialists" such as Robert Blatchford in England and Alexander Parvus in Germany "reveal many striking resemblances with subsequent Fascism".[27] In Italy, a number of prominent fascists including Paolo Orano were erstwhile revolutionary syndicalists, who saw their country's participation in WW1 as a moment of national redemption.[28] The early pseudo-socialism of Nazism, as articulated by the Strasser brothers, also borrowed from the "semi-Fascist conceptions of nationalism, imperialism and class-collaboration", which were long

---

26   Ibid., 235; 255.

27   Ibid., 157.

28   Zak Cope, *The Wealth of (Some) Nations: Imperialism and the Mechanics of Value Transfer* (Pluto Press, 2019), 180.

fostered by the chauvinist wing of social democracy.[29]

Within the western left of today, a reinvigorated class politics remains stuck in the social-imperialist cul-de-sac. Emblematically, in 2018 the prominent journalist Paul Mason—soon to publish a book on "how to stop fascism"—called for Jeremy Corbyn to advance "a programme to deliver growth and prosperity in Wigan, Newport and Kirkcaldy—if necessary, at the price of not delivering them to Shenzhen, Bombay and Dubai".[30] By pandering to nativism and anti-immigrant sentiments, social democratic and liberal parties throughout Europe and North America have continued to play into the hands of right-wing populism. Dutt should be recognised alongside the likes of Padmore, Sylvia Pankhurst, and Amílcar Cabral for demonstrating that the only effective counter to creeping fascisation lies in the path of anti-imperialism and socialist internationalism.

---

29  Dutt, *Fascism and Social Revolution*, 162.

30  Louis Allday, "Social Imperialism in the 21st century: Owen Jones, Paul Mason & the problem with the UK left", *Monthly Review*, 6 August 2018.

# Imperialism and the Deep State: Peter Dale Scott's *The Road to 9/11—Wealth, Empire, and the Future of America*

Patrick Higgins

> Now, what is victory? I say that victory is persuading the American people and the rest of the world that this is not a quick matter that is going to be over in a month or a year or even five years.
>
> Donald Rumsfeld, September 20, 2001[1]

As we approach the 20th anniversary of the September 11 attacks, the reputation of George W. Bush is undergoing a concerted resuscitation. The primary rehabilitators are the liberal Democratic establishment. Bush himself is also playing a role, rebranding as a conscientious defender of American decency against the depredations of Donald J. Trump, whose four years in the White House represent a supposed aberration from hallowed US political traditions. At about the middle mark of

---

1 "Pentagon Briefing on Aircraft Deployment", *The Washington Post*, September 20, 2001.

Trump's single term, a once-disgraced Bush emerged to denounce a series of easy targets: "bigotry in any form"; "bullying and prejudice in our public life"; and "conspiracy theories and outright fabrication".[2] These words were intended as a slight against Trump in a grand last stand of an old party loyalist against an infiltrating scoundrel. It was a performance, a victory of etiquette over substance. More crucially, it showed a new point of convergence between the Democratic and Republican Parties: namely their use of Trump as a convenient bogeyman against whom every sin and transgression could be forgiven.

It cannot be forgotten: Bush's presidency was *terrifying*—for the people of the US and the world. The terror hinged on the events of September 11, 2001. What followed that day was a new offensive that shredded through civil liberties and rights in a campaign whose intensity was in some ways unparalleled in history. New categories of "suspicious people" were watched, rounded up, deported, and imprisoned without trial in the United States and abroad. Effectively, the United States implemented martial law globally, granting itself legal jurisdiction just about everywhere in what could be called "imperial sovereignty". Wars of both high and low intensity followed, advanced through all manner of fabricated ties to the events of 9/11. The state, along with the corporate press, is now dedicated to vanishing any serious memory of this, an endeavour in which

---

2   "George W. Bush Bashes Bigotry, Bullying, and Lies But Doesn't Use Trump's Name", *New York Magazine*, 19 October, 2017.

Trump has proven to be a valuable asset. Antidotes to this coerced amnesia are sorely needed, and for a genealogy of 9/11 itself, few books are as important as Peter Dale Scott's much-neglected *The Road to 9/11: Wealth, Empire, and the Future of America* (2007).

The role Scott's book can now play is more substantial than feeding the usual left-liberal rebuke to Bush amnesia, which is to claim that the problem with Bush was simply that he "gave us Trump". It is not useful to imply that the Trump years were appreciably "worse" than the Bush era, nor is it instructive to insist the Bush presidency was simply a warm-up for Trump. More helpfully, Scott's book provides a serious political history of how the long-term institutions of US rule were unleashed in new ways during the Bush presidency. His work on 9/11 can thus help us to place that era into a broader historical timeline of US imperialism.

*The Strange Trajectory of the "Deep State"*

Among the strangest developments of the Trump years has been the appearance of the term "deep state" in popular culture. This phrase has become a bugbear for corporate journalists, who tend to view its use disdainfully, treating it as a sign of substandard intellect marred by conspiracy thought. What's amusing is that its use began on the political left. Peter Dale Scott—a poet and long-time English professor who also served as a Canadian diplomat between the late 50s and early 60s—has, at least since 2007, frequently used the phrase in his explanations of the workings of US imperialism, including his argument for how and why 9/11 and its repressive aftermath took place.

Scott himself adopted the phrase from an earlier source: the Turkish left, which needed a language to describe the networks undergirding the secretive, fascist paramilitaries the state used to repress, terrorise, and destroy Turkish Communists and the Kurdish national liberation movement.[3] Book-length studies have contributed empirical evidence of the activities of these networks in both Turkey and Western Europe, along with analyses of their *raison d'être*.[4] That is, as the postwar US sought to secure its supreme military and financial position in the world, it increasingly safeguarded its grip on vital resources and trade routes from Communist and working-class threats through covert, extra-legal, and manifestly violent means.

A common left riposte to speculations about the "deep state," especially since the term entered the lexicon of the right, has been to argue that there is no deep state, only a bourgeois state, or a capitalist state, or an imperialist state—choose your preferred argot. This response, however, eludes the main point, made by Scott and others about how political repression in so-called "democratic" systems functions. While it could

---

3   Some sources trace the initial use of the phrase "deep state" to Bülent Ecevit, the social democratic former Prime Minister of Turkey who got his start in politics with the Republican People's Party (CHP).

4   These include Daniele Ganser's *NATO's Secret Armies: Operation GLADIO and Terrorism in Western Europe* and Paul L. Williams's *Operation Gladio: The Unholy Alliance between the Vatican, the CIA, and the Mafia.*

be argued that the right's use of "deep state" has made the phrase more trouble than it's worth, it still remains necessary to name and analyse the vast infrastructure in an empire such as the US that remains hidden from public view and immune from even the pretence of democratic accountability.

Scott argues that the US deep state was a postwar creation. The 1947 National Security Act merged the Department of War and the Department of the Navy into the National Security Establishment; created the Department of Air Force; and perhaps most significantly, established the National Security Council and the Central Intelligence Agency. It is important to note that Scott's idea of the deep state transcends the formal bounds of the military and the national security establishment, such as the NSC, the CIA, and the Pentagon. Very often, personnel working within and through these institutions develop para-state relationships to procure the illegal movement of weapons, finances, and even narcotics.

For example, in the 1970s, after the United States began to "[oblige] the world's central banks to finance the US balance-of-payments deficit by using their surplus dollars to buy US Treasury bonds," Nixon's treasury secretary, William Simon, "negotiated a secret deal so the Saudi central bank could buy US Treasury securities outside the normal auction…Thus the biggest demand for dollars overseas [was] the need of oil-importing countries to maintain dollar reserves to pay for their oil."[5] As a result of the petrodollar arrangement, a number of other

---

5   Peter Dale Scott, *The Road to 9/11: Wealth, Empire, and the Future of America* (University of California Press, 2007), 36-37.

backdoor business relationships were initiated between members of the US and Saudi ruling classes, united by a common desire to turn profits and destroy nationalist and Communist challengers in the Arab region.

By mentioning connections such as these, Scott is making the point that the "parallel structures" that constitute the deep state largely escape public examination and make use of the state's infrastructure while also extending beyond formal state institutions. There is an important US domestic component to the development of these forces as well. The 1960s marked a major acceleration point. The twin, interconnected spectres of the Vietnamese and Black liberation movements deeply shook the US ruling class.[6] Engines of domestic repression were proffered, overwhelmingly in secret, as part of the total US war machine. After US Army paratroopers launched war on Black proletarians in the streets of US cities like Detroit and Newark in the late 60s, Lyndon Johnson convened the 1968 Kerner Commission to diagnose the cause of the US's so-called "civil disorders." The Pentagon responded to the commission by putting together Operation Garden Plot, which granted permission for the US armed forces "to respond to reasonable requests from the FBI for military resources for use in combatting acts of terrorism".

By the 1970s, the open, publicly visible arms of the state moved to absorb and, in some cases, respond to popular pressure from below. Scott's handling of the

---

6   Scott points to Marine Colonel Oliver North's belief that "the war effort in Vietnam was not lost on the battlefield; rather, it was lost in the streets of America." *The Road to 9/11*, 9.

Watergate investigation shows that he does not treat the deep state as a monolithic bloc with its various branches in perfect sync. There is no single cabal here, as bad faith critics often suggest. There are, however, a number of contending alliances, often shifting. Scott describes the Watergate scandal as the outcome of competing factions vying for control of the levers of the state. Particularly important during that episode was the tactical feud between a broad faction, led by Henry Kissinger and CEO of Chase Manhattan Bank David Rockefeller, which preferred an overall scale-down in Southeast Asia and a public détente with the Soviet Union in order to defeat Communism by more aggressive covert means, and another faction, "centered in but not restricted to the Joint Chiefs of Staff," which aimed "to win in Vietnam and put an end to Nixonian plans for coexistence with the Soviet Union".[7]

Watergate, combined with the popular protest of the Black liberation and anti-war movements, led to a series of Congressional reviews into the nature of covert operations. The 1975 Senate Church Committee publicly investigated the abuses of the CIA, NSA, FBI, and IRS. It had a counterpart in the House, the Pike Committee. These appraisals reconfigured the contours of the deep state, as hardline anti-communists in the intelligence agencies and national security apparatus now had to find alternative funding streams and novel means to destroy the Soviet Union. This search led directly to a set of new wars that would play a major role on the road to 9/11, namely in Afghanistan and Central Asia.

---

7    Ibid., 47.

## The Deep Origins of Al Qaeda

Essential to Scott's argument is the premise that Al Qaeda, despite its eventual all-purpose use as the purported target of the War on Terror, was a creation of deep politics. Its origins date back to Jimmy Carter's National Security Advisor, Zbigniew Brzezinski, who was obsessed with destroying the Soviet Union. He hatched the idea that "an arc of Islam could be mobilised to contain the Soviets."[8] He was joined by a team of people "who wanted to keep Soviet forces pinned down in Afghanistan and thus to avenge Vietnam."[9] Brzezinski enlisted the services of likeminded organisations including the Pakistani Inter-Services Intelligence Agency (ISI) and the Saudi International Islamic Relief Organization (IIRO).[10] The role of these agencies allowed the United States to outsource its war policy, something that had become more important in the wake of the war on Vietnam, the anti-war movement, and the ensuing Congressional reviews. In his own words, Brzezinski thought the "Islamic arc" strategy would offer the US "the opportunity of giving to the USSR its Vietnam War".[11]

---

8   Quoting State Department official Henry Precht. From Robert Dreyfuss, *Devil's Game: How the United States Helped Unleash Fundamentalist Islam* (Metropolitan Books, 2006), 240 (as cited in Scott, *The Road to 9/11*, 67).

9   Diego Cordovez and Selig S. Harrison, *Out of Afghanistan: The Inside Story of the Soviet Withdrawal* (Oxford University Press, 1995), 33 (as cited in Scott, *The Road to 9/11*, 68).

10   Scott, *The Road to 9/11*, 72.

11   Brzezinski interview with *Le Nouvel Observateur* (1998). Translated from the French by William Blum and David N. Gibbs. This translation was published in Gibbs, "Afghanistan:

Imperialism and the Deep State 37

This war policy carried on and even expanded into the next administration under the directorship of Reagan's chosen CIA head, William Casey, who used these right-wing fundamentalists—essentially the contras of Central Asia—to launch offensive wars into Soviet republics. The Bank of Credit and Commerce International (BCCI), on which Casey had relied in the early stages of the Iran-Contra affair, provided a channel through which CIA-backed contras, including those profiting off the heroin trade, could hold and send money.[12] US-based oil and gas multinational corporations played a role as well. Unocal, which had a large part in constructing the Trans-Atlantic Pipeline that ran through Afghanistan from the Caspian Sea to the Indian Ocean, stood accused, by the French journalist Olivier Roy and others, of working with the ISI and Saudi-based Delta Oil to "finance the Taliban's seizure in Kabul in 1996".[13]

The core of men who founded and led Al Qaeda did so under the policy of US support in Afghanistan. US intelligence agencies protected several of them for decades leading up to 2001. Shortly after the 9/11 attacks, the intimate, multi-decade business relationship between the Bush and bin Laden families through the Carlyle Group became nearly popular knowledge.[14] Less known and understood are the backgrounds of several other

The Soviet Invasion in Retrospect", *International Politics* 37:2, 2000.

12 Scott, *The Road to 9/11*, 99.

13 Ibid., 166.

14 "'Ex-presidents club' gets fat on conflict", *The Observer*, 23 March 2003.

major Al Qaeda figures such as Omar Abdel Rahman and Ali Mohamed. These men were involved in the Al Kifah Center at the Faruk Mosque in Brooklyn, which for years doubled as a recruitment facility for the US's covert war effort in Afghanistan.[15] The CIA specifically allowed Abdel Rahman,[16] who got his political start as part of the anti-Nasserist fundamentalist movement in Egypt and eventually served as an inspiration to the 1993 bombers of the World Trade Center,[17] to enter the United States even when he was on a State Department list of people with ties to "terrorist organizations".[18] The important point here is not to insist that the US should take a more hardline approach to its already militarised borders; it is to illuminate that US borders are controlled on a political basis, with decisions around entry and exit often made with specific goals in mind.

Ali Mohamed's US connections were even more direct and more extensively documented. In 1981, "he completed a program for foreign officers offered by the Special Forces school at Fort Bragg," where he "learned unconventional warfare—the same training given Green Berets." At the same time, he joined Egyptian Islamic Jihad, which would become absorbed into al Qaeda, to

---

15   Andrew Cockburn, "A Special Relationship: The United States is teaming up with Al Qaeda, again", *Harper's Magazine*, January 2016.

16   "C.I.A. Officers Played Role In Sheik Visas", *New York Times*, 22 July 1993.

17   "In 'Jihad for America', Food for Uneasiness", *New York Times*, 21 November 1994.

18   "Islamic Leader on US Terrorist List Is in Brooklyn", *New York Times*, 16 December 1990.

which he eventually offered the very training program that he received in the US Army. When one of his students was tried in court in 1995 for allegedly plotting a series of attacks on New York City landmarks, including the World Trade Center, Mohamed's presence was requested as a witness for the defense. He was allowed to avoid testifying for unknown reasons. What is known is that, in addition to working for the US Army at Fort Bragg, he served as a lecturer at the John F. Kennedy Special Warfare Center and School, was an informant for the FBI, and in the 1980s worked as a "contact agent" for the CIA in Germany.[19] He was eventually arrested over the 1998 United States embassy bombings in Kenya and Tanzania.

Scott goes on to show that the forces the US backed in Afghanistan played an important role in Bosnia against Serbian forces and in Libya against the Qadhafi government. More recently, long after the publication of *The Road to 9/11*, the US tapped similar networks to carry out assaults for a similar covert war on Syria. The incredulity many self-described leftists showed in the early stages of that war—disbelief that the United States could be backing al Qaeda—only demonstrates how urgent Scott's careful documentation remains, despite much of it having fallen from collective memory.

*CoG, Rex 84, and the Patriot Act*

*The Road to 9/11* reminds us how 9/11 led directly to three interrelated and sustained US assaults on humanity:

---

19   Scott, *The Road to 9/11*, 152-153.

the Patriot Act, the Global War on Terror, and the invasion of Iraq. The new legal framework of the first in many ways facilitated the latter two. Scott highlights the Patriot Act as a breakthrough for the US ruling class, the culmination of a number of extreme anti-democratic attempts, trends, and systems that had long been present. It was, in other words, years in the making.

The modern protocol for US "Continuity of Government" (COG) orders was hammered out under the Truman Administration to meet concerns around a "civil defense emergency" amid possible nuclear war with the Soviet Union. These orders established that the United States government would continue to run, and the stars-and-stripes would carry on waving, even after a nuclear attack. This continuity plan was actually activated after the September 11 attacks. Vice President Cheney and his team worked under the auspices of COG—dubbed a "shadow government" in the mainstream press—in the months after the attack, when they entered the secret compound of the Raven Rock Mountain Complex, an underground nuclear bunker located inside a hollowed-out mountain in Pennsylvania.[20] Scott suggests that this was likely the period when the details of the Patriot Act were discussed and enumerated—that is, a long distance out of public view.

Especially disturbing in *The Road to 9/11* are the many listed instances when Cheney and his closest associates, particularly Donald Rumsfeld, expressed the desire, long

---

20 "Here's the gigantic, not-so-secret Pennsylvania bunker 'where nuclear war in the US would begin'", *Philly Voice*, 24 August 2017.

before 9/11, to suspend the US Constitution, nullify the Bill of Rights, and find a pretext to gain public support for a major land war.[21]

Cheney's aspiration to invade Iraq preceded any public claims about "weapons of mass destruction." A Judicial Watch release revealed that an NSC document pertaining to a review convened by a Cheney-led task force and dated February of 2001, contained a map of Iraq with the "Southwest... neatly divided... into nine 'Exploration Blocks'" for Iraqi oil.[22] Cheney, Rumsfeld, and Bush's advocacy for war on Iraq in fact dated back to their time as part of the Project for the New American Century (PNAC) in the 1990s, when they openly stated their desired "process of transformation, even if it brings revolutionary change, is likely to be a long one, absent some catastrophic and catalyzing event—like a new Pearl Harbour".[23] As Scott puts it, "The Bush agenda, in other words, depended on 9/11, or something like it".[24]

This thought process of using a catastrophe for purposes of tyranny and war had deeper, more widely spread roots in US statecraft. Scott cites as precedent Operation Northwoods, a proposed false flag terrorist

---

21  Here the spectre of the Vietnamese Revolution haunts the US imperialist psyche once again: Cheney knew very well that the US public would be hard pressed to support another major war after what happened in Vietnam.

22  Linda McQuaig, *It's the Crude, Dude: Greed, Gas, War, and the American Way* (Thomas Dunne Books, 2006), 79-80 (as cited in Scott, *Road to 9/11*, 189).

23  "Were 1998 Memos a Blueprint for War?", *ABC News*, 6 January 2006.

24  Scott, *Road to 9/11*, 193.

attack on US soil made in 1962 by the Department of Defense and the Joint Chiefs of Staff that intended to frame the Cuban government to manufacture support for a war on Cuba. (John F. Kennedy, the US President at the time, nixed the idea.) There was also the case of Rex 84, or Readiness Exercise 1984, which contained a plan to detain a large number of people deemed to be "national security threats" in the case of a National Emergency—potentially including anti-war activists in the event the United States carried out a direct invasion of Central America.

When the Patriot Act passed, it brought several aspects of the COG and Rex 84 frameworks to reality. The state's use of secret evidence against Arab and Muslim suspects became the norm, as did indefinite detentions in undisclosed locations. Up to 1,200 non-citizens were rounded up without due process over the course of the six months following 9/11, to say nothing of the establishment of black sites across the world and the torture mill at Guantanamo Bay.[25] This new legal regime heralded structural changes much more akin to a "coup" than the brief takeover of the Capitol building on January 6 2021. The Patriot Act should also be re-examined in light of the Trump Administration and its aftermath. Its passage into law demonstrates that it is not deep division, but rather *consensus* and *unity* that often foretell the most frightening structural changes in the US. Reflecting imperialist points of consensus, Trump entrenched Bush's structural changes ever more

---

25 "US Muslims see their American dreams die", *Financial Times*, 28 March 2002.

thoroughly with his appointment of Brett Kavanaugh to the Supreme Court. While much attention was justly brought to Kavanaugh for the credible allegations of sexual assault brought against him, less remembered at the time of his confirmation hearings was his role as an associate council for George W. Bush, when he assisted in passing the Patriot Act.

## *Empirical Imperialism Studies: Notes on Scott's Method*

Perhaps the most provocative chapters of *The Road to 9/11* are those dedicated to the event itself. For some readers, Scott's main contention about 9/11 will seem explosive: he makes the case "that Vice President Cheney is himself a suspect in the events of 9/11 who needs to be investigated further".[26] This contention, however, does not dwell on World Trade Center Building 7 or the possibility of controlled demolition. Scott demonstrates there is no need for anybody to play amateur physicist to reasonably doubt the US government's official summation of events. He is focused elsewhere, on the glaring omissions, evasions, and cover-ups in the 9/11 Commission Report. He furthermore departs from other 9/11 researchers insofar as he does not claim the report was made purely of lies. Rather, he insists that the report is for the most part credible, well cited and researched. It is precisely this general clarity that makes its omissions so flagrant.

Scott's close reading of the report, alongside his attention to contradictory testimonies excluded from

---

26  Scott, *Road to 9/11*, 194.

it, is much too detailed to recount here. His objections to the report revolve around two basic areas. The first is about a Joint Chiefs of Staff instruction dated June 1, 2001. The order overturned a previous directive from 1997 regarding "Aircraft Piracy (Hijacking) of Civil and Military Aircraft". The revision insisted the National Military Command Center (NMCC) "forward requests for [Department of Defense's] assistance to the Secretary of Defense for approval". This change meant that any attempt to intercept off-course airplanes ("'intercept" does not necessarily mean to use force) had to be personally approved by Donald Rumseld first.

The other discrepancy, or rather long list of discrepancies, pertains to Cheney's behaviour and whereabouts on the day of September 11, 2001. Most disconcertingly, the Commission Report omitted testimony from Former Secretary of Transportation Norman Mineta, NSC member Richard Clarke, and even from Cheney himself that contradicted its own chosen story about which time Cheney entered the Presidential Emergency Operations Center (PEOC) that day.[27] These exclusions are not trivial. The time span in question would have been when two of the most important orders of the day were given: "a Stand Down order that got all the planes down on the ground... and a Shoot Down order, to shoot down any emaining hijacked planes".[28]

The issues with this part of the Commission Report

---

27 Ralph Lopez, "9/11 report testimony altered to hide Cheney role in Pentagon hit", *Digital Journal*, 2 February 2015.

28 Lecture delivered by Peter Dale Scott on JFK and 9/11 in Dallas on November 18, 2006.

Imperialism and the Deep State 45

only get more troubling from there, and readers are advised to approach these chapters from *The Road to 9/11* with an open mind. Corporate media have worked tirelessly during the 20 years since 2001, aided by the all-purpose pejorative of "truther," to make any questioning or scepticism about the official US story about 9/11 utterly radioactive to one's reputation. Often times, left-wing and right-wing lines of thinking get lumped together as targets of a larger assault on "conspiracy theories," which as a category has become shorthand uniting any and all forms of opposition to the US-led postwar order—or, as Twitter recently put it to justify one of its censorship sprees, those "undermining faith in the NATO alliance and its stability".[29] If powerful sectors employ the term "conspiracy theory" loosely and consistently enough, along with kindred terms such as "trutherism," anti-imperialist theories on one hand, and anti-Semitic and esoteric views on another, become equally condemnable under similar terms of engagement. The tactic ends up aiding the popularization of "the horseshoe theory" for the benefit of the very institutions chiefly responsible for the international inequality before us today.

The empirical record of the events of 9/11 remains pertinent on this front. In September of 2020, *The Wall Street Journal* linked "9/11 Trutherism" to "more recent conspiracist movements such as QAnon".[30] What is fascinating in this particular instance is the utter lack of

---

29 "Disclosing networks of state-linked information operations", *Twitter Safety*, 23 February 2021.

30 "9/11 and the Rise of the New Conspiracy Theorists", *Wall Street Journal*, 10 September 2020.

interest in any of the specific details in question. Under these standards, it is enough that one doubts official truths. *In what way* one doubts those truths, and *why*, is treated as irrelevant. What *The Wall Street Journal* and its co-presses thereby offer is a rigor-free denunciation made in the name of rigor. By this very standard, many of the mainstream corporate newspapers would have to be censured for irresponsible conspiracy theorizing. For example, in March of 2002, *The Guardian*, which on the whole egregiously aided and abetted the Anglo-American invasion of Iraq, published a piece mocking "Uncle Sam's lucky finds", rightly insisting that the US's claim to have found Mohammed Atta's intact passport in the post-inferno rubble of the World Trade buildings was plainly ridiculous.[31] Twenty years of propaganda has ensured that even the self-described political radicals of today rarely doubt the US empire's claims about 9/11 as brazenly as a liberal *Guardian* writer did at the time.

The question often arises as to whether establishing the truth of 9/11 is even important. Scott's research method and intellectual project depends on the idea that, yes, the empirical record of what happened on 9/11, and other casus belli like it, very much does matter. Scott comes from a school of thought in which *facts* are deemed essential, even if they are not in themselves conclusive. Even figures such as Noam Chomsky, who worked with Scott on a collection about the Pentagon Papers, and Alexander Cockburn, both of whom would affirm in theory that empirical research is important in laying bear the record of imperialism's assaults on humanity, have

---

31 "Uncle Sam's lucky finds", *The Guardian*, 19 March 2002.

argued that some of Scott's preoccupations constitute intellectual and political rabbit holes. This debate swirled before 9/11, around the topic of the JFK assassination, another one of Scott's objects of inquiry. In the 1990s, when the debates about JFK reached a fever pitch, Michael Parenti harshly rebuked both Chomsky and Cockburn's eye rolling:

> What is so compelling about the JFK assassination is how nakedly the gangster nature of the state is revealed. It is an awakening. And to know the truth about the JFK assassination is to create a delegitimizing force that calls into question the entire state system and the entire social order it represents.[32]

If these principles are then applied to 9/11, establishing a truthful, accurate record of the day's events should only become *more* important, not less, especially in light of the magnitude of the wars launched afterwards. After all, exposures of the outright fabrications of the Gulf of Tonkin incident proved hugely important to the growth of the movement against the US war on Vietnam.

It is important for as many people as possible who notice official lies and spot signs of conspiracy to see that the political left is honest and courageous enough to acknowledge them. The state, after all, really does lie. The media do lie. Moreover, these entities conspire together. And the average person at least knows enough to know the media are liars. This is why anti-capitalist critique should never be limited to analysing abstract processes.

---

32   Michael Parenti, "JFK Assassination & the Gangster State", *KBOO Radio*, 21 November 2017.

Individuals, specific institutions, and concrete plans and funding streams punctuate how people experience the rule of capital, just as they provide movements with strategic targets.

*A Final Critique*

It is possible for Scott's findings to be misappropriated, as part of a larger phenomenon in which right-wing media obfuscate accurate reports of imperial conspiracy, a process wherein the principal *targets* of these conspiracies become recast as *accomplices* to them. Through this trick of reversal, what should be explained by class analysis instead becomes an attempt to promote racist hostilities.

For an example of how this phenomenon works, look no further than the radio show host Alex Jones, who went from the margins of public access television in Austin, Texas, in the 1990s, to being a nationally known quantity and invited press guest of the White House during the Trump presidency. For years, Jones propagated the idea that the Federal Emergency Management Agency (FEMA) was planning to imprison Americans in concentration camps after the US declared martial law in the wake of a national disaster or emergency. According to Jones' variation on this theory, the targets would be people like him, "constitutionalists" and "patriots." In his reference to "FEMA Camps," Jones was in fact inverting a true story—one Scott details at the end of *The Road to 9/11*. With Operation Endgame, the Department of Homeland Security "envisaged a plan for FEMA to round up and detain four hundred thousand imaginary 'refugees,' in the context of 'uncontrolled population movements' over the Mexican border into the United States".[33] The plan was chartered in September 2001; it was ultimately co-organised with US Immigration and Customs Enforcement (ICE), another creation of the War on Terror. In other words, the camps were real, and Alex Jones and his ilk became ardent defenders of them once Trump was their steward; the targets were to be the working-class victims of US wars and plunder.

The answer to this problem cannot be to forego forensic probes into imperial conspiracy. It is important, rather, to add theoretical depth to the study of deep politics as it pertains to class. Scott is an honest liberal—and not a Marxist. He does attest that he over time became convinced that the deep state networks he was following were acting in the interests of private profit. Such an affirmation does not itself, unfortunately, adequately grapple with the classic questions around how profit is accumulated: surplus, use and exchange values; labour time; and resource and land use. This absence causes serious errors of judgment in both Scott's descriptions and prescriptions of the US.

In terms of description, Scott's suggested turning points, whether dated 1945 with the emergence of the National Security Establishment, or 1963 with the Kennedy assassination, are relatively late developments compared to the very establishment of the US involving chattel slavery and the violent eradication of the Native peoples. There are serious ramifications to such a slight, such as severing the connections between the modern

---

33  Scott, *Road to 9/11*, 240-241.

and early US war states. The empire began with a war for land well before 1945. Consequently, the architects of the postwar national security establishment were overwhelmingly family beneficiaries of colonial industries. The Bush family, the object of some of Scott's gravest charges, seized their primitive capital through the slave trade in the merchant-run northeast before re-establishing themselves as Texas oil cowboys.[34]

These necessary criticisms of Peter Dale Scott's work are more so suggestion for *how* it is best read: alongside Marxist theorists of imperialism and global value transfers such as Arghiri Emmanuel and Samir Amin; and anti-colonial and anti-imperialist theorists of revolution such as Amilcar Cabral and Walter Rodney. Otherwise, Scott's corpus as a whole, but especially *The Road to 9/11*, serves as an essential anchor for any serious curriculum addressing the crimes of US imperialism, complete with the necessary courage to doubt and militantly rebuke state lies as they are being told. And his work is self-sufficient on at least one front: it provides all one needs to refute any propagandistic attempts to isolate the legacies of US presidential administrations from the other, or from the systems in which they all operate.

---

34   "The Ancestral Link Between the Bush Family and the Slave Trade Is Confirmed", *The Atlantic*, 20 June 2013.

# Mutiny in Vietnam: Richard Boyle's *Flower of the Dragon: The Breakdown of the US Army in Vietnam*

Marlon Ettinger

The American journalist Richard Boyle witnessed combat for the first time in South Vietnam. It was 1965 and he was, by his own admission, simply a reporter looking for stories of heroism. For Boyle, the Green Berets were perfect: ready, tough, brave, idealistic. They were the archetypal American heroes. And they made good copy.

So too did the Rangers in the Army of the Republic of Vietnam (ARVN). "Crack professionals, mercenaries in psychedelic rainbow-patterned helmets and day-glo red scarves," they "had power and they knew it." That power came from their backing by the United States, whose military advisers and material kept the puppet regime in the South in power in the face of mass public discontent. Boyle went out with them in February 1965. In the Mekong Delta, the Rangers stormed a village in Bạc Liêu, taking all military aged men as prisoners.

An ARVN Ranger captain and an American adviser

started interrogating the prisoners. They were all about 14 or 15 years old, and they wouldn't talk. One of the Rangers kicked the boy in the head hard, bringing blood to his mouth. He wouldn't talk. He was kicked again. He still wouldn't talk. A sergeant had two rangers hold him while he stuck his bayonet into the boy's belly. The boy whimpered but didn't say anything. He wouldn't talk. A sergeant hacked away with his blade until the boy died. But he didn't give up a scrap of information.

"If I had paid more attention to the faces of the Vietcong prisoners at Bac Liêu or to the way the young men died there, I might have seen things differently," Boyle reflected in his 1972 book *Flower of the Dragon: The Breakdown of the US Army in Vietnam*. "But as America marched off to war against the 'little people,' I marched with her."

He'd managed to snap a picture of the soldier standing over the dead boy, captioned "VIETCONG PRISONER KILLED BY RANGERS," but nobody would buy it.

"Later, back in the States, I sold the photograph with a different caption: 'RANGER KILLS VIETCONG IN FIREFIGHT.' It was my first copout of the war."

*Foreign Correspondent*

Richard Boyle was an archetypical American war reporter. He'd watched Jimmy Cagney movies as a kid and wanted to be a journalist when he grew up. He'd learned on a series of small newspapers early in his career that the worst thing a reporter could do was get involved in his story. And he'd wanted to see what war was like. So he'd saved up his "meager reporter's pay" and gotten a visa to go play war correspondent in Vietnam.

There, the US military was the source of almost all stories that American correspondents wrote. As long as you played along, didn't take pictures of prisoners being tortured, and kept your mouth shut, you'd keep your press card. Without it you couldn't get on Army bases or rides on helicopters, and you'd be stuck, and you couldn't work.

"If you went along with the Army it was a good life..." wrote Boyle. "So I went out, took pictures of people dying, came back and sold them, took my money, and went out again. The more suffering, the better the pictures."

Boyle's eventual conversion against the war wasn't the result of anything monumental. He left Vietnam in 1965, hospitalised with hepatitis. He opened a magazine and saw a story about a good soldier friend of his who had been killed. Another war correspondent friend was killed by a landmine around the same time. This made him angry. But it didn't turn him against the war. Instead, he began speaking out in favour of the war. "I was a hawk," wrote Boyle, "and I stayed a hawk until 1969, when I returned to Vietnam."

Before his return, Boyle was peddling an early version of the reactionary spit-on-veteran myth, in which the war was supposedly lost because of dirty hippies jeering at iron-jawed vets betrayed by their country and the crazy kids who greeted them with free love, drugs, and the pill.[1]

---

1   This was a fabricated narrative, invented to drive a wedge between the GI movement and the public. In the 1988 book *The*

Yet, between the liberal shoot and cry stories on one side and the spit-on-veteran myth on the other, in *Flower of the Dragon*, Boyle gives an excellent and deep introduction into a third trend within the largely conscripted Army that was sent to Vietnam. It's a history that's been obscured.[2]

When Boyle returned, he started hearing about Ben Het, a Special Forces camp deep in the Central Highlands, where Cambodia, Laos, and Vietnam met. The 66th Vietnamese regiment, one of the North's most elite units, was laying siege to this outpost. By 1969, a year after North Vietnam's successful Tet Offensive,[3] Vietnamizaton was in full effect - so it was the ARVN fighting to hold Ben Het, with just a handful of American troops with them.[4]

---

*Spitting Image*, the sociologist Jerry Lembcke documented how this narrative was spread in Hollywood and the print media, with the backing of the Nixon administration, despite there being no substantiated media accounts of a veteran ever being spat upon. Lembcke instead documents accounts reported in the media of pro-war activists spitting on anti-war demonstrators, and cites a 1971 poll that shows that 94% of Vietnam veterans reported a "friendly" welcome when they came back to the United States.

2   Joel Geier, "Vietnam: The Soldier's Revolt," *International Socialist Review*, Issue 9 (August-September 2000).

3   So-called because it was launched to coincide with the 1968 Lunar New Year celebrations when most South Vietnamese soldiers would be on leave. The campaign inflicted many American casualties and turned the tide of American public opinion against the war.

4   This policy was provoked by domestic discontent about American deaths in the war. In response, Secretary of Defense Melvin Laird introduced a policy to "expand, equip, and train South Vietnam's forces and assign to them an ever-increasing

Boyle went to Ben Het to find the same types of stories he'd looked for when he'd been in the country four years earlier.

But *Flower of the Dragon* isn't filled with copy about those "lantern-jawed" Marines and their exploits of American heroism. Instead, he found soldiers exhausted with the war and no desire to fight.

"Hey," one shouted to him. "Tell the people back home to get us out of here. We're losing too many people in this stupid, useless war."

"It was hardly what I expected American troops to say," wrote Boyle.

He gathered around a dozen troops to see if this was the general sentiment or just the opinion of one man.

"Does what he says go for all of you?" Boyle asked.

"'Sure does,' said another, and the rest of them nodded."

*Class Struggle*

Boyle kept collecting stories of the side of the war that the Army was eager to keep out of the press. One recurring theme was the "grunts" vs. the "lifers"; the conscripted men and the officer class fighting a low-level shadow war, mounting in intensity year after year.

These eruptions against the ruling officer class began with simple insubordination, but accelerated into combat refusal, striking officers, even killing them, and a rising sense of mutiny. There was a similar sentiment from the

---

combat role, at the same time steadily reducing the number of US combat troops." This reduced American deaths drastically, with casualties dropping by 95% over three years.

side of the officers—if the soldiers were getting ready to fight against them, they'd hit back just as hard. They were already notorious for not caring whether their infantrymen lived or died. Because the path to a plush Army career required combat time for promotion, and because there was such a glut of officers in Vietnam, desperate for a conventional war to advance their careers, they would send conscripted men into battle as fast as they could during their tours.

Combat refusal began, officers were hit, and desertion started to rear its head. A series of court-martials were drawn up to try to suffocate this movement in the crib. Boyle went to report on a series of these proceedings and found that this sentiment was widespread. Even the Army lawyers prosecuting the court-martials hated the war and the Army hierarchy. "It all added up to one thing," Boyle wrote. "They'd had enough."

"'You know,' General Theodore Mataxis told Boyle, 'our army is like the army of the Austro-Hungarian empire in 1917.' As defeat loomed, that army, made up of various ethnic minorities - Czechs, Slavs and Poles as well as Austrians and Hungarians—began to break up into bickering and rebellious factions. There was an obvious parallel, Mataxis seemed to be saying, with the rise of the black liberation movement in the US Army."

One GI at the Southern coastal city of Nha Trang told Boyle that the basic division within the Army pitted the "heads"[5] and the black GIs against the lifers on the

---

5   This was a reference specifically to the White GIs who did drugs, but was also a general catch-all term for any of the white soldiers with a countercultural, anti-war, or otherwise subversive perspective.

other side. "The revolution is coming. There is no way to stop it," he told Boyle. "This place is going to blow, the only question is when. And when it does, every GI is going to have to take a stand. Either with us or with the lifers."

*South Vietnam*

One of the virtues of Boyle's book is that, while it focuses on the GI movement, it doesn't leave out the South Vietnamese anti-war movement. Instead, it makes a connection between the two and a compelling case for their importance in ultimately ending the American invasion.

In 1971, the class struggle was intensifying across South Vietnam. A massive student protest movement was rising up against the American puppet dictator Nguyen Văn Thieu, who was running in elections he had rigged to exclude any opposition. His government was run in the service of the landlords, and enjoyed essentially no support from anybody outside of this rentier class. A seething, raw component in the South Vietnamese peace movement was the veterans who had come home from the front. The class struggle in the ARVN was intense.[6] In the first half of 1966, over 81% of personnel losses in the ARVN were from desertion.[7] Whole battalions would melt away after combat, with the conscripted men

---

6   A 1966 CIA Intelligence Memorandum observed that "the nearly continuous rise in military desertions, dating from at least 1962, constitutes the most serious manpower problem…of the South Vietnamese Armed forces".

7   CIA Intelligence Memorandum, 1966, 15.

leaving only officers and NCOs behind.

Thieu responded to the growing uprising the only way he was able to: with massive repression. There were some 200,000 political prisoners in the country - in the notorious Con Son prison they were stuffed in so-called "tiger cages," where twelve people would share a single cell.

Boyle describes how deserters from the ARVN led their own movement against the war, organizing protests in Saigon, and reaching out to active soldiers urging them to desert too. Ahead of 1970, a Christmas Eve peace march was organised to call for an end to the war on February 5th, the date of Tet, the Lunar New Year in Vietnam.

> The risks, of course, were great. The American Army brass would do everything it could to stop it… there had never before been a demonstration of both GIs and South Vietnamese. If the Hoat Vu [Thieu's secret police] or National Police fired… and shot American soldiers, the repercussions would be enormous.

Despite a military media blackout from *Stars & Stripes* and AFVN, the Army television channel, about 15 uniformed GIs showed up, along with a dozen other Americans. Boyle came not as a reporter but as a participant. The role of the GIs was critical for the march. The South Vietnamese anti-war movement needed news cameras, and only American participants would bring them. The GIs and the newsman's cameras would provide some small protection to the demonstrators. The American military knew this, so they brought military police to disperse the GIs.

The American press corps at the march ignored the demonstration, or if they did report it they were censored. But the South Vietnamese press printed it boldly, as they started mounting more and more open resistance to the Thieu regime.

In defiance of the media blackout, an Army broadcaster named Bob Lawrence reported on the cover up of the demonstration. He was court martialled on a trumped-up charge, but the broadcast brought more GIs into the anti-Thieu movement, which heated up and, following an abortive student-led demonstration in January, led to widespread rioting in the spring of 1970.

The country was ready to boil over. The North Vietnamese Army was ready to take advantage of the situation. General Võ Nguyên Giáp, the military genius behind the North's strategy, prepared an offensive down Route 22 towards Saigon. The offensive was to coincide with Thieu's sham elections.

*The Road to Saigon*

There were three hurdles the North Vietnamese forces would need to clear on their way to Saigon: Krek, Tây Ninh, and Firebase Pace. If any link of this chain broke, they would have an open road to Saigon. Firebase Pace, defended by four long range American artillery rifles, just 300 meters from the Cambodian border, was the most important to defend. The Americans were desperate to prevent it from falling. But if they sent too many American troops to hold the base, high casualties were inevitable, and they weren't willing to stomach the domestic unrest this would produce.

This was the impact of the anti-war movement, and its effect on North Vietnamese strategic considerations was significant. A document captured in 1969 by the Pentagon's Systems Analysis Office laid out this logic. The 1969 spring offensive, it said, had been "a significant and great strategic victory... we killed more Americans than we did in the 1968 spring offensive. [It] upset Nixon's plan, because US forces were heavily hit and their weakening puppet army could no longer provide support for the implementation of neocolonialism. The anti-war movement in the US flared up again strongly demanding the withdrawal of US troops... For each additional day's stay the US must sustain more casualties...".[8]

South Vietnamese troops were supposed to defend the base, but there was little evidence that they had much commitment to fighting either. The American officers were worried. They knew that they couldn't get the South Vietnamese conscripts to fight. Still, they figured they would be able to get their own men to go, as long as they didn't lose too many. But the North Vietnamese troops were battle-hardened and hunkered down. Taking tunnels was a suicide mission with little chance of success. Nevertheless, the officers decided to send out fifteen men. If the radar reports were accurate, they were probably going out against thousands of North Vietnamese troops.

The standard story of heroism would have the troops

---

8   William Shawcross, *Sideshow: Kissinger, Nixon and the Destruction of Cambodia* (Simon & Schuster, 1987), 109.

go out, doomed and aware that they were doomed, to wipe out the North Vietnamese mortar teams. Then the South Vietnamese would be rallied by the courage of the American example, and lay their lives down defending the base against the communists.

But Vietnam wasn't a movie set. It was a real place with real people—and that is what's perhaps most refreshing about Boyle's book. He wrote it when it was happening, and the realism it portrays is not the phony profundity of Hollywood's depiction of the war, where morally uncertain, dark and confused fare passes for high verisimilitude. Boyle chose instead to look at what he saw and print it, and crucially, he took a side. The officers were monsters, the war effort was murderous and genocidal, and there's nothing heroic about outnumbered Americans defending a position in service to imperialism and landlordism. What happened next, though, was heroic in a way.

*"I Ain't Going"*

As the fifteen men who had been chosen to go out into the night were being given their orders, one of them, named Chris, didn't listen to the instructions. "Go fuck yourself," he said. "I ain't going."

Five of the other soldiers joined. That crippled the mission. They couldn't send 9 soldiers out into the night. A court martial was drawn up against the six refusers. But 30 other soldiers got together and voted on it - they weren't going to let that happen. A veteran soldier with a Zapata moustache, Al Grana, told Boyle "We ain't lettin' the lifers fuck over those guys." They drew up a petition to send home with Boyle to explain why they weren't fighting. Then they set about getting the signatures of the majority of the company. When the officers tried to reassert discipline, they were met with bored insubordination. An officer tried to get them to clean their guns. "Oh shit, who needs this," one of the grunts said, then left. The rest of them followed, until the officer was left standing alone awkwardly inspecting his own rifle.

"I wish we could let them know we have nothing against them," said a grunt about the North Vietnamese soldiers. So they decided to stop fighting. "The men agreed, and passed the word to the other platoons: nobody fires unless fired upon. As of about 1100 hours on October 10, 1971, the men of Bravo Company, 1/12, First Cav Division, declared their own private ceasefire with the North Vietnamese. For the first time since they got to Pace, it was all quiet on the Cambodian Front."

"To the grunts, it wasn't the North Vietnamese who were the enemies, it was the lifers… the grunts had the power." Just like the South Vietnamese soldiers, they weren't fighting anymore. "The grunts… had the machine guns, the light assault weapons. The grunts outgunned the lifers by about 30 to 1… If it came down to it most of them might join the Bravo Company rebellion rather than side with the lifers."

A conscript mused about the success of their informal ceasefire. "Today we haven't done nothin' but sit here and wait, and they haven't done anything either. It makes you kind of wonder…"

By this point, the rebellious soldiers had gained the support of most of the other soldiers in their company. Over 50 percent of them were bordering on open mutiny and had signed the petition. Boyle went back to the United States and got the story out to the international press. When the story broke, the Army pulled Bravo company out and relented on the court martials and rotated Delta Company onto Firebase. But then Delta Company heard about the revolt. When a patrol was ordered, 20 men refused to go out. The Army was forced to abandon their base. The road to Saigon was open.

*Fragging and Domestic Revolt*

While the mutiny at Firebase Pace is perhaps the most dramatic example in Boyle's book, resistance took all sorts of forms. The most notorious and widespread way that this manifested was in the ubiquitous practice of fragging. Fragging was a way for soldiers to institute discipline on officers who were sending them off to fight when they didn't want to. They were a semi-formal process of soldier enforced discipline: officers were warned before the fragging took place and given a chance to change their orders. Then, a smoke grenade would be rolled under their bed as a final warning.

In 1972, an Army judge named Capt. Barry Steinberg told Eugene Linden in the *Saturday Review* that this way of controlling officers was "deadly effective."

"Through intimidation by threats—verbal and written—and scare stories, fragging is influential to the point that virtually all officers and NCOs have to take into account the possibility of fragging before giving an order to the men under them," concluded Linden.[9]

GI underground papers at home played a role too: one told conscripted soldiers not to desert. Instead, it urged them to "go to Vietnam and kill your commanding officer."

The anti-war movement at home also didn't confine itself to nonviolent tactics. In response to Stanford University voting to allow a Reserve Officers' Training Corps program on its campus, riots caused $200,000 in damage to buildings. A militant group on the West Coast carried out large-scale armoury thefts against army bases in Oakland. And three soldiers were indicted in 1970 for dynamiting the telephone lines, power plant, and water works of a base in Wisconsin.[10]

The story about the informal ceasefire at Firebase Pace was a representative and dramatic moment, but by no means unique. In 1969, a company in the 196th Light Infantry Brigade sat down on the battlefield. Later in the year, a rifle company in the 1st Air Cavalry Division refused to go forward on a dangerous trail, in a dramatic moment aired on CBS-TV.[11] At the Paris Peace Talks in 1971, the North Vietnamese released a statement that they had ordered their own units not to engage with American units that didn't attack them. And they also claimed that they had American defectors who had

---

9   Eugene Linden, "Fragging and Other Withdrawal Symptoms," *Saturday Review*, 8 January 1972, 12.

10   Col. Robert D. Heinl, Jr., *Armed Forces Journal*, 7 June 1971, 30-38.

11   Ibid.

joined their ranks.[12]

*Conscript Soldiers, Imperial Shadow Wars*

In a frank interview with General Mataxis, Boyle received a grim diagnosis of the effect the breakdown of morale and the rise of insurrection had on the American Armed Forces. "We had a good army then," Mataxis said of the beginning of the war in 1965. "It's been the opposite of Korea. There we went in with a bad army and came out with a good one. In Vietnam we went in with a good army and came out with a bad one."

Mataxis also confirmed to Boyle that the fragging campaign against the officers—conscripts against the lifers—had reached such a worrying tempo that the officer class began taking matters into their own hands. A counter-fragging offensive was launched. GIs that had attacked the officers were targeted for reprisal. The campaign began taking on the character of a low level hot civil war, a smouldering insurrection at the heart of the American armed forces.

"What Mataxis was saying was something else" from just scattered reprisals though, said Boyle. "He strongly hinted at a sort of underground movement of lifers, a kind of white guard like the secret organization of Czarist officers who fought the Bolsheviks during the Russian civil war. The lifers knew who the leaders of the GI anti-war movement were, Mataxis said, and his own junior officers knew "whom to get."

Mataxis also spoke about the fear the generals had

---

12   Ibid.

about the anti-Americanism in South Vietnam. It was, Boyle wrote, at "an all-time high... nobody knew if the ARVN could really be counted on to help." This worry was so significant that at the time of Thieu's sham elections, US high command ordered American troops be confined to their bases, for fear of a massacre by the South Vietnamese people.

## *The United States vs. Vietnam Vets*

There were also worries about how the mass of disillusioned veterans would behave at home. Boyle reported some of the sentiment they shared with him when he was back in Washington D.C.

"I killed three hundred VC, man," he told me, "and you know what I found out when I got back here? I killed the wrong people. Ain't *that* a mind blower?"

Then there was Jim, who'd had a chunk blown out of his leg. He told Boyle he felt betrayed by the United States, "sent to bleed in a war to make millionaires richer."

"There's something happening, man, it's in the air, I swear it," Boyle wrote. "There are about two million vets all over this country, and a hell of a lot of them are getting it together."

He related a conversation he'd heard from a few bitter veterans at home named Cheyenne, Beagle, and Jim.

"'Shit, man,' Cheyenne said, 'Nixon's the same as King George.'"

"'Right on,'" Beagle replied. "'The people of this country have been fucked over, cheated, and lied to by all of them. Johnson's the same as Nixon, and Nixon's the same as Muskie or Humphrey: they all want to screw you."

"'That's what this whole war was,' Jim said, 'a big ripoff. Fifty-five thousand guys died to make some people rich.'"

Boyle reflects on this at the end of his book. "It was the troops who pulled off the French Revolution," he muses, "and it was rebelling soldiers and sailors who stormed the Winter Palace in Russia in 1917. If there are too many more Kent States, or Jackson States, or Atticas, and the people revolt, I think the grunts are going to be with the people, not with Nixon and the lifers. And I think the Pentagon knows it."[13]

---

13  On May 4th, 1970, 4 students were killed and 9 injured at Kent State University during a protest against the US invasion of Cambodia. They were shot and killed by National Guardsmen in a premeditated act. 11 days later, just after midnight on May 15th, Mississippi highway patrolmen and municipal police shot at students protesting in front of a girl's dormitory at Jackson State College, a predominantly black school. They were protesting racism in the state government and the US invasion of Cambodia. One college student and a local high school senior were killed, and 10 others were wounded. The street they were shot on was called Lynch Street. A year later, on September 9th, 1971, at the Attica Correctional Facility near Buffalo, New York, a prison revolt began which demanded better conditions and the removal of the racist warden. The prison, whose inmates were 54% black, was staffed by all-white prison guards, notorious for their racism and mistreatment of the inmates. Five days after the revolt began, Governor Nelson Rockefeller launched a "military attack" to retake the prison. 31 prisoners and 8 guards were killed in an assault led by a heavily armed 1000-strong force of National Guardsmen, prison guards, and local police. News reports initially claimed that the guards' throats were slashed by prisoners, but autopsies showed that it was gunfire from Rockefeller's assault force which had actually killed them.

Maybe this was where the twin narratives of the stab in the back and the spit-on-vet came from: the fear from the US ruling class of a mass of embittered, disillusioned young men with military training who'd developed, in the jungles and mountains of Vietnam, a class consciousness which crystallised the antagonisms the United States and the world was (and remains) riven by into a simple formula: lifer vs. grunt. Conscript vs. officer.

Back home there were a bevy of obstacles erected against the furthering of this political education. The spit-on-veteran was a myth, but one targeted at rupturing growing bonds between the G.I. movement and the rest of American society. And it wasn't hippies or the New Left who "betrayed" the GI movement by pushing class conscious and politically developed veterans out of their ranks. Boyle writes in his book how radical veterans were viewed as politically unreliable to the prerogatives of a thoroughly bourgeoisified US society. In New York State, the Chamber of Commerce printed a pamphlet instructing businessmen not to hire veterans. The pamphlet claimed this was because veterans were all junkies.

But maybe this wasn't the reason. Maybe so many Vietnam veterans were pushed into homelessness and addiction, out of jobs and onto the streets, because they represented a huge mass who hated the war and were ready to revolt.

And maybe it was because they represented a disillusioned, oppositional force that might not be able to be whipped into the discipline of the labour regime back at home.

A March 1978 article in *The Atlantic* called "Soldiers of Misfortune" detailed how the administrative apparatus of the state ensured that these potentially revolutionary subjects were immiserated, isolated, and alienated.[14] In the fall of 1974, Vietnam-era veterans accounted for a full ten percent of prison inmates. Up to 150,000 men were given dishonourable discharges, a highly undesirable status for most employers. Anything but a fully honourable discharge made businesses wary. The most common reason for a general or dishonourable discharge was "character and behaviour disorders."

Even soldiers who received fully honourable discharges could be designated a "misfit" if their discharge forms were stamped with the code "SPN," marking around 200,000 veterans politically unreliable and potentially subversive. The military claimed these codes were used only for internal military use, but the *Atlantic* reported there was "overwhelming evidence that the key to deciphering the codes fell into the hands of many civilian employers."

Not only did the SPN number ward employers off from hiring politically unreliable GIs, but it also denied them access to treatment and education. SPN marked GIs weren't allowed access to VA drug treatment facilities, they weren't able to go to school on the GI bill, and they were excluded from VA hospitals. If the vision of the Vietnam vet in popular culture is a drug addict huddled on the street in a heap of rags, it's more likely than not that he'd be the recipient of an SPN.

---

14   Tracy Kidder, "Soldiers of Misfortune", *The Atlantic*, March 1978.

What this all meant was that, in Vietnam, the US military saw subversive soldiers as a threat to their anti-communist mission. As links were forged between the North Vietnamese Army, the peace movement, and the GI movement, America's calculus in Indochina shifted, with the threat of mutiny among the enlisted men significantly constraining the operational capacity of the officer class. Then, back at home, anxious about the possibility of soldier revolts and a militant black power movement, GIs were caught up in the drug war launched against black radicals by the state,[15] and were further excluded from the national body by administrative coercion.

*Lessons Learned*

The war ended, and the United States learned their lesson. Never again would they trust a conscript army in a colonial war. Paul McCloskey, a nominally anti-war California Republican who entered Richard Boyle's record of the Firebase Pace grunts into the Congressional Record, articulated well the fear that the GI soldier revolts represented to the US ruling class.

"There is a growing danger of confrontation between American troops and their officers," McCloskey told a press conference at the Capitol building in 1971, "which could prove ugly and disastrous."

Ugly and disastrous for the American Empire, no doubt. Reading Boyle's book helps us excavate a moment in the history of the American military

---

15 "Aide says Nixon's war on drugs targeted blacks, hippies", *CNN*, 24 March 2016.

where its commanders were terrified that a growing consciousness in its conscripted members could be hitched to the ideological leadership of a movement ready to cut off the head of the snake of the American Empire. All successful revolutions are marked by the mass breakdown of discipline within the national or Imperial armed forces. The United States military read its history, and knew the danger that a conscript revolt in a colonial war could pose. The American ruling class applied these lessons and managed to hold off a similar process from being carried out in America's Indochinese twilight. Boyle's book is a remarkable document of just what it is they were so afraid of.

# Penetrating Curtains of Deceit: I.F. Stone's *The Hidden History of the Korean War*

Tim Beal and Gregory Elich

When the American journalist, I.F. Stone, published *The Hidden History of the Korean War* at the height of the military conflict in 1952, its message did not find a warm welcome at home. In a period of unhinged anti-communist fervour, mainstream media took little or no notice of such an iconoclastic work, and whatever impact it had would have to wait for a later time, when the Vietnam War encouraged more scepticism about the motives underlying US war-making. Even so, mainstream receptiveness to critical analyses of US war-making in subsequent decades has not substantially improved, and Stone's book has spent far more years in out-of-print oblivion than in ready availability.[1]

As Stone explains in his book, he realised that he could be persuasive to a domestic audience only if he "utilised material which could not be challenged by

---

1 Originally published by Monthly Review Press it has appeared in various editions, including a Kindle one.

those who accept the official American government point of view".[2] Consequently, Stone limited his sources to official US and UN documents and American and British newspapers. The approach he adopted was to compare sources and take note of discrepancies, omissions, emphases, and framing to arrive at a more accurate assessment of events. For alert readers, the book continues to serve as an object lesson in analysing mainstream media, particularly regarding America's continual war-making.

Stone illustrates how the eruption of full-scale war on the Korean Peninsula advanced US geopolitical interests and those of its key Asian clients. The country had been unnaturally divided by the US in 1945 in order to protect its control of Japan and to provide a beachhead on the Asian mainland. The division was carried out without any consultations with the Korean people and was opposed across the political spectrum, which made the resulting reunification war virtually inevitable. The conflict itself boosted President Truman's "get tough policy", which Stone points out "required the maintenance of tension at home and abroad, in order to make politically possible the imposition of a heavier burden of armament and taxes, the rearmament of Western Germany and Japan, and the imposition of ever greater restrictions on trade with the Soviet bloc".[3] The war also provided the pretext for Truman to quadruple the military budget and create a militarised economy and foreign policy that remain with

---

2   I.F. Stone, *The Hidden History of the Korean War* (Little, Brown & Company, 1988), xxi.

3   Ibid., 104.

us to this day.

The war made permanent the US military presence in the Asia-Pacific, thereby removing any prospect of Taiwan's reunification with China. It also encouraged the deposed Chinese nationalist leader Chiang Kai-shek to lobby conservative American political figures to support his goal of launching a cross-channel attack on the mainland from his base on Taiwan. For South Korean President Syngman Rhee, US involvement meant that he could continue in office in the southern part of Korea with the prospect of taking over the northern part, despite his deep unpopularity.

One of the book's central themes concerns US policy towards the socialist bloc, where conservative politicians and General Douglas MacArthur pursued goals that clashed with Truman's. "Truman wanted something which was neither war nor peace [with China and the Soviet Union]. MacArthur wanted war".[4] MacArthur's habitual insubordination frequently crossed the line into acts intended to present Truman with a fait accompli of a political nature that would be awkward to undo. "It cannot be said that MacArthur hid his views", Stone writes. "His view was that the time had come for the US by military force to oppose Communism everywhere in Asia".[5] Stone documents MacArthur's myriad machinations in eye-opening detail, noting that he "was trying to drag the US and United Nations into war with China and Russia. He was trying to start World War III".[6]

---

4 Ibid., 106.

5 Ibid., 92.

6 Ibid.

One of McArthur's more provocative actions came in August 1950, as US and British airplanes crossed over into Chinese territory to strafe airfields and railways. A month and a half later, American fighter planes attacked an airport in Soviet territory. The US formally refused to accept the Soviet letter of protest, responding that it was a question for the United Nations to consider, as MacArthur ostensibly operated under the name of the UN, even though that organization had no say in any of his actions.[7] Similarly, when eleven American fighter planes shot down a Soviet bomber flying on a training mission over its own territory, the US refused to accept a protest note, using the same bogus argument.

MacArthur's headquarters repeatedly issued alarmist reports about the disposition and strength of Chinese forces in Korea, wildly inflating estimates of its military capability. Units based in China were continually portrayed as being on the verge of crossing the border in support of those fighting in Korea. As one of MacArthur's reports put it, China "might have as many as 500,000 men... capable of reinforcing the Communist forces in Korea". These units, it added, are "immune from attack on the Manchurian side".[8] Stone notes that "this emphasis on Manchuria's "immunity" to attack was to become a constant theme of MacArthur Headquarters".[9] Indeed, MacArthur never relented in

---

[7] The Korea Policy Institute and Jang-hie Lee, "In Name Only: The United Nations Command and US Unilateralism in Korea", *The Korea Policy Institute*, 2020.

[8] I.F. Stone, *The Hidden History of the Korean War*, 181.

[9] Ibid., 181.

lobbying the Truman administration for permission to launch widespread bombing attacks on Chinese territory, fudging the distinction between Chinese units fighting in Korea and those who remained stationed at home. The aim behind McArthur's persistent threat inflations was the same as with most of his public statements and many of his military moves. He wished to inculcate the American public and officials with a belief in the necessity of taking the war into Chinese, and ideally also Soviet, territory, and turning the localised Korean War into a world war in a grand campaign to crush the socialist bloc. The many millions of people who would lose their lives in such an endeavour never merited consideration.

In general, American newspapers ignored the more sober-minded assessments that other US officials provided and instead ran with MacArthur's fear-mongering claims in their headlines. Regardless of the reality on the ground, what newspapers fed the American public was a steady diet of MacArthur's fabrications. Such stories began to produce the desired political effect. Stone reports that by January 1951, increasingly loud demands were being made in Congress to open a second front in China, to be led by a cross-strait attack by Chiang Kai-Shek's forces. Pressure continued to mount in Washington, but never enough to sway the Truman administration into following MacArthur's desire to light an international conflagration.

The one area where MacArthur and other rabidly anti-communist US politicians did march in lockstep with the Truman administration was in harbouring the conviction that peace on the Korean Peninsula was to be avoided. That aim was shared by "the German and Japanese military who wanted to rearm, and for Chiang Kai-shek whose only hope was a new world war".[10] Peace could have come early in the first year of the war when US and South Korean forces had essentially reached the 38th parallel that divided the two Koreas. It could also have come later that same year when US and South Korean forces had taken most of North Korea. On both occasions, the Soviet Union and China advocated a peaceful settlement. "Whenever peace came within talking range a common bond seemed to appear between Truman and [Secretary of State] Acheson on the one hand and MacArthur and [special advisor John Foster] Dulles on the other. While only the latter seemed bent on widening the war, none of them seemed eager for peace".[11]

The US pursued a scorched earth policy in Korea, as ground troops routinely burned villages and warplanes rained down death and destruction. Stone observes, "one of the problems which began to trouble the [US] Air Force in Korea, judging by the communiqués, was that there was nothing left to destroy. These communiqués must be read by anyone who wants a complete history of the Korean War. They are literally horrifying".[12] Stone proceeds to provide several quotes which amply illustrate his point, with villages being attacked by rockets, strafing, and napalm saturation bombing. Typically, the tone of the reports demonstrated a "complete indifference to

---

10   Ibid., 104.

11   Ibid., 201-2.

12   Ibid., 256-57.

non-combatants", which Stone rightly found disturbing.

> There were some passages about these raids on villages which reflected, not the pity which human feeling called for, but a kind of gay moral imbecility, utterly devoid of imagination—as if the flyers were playing in a bowling alley, with villages for pins.[13]

One of the examples listed is from a captain who led a group of four planes, whose mission report concluded, "You can kiss that group of villages good-bye".[14] This destruction is all the more tragic as in the five years prior to the outbreak of war, a popular revolutionary movement in the north had begun to make substantial improvements in the lives of its villagers through land reform, popular literacy programs and other initiatives.[15] Ironically, one of the victims of this scorched earth policy was Seoul itself, as the US bombed it in 1950 to slow the North Korean advance. At least 1,500 civilians were killed,[16] but an investigation into this bloodbath, along with many others, was later covered up by the Lee Myung-bak administration in 2010.[17]

Stone is enlightening in his description of how the US undermined peace negotiations to ensure the

---

13   Ibid., 258.

14   Ibid., 259.

15   Gregory Elich, "Construction the North Korean Revolution", *MRonline*, 2014.

16   Gil Yoon-hyeong, "US's Yongsan bombing of 1950 caused 1,587 civilian deaths", *Hankyoreh*, 2010

17   Charles J. Hanley and Hyung-Jin Kim, "Korea bloodbath probe ends; US escapes much blame", *Boston.com*, 2010.

continuation of the war. At one point, late in 1951, an "almost hysterical fear of peace made itself felt when the shooting stopped" after an agreement was reached on a ceasefire line, where "Red troops played volleyball within range of UN trenches".[18] President Truman was insistent that fighting should continue until every point of disagreement had been negotiated. Progress, however, failed to materialise due to American intransigence. "One could almost feel the relief in Washington as the truce talks bogged down again in an endless wrangle over air bases and the exchange of prisoners".[19] US negotiators succeeded in drawing out the process for another year after the publication of Stone's book, as tactically pointless conflict added to the death toll, all to serve Washington's geopolitical ambitions and the machinations of Syngman Rhee and Chiang Kai-shek.

The *Hidden History* was published nearly 70 years ago but wears its age remarkably well. As Bruce Cumings points out in his 1988 preface, the book concludes with "tantalizing uncertainty" and "many still-unanswered questions".[20] That is one of its strengths; Stone eschews glib certainties and doesn't claim to know more that he can know. Later investigators have access to information not available to Stone, such as archival records, but more importantly they know what came next so they come at the issues with a different perspective. However, it is more than a matter of fresh information coming to light. Stone follows Socrates in focusing on the question

---

18  I.F. Stone, *The Hidden History of the Korean War*, 346.

19  Ibid., 346.

20  Ibid., xix.

even if that does not lead to a definitive answer. We cannot know what public figures such as Acheson really thought, we can only surmise from what they do and say. Uncertainty is never completely vanquished and the questioning must go on.

There are at least four major reasons that make Stone's book enduring: the crucial role of the Korean War, the concept of "limited war" as a proportional instrument of imperial power, the role of local clients within the broader canvas of imperialism, and the false narratives of imperialism that validates the book's title of "Hidden History".

*The Korean War as a Pivotal Event*

The Korean War was a pivotal event, bedding down the Cold War, establishing the permanent war economy and putting imperialism at the centre of US foreign policy. It was the moment when the business of America moved from commerce to war.[21] The Military Industrial Complex, despite Eisenhower's valedictory warning, became a major economic and political pillar of the US state, if not its keystone.[22] The military carved out a hallowed place in American society and for years has been the most trusted institution in the country.[23]

Although the fighting on the Korean Peninsula has

---

21   Ellen Terrell, "The Business of America is Business", *Library of Congress*, 2019.

22   Louise Uchitelle, "The US Still Leans on the Military-Industrial Complex", *New York Times*, 2017.

23   Niall McCarthy, "The Institutions Americans Trust Most And Least In 2018", *Forbes*, 2018.

been suspended by an armistice, the US continues to wage war on North Korea, mainly through the use of sanctions, causing economic distress, food insecurity and malnutrition.[24] The war continues because the US wants to preserve its monopoly, vis-à-vis small countries, on nuclear weapons ("non-proliferation") and its forward military position against China. Korea remains America's longest war (1950 to the present) and the peninsula is the likeliest place for war between the US and China to break out.

*Limited War and Imperial Power*

Both "World Wars" were just that—wars unlimited by geographical constraints. The Soviet breaking of the US monopoly on the combination of nuclear weapons and long-range missiles, together with its support for anti-colonialism, raised the spectre that a local war against a country which could not retaliate would become not merely a global war, but one in which, for the first time, the US would be vulnerable. The rise of China has compounded that danger. The opposition of Truman and the Joint Chiefs of Staff to MacArthur's desire to extend the war to China resonates in Washington today: while planning to win a war with China remains necessary, it is no longer sufficient, the US must also consider how to limit war and its costs.[5]

The Korean War took total war, that involving all of society with no distinction between military and civilian

---

24  Edith M. Lederer, "UN investigator: 11 million North Koreans are undernourished", *Associated Press News*, 2019.

components, to new extremes, particularly through the use of indiscriminate mass bombing that was worse even than that of the Second World War,[25] but it also marked the end of US invulnerability and hence delineated the limits of its global power. This was particularly evident in the Vietnam War, where the US was very careful not to provoke Chinese intervention.[26] It is also the main reason the US has not invaded North Korea since the armistice.[27]

## The Role of Clients in Imperialism

Throughout history, imperialist expansion and rule have been based on much more than the deployment of overwhelming, brute force. They have always involved an alliance between the imperial power and local clients. The alliance is unequal of course, but is nonetheless subject to constant negotiation. Stone brings the role of local agents, Syngman Rhee and Chiang Kai-shek into focus. They served America but with their own agenda in mind. Chiang Kai-shek had far more substantial credentials than Rhee. He was a genuine national leader but was incapable of solving China's problems. Having lost both popular support and then the civil war, he looked to Washington to rescue his fortunes. The Chiefs

---

25  Tim Beal, "The Continuing Korean War in the Murderous History of Bombing", *Monthly Review*, 2021.

26  Erik B. Villard, *Staying the Course: October 1967 to September 1968* (Center of Military History, United States Army, 2017), 5.

27  Barbara Demick, "Escalating tension has experts simulating a new Korean War, and the scenarios are sobering", *Los Angeles Times,* 2017.

of Staff were too canny to attempt to restore him to power, but they did afford him protection on Taiwan and that separation from the mainland continues up to today. The "Taiwan issue" faded from prominence after Nixon's rapprochement with China, but has resurfaced as the US confrontation with rising China has intensified.

Syngman Rhee was of less standing as a national figure but more central to US involvement in Korea. He was brought in by the US and airlifted out by the CIA in 1960 when popular opposition made him too much of a liability. The history of South Korean leaders since then has been a checkered one. Dictators such as Park Chung-hee have been more successful in handling US pressure than the progressive democratic ones such as the present incumbent_Moon Jae-in.[28] Despite having been swept into power by the Candlelight Revolution, which toppled Park's daughter, Park Geun-hye, and the opportunities presented by Kim Jong Un's peace offensive in 2018 and Trump's fumbling willingness to engage with Pyongyang, he has been too weak to stand up to American pressure and will finish his term of office with little achieved in respect of peace with the North.[29] The role of President of South Korea has always been a limited one because of US dominance, but as Kim Dae-jung and Roh Moo-hyun demonstrated, there is some potential to nudge the US towards peace.

---

28  Gregory Elich, "Will South Korea's Moon Defy Trump and Improve Relations with North Korea?", *Counterpunch*, 2020.

29  Tim Beal, "A Korean Tragedy", *The Asia-Pacific Journal*, 2017.

*Hidden War—Deceptions, Machinations and Obscured Motivations*

All war utilises deception but American imperialism positions it at the epicentre. Duplicity is America's very essence, if for no other reason that it denies its imperialism.

Too often even critical reassessments of US foreign policy take the line that it was a matter of good men, with the best of intentions being misled by faulty intelligence and over-confidence:

> …we escalated the war in Vietnam on wrong information, on mistaken and misinterpreted reports of torpedo attacks. In 2003, we launched a preemptive war on the grounds that Saddam Hussein had weapons of mass destruction at the ready. Wrong again. Today the fog of this war is also lifting…[30]

Stone generally goes beyond this superficiality, though he is not immune from it. Truman he sees as an "honourable and decent specimen of that excellent breed, the plain small-town American" who wanted peace but was constrained by domestic considerations—the charge of appeasement:

> … how to fight off the Red-scare bogey at home, if one was also open to attack for making an agreement with Moscow? The difficulty of dealing with the Russians was clear enough, but even clearer was the political danger at home. How negotiate without

---

30  Ellen Goodman, "Dispersing the fog of war, from Vietnam to Iraq," Baltimore Sun, 2 February 2004.

give-and-take? But how give anything at all without being charged with "appeasement"? To "get tough," to avoid negotiation, to carry on a sniping campaign just short of actual warfare-this was the line of least political resistance.

His analysis of the domestic constraint is astute enough; it remains a basic reason why the US finds it so difficult to negotiate, and to keep to deals—what the Russians have labelled "not-agreement-capable".[31] It manifests itself in respect of Korea today but is a more general problem of governance. However, Truman is the president who started the Cold War, so Stone's assessment of him here is inadequate. Truman was also deeply racist.[32]

With the passage of time and the exigencies of power—it was Truman who desegregated the US military[33]—his racism was muted though "even after blacks hailed him as their champion, he continued to sprinkle his private conversation" with crude racial slurs.[34] It is reasonable to assume that Truman, along with other American leaders then, and now, were more willing to accept the carnage deployed on Korea, as with

---

31   The Saker, "Why the recent developments in Syria show that the Obama Administration is in a state of confused agony," *The Saker*, 23 September 2016.

32   William E. Leuchtenburg, "The Conversion of Harry Truman," American Heritage, November 1991.

33   DeNeen L. Brown, "How Harry S. Truman went from being a racist to desegregating the military", *The Washington Post*, 2018.

34   William E. Leuchtenburg, "The Conversion of Harry Truman".

Japan before and Indochina later, than they would have against Europeans.

Stone was a man of his times, who had to make a living, with inevitable compromises, but who in general stands out as a beacon of good journalism. How he styled his name illustrates some of the issues he faced. Born Isidor Feinstein Stone he was persuaded in 1937 to call himself I. F. Stone to hide his Jewishness; we tend to forget how prevalent anti-Semitism was in America before the postwar rise of Jewish political power made it unfashionable in public. "Jew" and "Communist" were often used interchangeably. But he personally called himself "Izzy" and was very active in left-wing politics. He was not lacking in courage.

It is not that Izzy Stone provided conclusive answers to these four themes and the other topics covered in his book. How could he? What he does, however, is far more important. He starts the process of investigation, of challenging conventional wisdom and in so doing, provides empirical evidence upon which Marxists and anti-imperialists can build subsequent analysis. He followed in the footsteps of radicals such as Mark Twain, Jack London, and Upton Sinclair but reached further into foreign affairs. He has been followed by others, but far too few, with most people working in mainstream media or academia being either stenographers, mindlessly (but safely) regurgitating the official line, or megaphones, spewing out propaganda to serve some hidden objective of the ruling elite.

We would well do with more Izzy Stones—they are a rare breed—but perhaps the real solution lies within ourselves. *The Hidden History* is not the product of access to secret stashes of information. He used what is now called open-source materials and that is accessible to us, much more than it was in his day. This surely means that Stone's most important lesson is that we can all try to do what he did—read carefully with a critical eye. There are plenty of other histories hidden behind curtains of deceit.

# Socialist Construction in Korea: Suzy Kim's *Everyday Life in the North Korean Revolution, 1945-1950*

Ju-Hyun Park

Few countries on earth have been subjected to a propaganda campaign as relentless and far-reaching as the Democratic People's Republic of Korea. Although demonization of the DPRK can be traced back to its founding in 1948, "North Korea" has occupied an unenviable position of regular vilification in contemporary western media since George W. Bush denounced it as part of the "Axis of Evil" in 2003. The anglophone archive on the DPRK is a bleak record of imperialist slander, replete with the most lurid and theatrical tales of passively suffering masses and the flamboyant pseudo-socialist "regime" that supposedly keeps them in a state of total servitude. Between hypocritical fears of its nuclear power and conscience-rattling anxieties over the alleged condition of human rights within, the DPRK looms as a symbol of the negation of liberal freedoms. It is within this context that Suzy Kim's *Everyday Life in the North Korean Revolution, 1945-1950* must be considered.

The figure of the "North Korean" in English-language scholarship is marked by contradiction; she is, at once, overrepresented, and yet she cannot speak. Driven by the demands of US geostrategic interests, 21st century anglophone knowledge production on Korea can be located along two poles. On one end, national security think tanks and human rights organizations, in collusion with the US and Republic of Korea (south Korean) governments, generate a ceaseless deluge of material on the barbarity of the Kim "regime." On the other, a smattering of historians and journalists attempt to shift the focus towards the originating brutality of the ongoing US war on Korea,[1] often acquiescing to, or at least not contesting, the right's characterization of the DPRK as a fundamentally totalitarian project. Speaking in the most general terms, Koreans themselves (notable exceptions notwithstanding) often occupy subordinate positions across this spectrum. They contribute as junior associates, research assistants, lesser-known scholars, rarely-acknowledged spouses, and most significantly, as primary sources, whether as defector "activists" or survivors of US and ROK state terror. While Koreans are the subjects of the story (or perhaps more honestly, its objects), they are rarely its narrators, and certainly not the architects of the terms on which these stories are told.

Published in 2013, Kim's book offers an important intervention in the field described above. Drawing primarily on DPRK documents captured by the US

---

[1] Tim Beal, "The Continuing Korean War in the Murderous History of Bombing", *Monthly Review*, 2021.

Army in the early 1950s from Inje County, an area just north of the 38th parallel which is now mostly under ROK administration, *Everyday Life in the North Korean Revolution* offers a rare glimpse into socialist construction as a mass project in north Korea. Eschewing a "top-down" historical account, Suzy Kim emphasises the role of the masses in the actual construction of the DPRK and the implementation of the revolution in "everyday" life by "everyday" people. What follows is a mosaic representation of the revolution as it was experienced—and enacted—by the men and women, peasants and workers, elderly and youth of Inje County and beyond. Rather than giving "voice to the voiceless," Kim's project peels back the layers of silence imposed by imperialist academic, media, and state interests, demonstrating that the "voiceless," are, in fact, per Arundhati Roy's observation, actually just the "deliberately silenced, or the preferably unheard."[2] In doing so, Kim presents her readers with an opportunity to engage the origins of the DPRK on its own terms.

*Revolutions in the "Everyday"*

> What is missing... from most studies on North Korea, is the everyday life of local villages undergoing a major transformation, instituting hands-on the radical changes in a revolution that no Soviet official could have orchestrated.[3]

---

2   Arundhati Roy, "Peace and the New Corporate Liberation Theology", 2004 City of Sydney Peace Prize Lecture.

3   Suzy Kim, *Everyday Life in the North Korean Revolution: 1945-1950* (Cornell University Press, 2013), 7.

Kim's book is neither polemical nor evangelical, and this is evident from the outset. An historian by training, Kim frames her text by flipping the script on the Foucauldian critique of modernity as a disciplinary project of state power undifferentiated by the class character of government. In contrasting Korea's experience of colonial modernity under Japan, along with socialist construction in the north after WWII, Kim poses the north Korean revolution as a self-determined project of the Korean masses to build an alternative, *socialist* modernity to overcome their material dispossession under Japanese colonial-capitalist modernity. In doing so, she establishes the "everyday" as a framework through which the agency of "everyday" people enacting revolutionary change in the time and space of their own lives can be reclaimed. By recentring the north Korean masses as historical and revolutionary subjects, Kim breaks with dominant academic narratives that render the people of the DPRK as bystanders in their own story.

Kim begins with a detailed look at the development of class society and consciousness under Japanese colonialism, while paying special attention to how Japanese land and agricultural policies shaped peasant life and peasant resistance. While some industrialization did take place, particularly in the north beginning in the 1930s, Korea's greatest value to Japan was in the production of rice and the export of labour power and consequently it remained a predominantly agrarian society throughout the colonial period. Immediately after annexation in 1910, the Japanese colonial authorities conducted a land survey of the peninsula that solidified the power of the landlord class while appropriating lands that were once owned by the palace (Joseon Korea's largest landowner) for state management through the monopolist Oriental Development Company. Tenant-farming or sharecropping, a phenomenon that became increasingly common throughout the 19th century, formed a key component of the colonial matrix of control. The precarity of Korean peasants not only facilitated the seizure of virtually all Korean rice for the Japanese market, but also enabled colonial control of production down to the level of what plant varieties should be planted per square foot. The crises of hunger and poverty manufactured by the nexus of colonial and landlord domination resulted in the separation of masses of people from their means of subsistence and production. The emigration of one in seven Koreans to Japan and Manchuria following their expulsion from their lands is a powerful illustration of the devastation wrought in the countryside by colonialism.

The material conditions of Korea's peasantry provided the social basis for anticolonial movements, and eventually the north Korean revolution. Kim recounts the radical history of the Red Peasant Unions in 1930s northern Korea—alliances of tenant farmers and owner-cultivators that organised hundreds of night schools for the politicization of the peasantry, and led fierce and often violent struggles against colonial agrarian policies. While most organised resistance was driven underground or overseas by 1940, the radical political experience of peasants themselves informed developments in Korea following WWII.

*Constructing Socialism, Enacting Decolonization*

As the Japanese colonial order crumbled, the Korean masses established self-governing People's Committees across the peninsula. Initially organised through the liberal nationalist Lyuh Woon-hyung (Yuh Un-hyung)'s Committee for the Preparation of Korean Independence, the People's Committees served as the basis for a sovereign Korean state, the People's Republic of Korea (PRK), founded on September 6, 1945. With the arrival of the US military in southern Korea on September 8, the PRK was dissolved, and the US outlawed and violently disbanded the People's Committees. In the south, the new US military government absorbed the old Japanese colonial bureaucracy, and ruled through terror in alliance with local bourgeois and landlord elements; in the north, the People's Committees continued as the foundation of a state-building project enacted by the people themselves. The titular "north Korean Revolution" began with an agenda for decolonization determined and realised by the masses themselves.

Kim examines the character of this revolution by focusing on three major aspects of the social transformation that took place: land reform, literacy campaigns, and women's equality. Although peasants in some areas wasted no time expropriating land from Japanese colonisers, no centralised apparatus existed in August 1945 to ensure a consistent redistribution of land across the whole society. A Provisional People's Committee (PPC) was established as a temporary national structure representing all local People's Committees. The following spring, the PPC responded to a three million-strong peasant mobilization in support of agrarian reform by passing a land reform law. Within a mere 25 days, local People's Committees seized over 2 million acres of land from landlord and colonial control and redistributed it to over 700,000 peasant families. Prior to land reform, some 75% of Korean peasants were tenant farmers with less than 2.5 acres of land to produce adequate subsistence for their families. For them, the revolution was not an abstract concern imposed from above, but a material process that engaged them as subjects in the actual transformation of feudal and colonial property relations.

Beyond satisfying the peasants' centuries-old hunger for land, the revolution universalised education and transformed gender relations, arguably as part of a singular process. Some 80% of the Korean population had no formal schooling by the end of the Japanese colonial period, and 90% of women could not read. Women's participation in society was curtailed by the dominance of patriarchal ideology, in addition to the material exploitation of their productive and reproductive labour. In addition to Korea's first public education system, some 12,000 literacy schools were established across the north, with corresponding literacy eradication teams in each locale tasked with democratizing knowledge. By 1948, literacy rates stood at 92%. A series of gender equality laws passed in 1946 and 1947, sought to raise the status of women and simultaneously eliminate social practices that prevented their full participation in society. Women's equal political rights were enshrined for the first time, including their right to equal pay and suffrage. Women were guaranteed parental leave and nursing breaks across all industries. Child and forced marriage, polygamy, and prostitution were outlawed; in Korea, these practices had been connected in a matrix of gendered oppression established by and for the perpetuation of feudalism and colonialism, most infamously in the Japanese system of wartime sexual slavery in which some 200,000 Korean women were conscripted. By the end of 1946, over 1 million women had joined the Democratic Women's League, a mass organization that represented a third of all adult women in the north between the ages of 18 and 61. In a chapter titled "Revolutionary Motherhood," Kim examines how motherhood itself was enshrined as an ideal for both men and women to aspire towards, and in doing so elaborates on women's mass and heterodox participation in politics within the specific construction of gender in socialist Korea.

While refusing to understate the significance of these transformations, Kim is also careful to illustrate how contradictions persisted in this new society. Adult learners often struggled to retain their newfound literacy. Peasants sometimes coddled their former landlords—at least one person in Inje County continued paying rent to their landlord out of pity. Although the land reform reduced rents from 50-70% of peasants' crops to an agricultural tax-in-kind of 25%, some remained dissatisfied. Women became equal subjects under the law and played an unprecedented role in public life, but patriarchal social relations persisted. Kim tells the story of a local People's Committee publicity director who was "expelled from the party for making her husband clean and fetch her bath water." Many women were initially reluctant to take on greater public roles, already burdened by work in the home, and sometimes held back by internalised oppression. Facing such circumstances, various women published a barrage of criticisms of male chauvinism and exhortations for men to correct their attitudes and behaviour. Criticisms of men in positions of power's failure to adequately recruit women into politics (and later, only their wives) abounded, as did denunciations of men's continued habits of ignoring their childrearing and housekeeping responsibilities. Critics might seize on such details as evidence of the revolution's failures or limitations; in reality, these facts only reflect that the new society of the north Korean Revolution is a living and dialectically developing one like any other. In their everyday acts of building a socialist future, everyday people perpetuated the still-existing contradictions of the colonial and feudal past. They reflected on and wrestled with these contradictions, as Kim demonstrates on numerous occasions, including in a chapter analysing the autobiographies of various rank-and-file party members. The present society was no utopia, but that was precisely because of its mass character—an aspect neither any previous Korean society nor the contemporaneous south could ever claim.[4]

---

[4] A note from the editors: the author has amended this passage slightly from the version that originally appeared on the Liberated Texts website to more accurately reflect their interpretation of Kim's argument.

## *Democracy for the Masses, by the Masses*

The mass character of the north Korean Revolution would not have been possible without democratic participation. The first People's Committees organised after the end of WWII were hastily constructed. Most representatives had been locally determined on an ad-hoc basis. In light of this, the People's Committees were reconstituted through Korea's first free elections, operated on the principles of the secret ballot and universal suffrage. With election days treated as holidays, over 99% of the electorate participated. Lt. Col. Walter F. Choinski, a US Army liaison stationed in Pyongyang at the time of the village and township elections, offers a rare eyewitness account of procedures:

> [After receiving a ballot] The voter then retired to a table in another room, where he indicated his choice, folded the ballot and deposited the ballot in one of two boxes... In order to guarantee secrecy and protect the voter many polls placed low fences in front of the two boxes and cut an arm-size hole in the fence midway between the two boxes. This permitted the voter to stick his arm into the hole... and observe, without being observed, the hole into which he was casting his lot.[5]

Prior to the elections themselves, the People's Committees undertook public education campaigns to ensure the equal participation of all members of society. Candidates for each position were selected by the three parties of

---

5  Ibid., 83.

the Democratic National United Front through a public participatory process in which workers and peasants nominated and debated the merits of their peers. As one woman miner explained it to Anna Louise Strong, the only US journalist that reported from the DPRK prior to the Korean War, candidates were nominated on the basis of their existing relationships to their communities. Those who failed to achieve at least 50% voter turnout would not be elected, and candidates who could not secure at least 90% of the vote usually resigned in shame. When Strong asked her interviewee whether such a process could truly be democratic if the elections were not competitive, the woman retorted, "I don't see what the Americans have to say about it, anyway!"[6]

Village, township, county, city and provisional People's Committees were directly elected. The provincial People's Committees convened in 1947 to elect among themselves a national 237-member People's Assembly endowed with the authority to enact laws, and appoint the cabinet and Supreme Court. Although Workers Party members were represented among the candidates, they did not hold a monopoly on elected positions. Independent candidates and candidates from other parties constituted the majority of those elected to the People's Assembly and all People's Committees, with the exception of those at the village level—where the popularity of land reform among the peasantry resulted in a Workers Party majority.

Impressive as these electoral achievements were, mass participation in politics was not limited to the ballot box. Following land reform, enthusiastic peasants

---

6   Ibid., 89.

swelled the ranks of the Workers Party to more than 700,000 members by 1948. Those who were not full-fledged party members participated in determining and constructing socialism through the mass organizations. In addition to the aforementioned Democratic Women's League, similar organizations existed for youth, peasants, workers, artists, intellectuals, and numerous other social configurations. These mass organizations took an active role in governance, the best example being the Peasants' League, which by early 1948 counted 2.5 million peasants out of a total of 6 million among its membership. The Peasants' League provided the vehicle for the political transformation of the peasantry, not only through their engagement with national politics, but also through their collective management of agriculture. In contrast to the bourgeois democratic tradition, which claims mass participation on the basis of votes alone, the north Korean Revolution constructed a new system in which everyday people could transform their everyday lives through multiple avenues, both within and beyond the state apparatus proper.

*Reclaiming History*

Though Kim limits her text to the years 1945-1950, providing little information on events following the Korean War, *Everyday Life in the North Korean Revolution* is nevertheless an indispensable study. By focusing on a period neglected in most accounts of Korea's recent history, Kim provides crucial contextual information for contemporary events, and in doing so claims the "North

Korean" as an historical actor. The imperialist narrative seeks to deny Koreans a place in history. Kim counters this—not through didactic refutations, but by letting real people's stories speak for themselves. Whether through autobiographies of the party's rank-and-file, testimonies recorded in historical documents, or interviews with living former political prisoners of the ROK, Kim has curated a vibrant account of the revolution from those who made it real.

In recent years, the reality of the US's unfinished war on Korea has awakened a few conscientious persons to the anti-imperialist necessity of defending the DPRK. This development has progressed alongside the return of a semblance of socialist politics to the countries of the imperial core. A reader in search of a definitive guide to the DPRK will not find one here; what Kim offers instead is something perhaps more significant—a chance to see history as something "North Koreans," too, have made. The importance of this lies not in "humanizing" Koreans; our humanity is prior to any attempts to degrade us. Rather, what Kim has done in reclaiming history for north Koreans is given her readers the chance to rediscover their own humanity. As James Baldwin once observed, "anyone who insists on remaining in a state of innocence long after that innocence is dead turns himself into a monster." This book offers no deliverance, only the opportunity to betray one's own monstrosity, and maybe reclaim the future as the collective effort of everyday people. Perhaps this is the final table Kim turns—in the end, it may just be the north Koreans who save you.

# Revolution as Historic Necessity: Edgar Snow's *Red Star Over China*

Lewis Hodder

That *Red Star Over China* (1937) has not made the same impact on revolutionary literature as John Reed's *10 Days that Shook the World* (1919) isn't due to a lack of provenance; while Lenin personally recommended Reed's account of the October Revolution to "the workers of the world" in his introduction to the book, *Red Star Over China* sees far greater involvement by Mao himself. Rather than just remaining a revolutionary figure throughout the book, ratified after-the-fact, Mao sits down with Snow to recount his childhood, the conditions that necessitated the revolution, its tactics and how it must move forward against Japanese imperialism. But the revolution wasn't yet successful. It didn't involve an industrial working class identical to the proletariat of the advanced capitalist countries; its experience was not one event in Petrograd that was "almost exactly duplicated" throughout the country,[1] as Reed simplistically portrayed events in Russia.

---

1   John Reed, *10 Days that Shook the World* (Penguin Books,

It was a movement of intense offensives, retreats, and fronts over thousands of miles of Chinese countryside.

There is less mythology around Snow than Reed. *Insurgent Mexico,* Reed's first book, recounted his experience of the Mexican Revolution in 1910 and was met with critical acclaim as it encapsulated the supposedly exotic *flavour* and *spirit* of the revolution. But this was at the expense of accuracy. Rather than an American with a penchant for the n-word as his companion as was the reality, we read about a fictional Mexican officer who tested Reed's masculinity and threatened to shoot him before accepting him as a blood brother. His biographer, Robert A. Rosenstone, doubts whether Reed really "downed half a bottle of *sotol* while members of a guerrilla band cheered him on".[2] By contrast, in Snow's single volume, with prefaces and appendices from later decades including further conversations with Mao amid the development of the revolution, we find an inquisitiveness altogether more fruitful than Reed's accounts—even if at times more naïve. When he entered Red territory for the first time, Snow admitted that he "did not know what 'communism' might mean to these men in practice", as he prepared to have his scant belongings (bedding, two cameras, 24 rolls of film, and a little food) "requisitioned".[3]

"Did they read *Capital* and the works of Lenin?", he

---

1974), 9.

2 Robert A. Rosenstone, *Romantic Revolutionary: A Biography of John Reed* (Penguin Books, 1975), 150.

3 Edgar Snow, *Red Star Over China: The Classic Account of the Birth of Chinese Communism* (Grove Press, 2018), 59.

speculated. "Had they a thoroughly socialist program? Were they Stalinists or Trotskyites? Or neither? Was their movement really an organic part of the World Revolution? Were they true internationalists? 'Mere tools of Moscow,' or primarily nationalists struggling for an independent China?".[4] The Nationalist government of the Republic of China, the Kuomintang, had surrounded Red territory creating a blockade so that no information could reach the outside world. Even Snow himself was reported as having been killed by bandits.[5]

On his way to the front, Snow found himself discussing the political situation in China with a young man on a train. Afraid that he wouldn't be able to return home after seven years because of the threat of bandits, Snow asked "You mean Reds?" "Not Reds, although there are Reds in Szechuan, too. No, I mean bandits." Curious, Snow asked whether these were one and the same, but the young man replied that the newspaper editors must call them bandits because they're ordered to by the government; to call them communists or revolutionaries would be a sign of sympathy. "But in Szechuan don't people fear the Reds as much as the bandits?", Snow finally questioned. It depends, the young man answered.

> The rich men fear them, and the landlords, and the tax collectors, yes. But the peasants do not fear them. Sometimes they welcome them... My father wrote to me that they did abolish usury and opium in the Sungpan [Szechuan], and that they redistributed land

---

4   Ibid., 36.

5   Ibid., 39.

there. So you see they are not exactly bandits. They have principles, all right. But they are wicked men. They kill too many people.

An old man who sat beside them, listening intently to the conversation, suddenly interrupted: "They don't kill enough!".[6]

In the decade after 1927, the Kuomintang's betrayal of both the Communist Party and the peasantry in its refusal to enact agrarian reform led to worsening poverty among the rural population, where "reports came in daily of catastrophes which in China were considered more or less routine." Even as he was writing the book, Snow noted, "famine conditions continue to be reported in Honan, Anhui, Shensi, Kansu, Szechuan, and Kweichow." Szechuan had been one of the provinces where taxes had been collected sixty years in advance, leaving thousands of acres of farmland abandoned as farmers were unable to pay rent or the exorbitant interest in loans, and Snow highlights a survey that reported "30,000,000 people are now in the famine belt of that province", where its peasants had resorted to eating bark and balls of mud and straw to stave off hunger.

*"What is a communist?"*

Once Snow was smuggled into Red territory, he found himself speaking to one young peasant who had joined the Red Army. He told Snow that when the communists came to his village they were welcomed; villagers brought them hot tea and made them sweets while the Red Army

---

6   Ibid., 42.

put on plays. "It was a happy time. Only the landlords ran."[7] But this was someone who had already joined the Red Army who described it as a happy time. And so, stopping in a village where children soon came to look at "the first foreign devil many of them had seen", he decided to question them to see what they thought. "What is a communist?", he asked them. The peasant children replied that a communist is someone who fights the White bandits of the Kuomintang and the Japanese imperialists. Another chimed in to say that they help to fight against landlords and capitalists. Prodding them again, Snow asked whether there were any landlords or capitalists in the village. "No!", they all shrieked. "They've all run away!"[8]

Any negative connotations surrounding the Red Army were lost on both the peasants and the soldiers. The latter were "perhaps the first consciously happy group of Chinese proletarians I had seen," according to Snow. At times, he remarked, when he was with the Red Army he felt like he was among schoolboys who, rather than taking an interest in football or love, found themselves in a protracted guerrilla war. "I could scarcely believe that it had been only this determined aggregation of youth, equipped with an Idea, that had directed a mass

---

[7] Repeatedly, Snow encounters these stories of landlords fleeing at the news of the Red Army's imminent arrival. Ho Lung, an infamous leader of peasant rebellions who later joined the communists and was said to have established a Soviet district in Hunan in 1928 with just one knife, inspired so much fear in the landlords that reports of him being as far away as 60 miles would cause landlords to flee.

[8] Ibid., 85.

struggle for ten years against all the armies of Nanking." Speaking at the communists' own university outside of Pao'an, the Red Army University, he soon exhausted his knowledge of current events in Europe and America amid the students' questions. They asked: "why is it that, although the Communist Party is legal in both Great Britain and America, there is no workers' government in either country?" "What progress is being made in the foundation of an anti-Fascist front in England? In America?" "What are the results of the NRA policy in America, and how has it benefited the working class?" "Why has the League of Nations failed?"[9]

*Conversations with Mao*

It was here, in Pao'an, after riding through miles of Red territory on horseback—closely followed by White bandits before the Red Guard could rout them—that Snow finally met Mao. In a bare cave-dwelling with maps covering the walls, where their "chief luxury was a mosquito net",[10] Snow found Mao remarkably well read, not just on historical events and the ancient Greeks, as well as Spinoza, Kant, Goethe, Hegel, and Rousseau, but also on contemporary events across the world.

> Even on the Long March, it seems, the Reds received news broadcasts by radio, and in the Northwest they published their own newspapers. Mao was exceptionally well read in world history and had a realistic conception of European and social and

---

9  Ibid., 116.

10  Ibid., 93.

political conditions. He was very interested in the Labour Party of England, and questioned me intensely about its present policies, soon exhausting all my information. It seemed to me that he found it difficult fully to understand why, in a country where workers were enfranchised, there was still no workers' government. I was afraid my answer did not satisfy him. He expressed profound contempt for Ramsay MacDonald, whom he designated as a *han-chien*—an archtraitor of the British people.[11]

Snow noted that these interviews with Mao came to over 20,000 words.[12] They covered his childhood and how his parents came to be rich peasants, his early schooling and work, his political inspirations and development—even a brief anarchist period where he would discuss with a friend "its possibilities in China"—through the creation of the New People's Study Society, the formation of the Communist Party and its alliance and antagonisms with the Kuomintang. Throughout these interviews Mao slowly fades into the background as politics overtakes him, removing himself from the narrative as he recalls the setbacks faced by the Communist Party in 1927 and after. Snow repeatedly encouraged Mao to discuss his role in these events in vain. Surprised that anyone would be interested in his personal life, Mao only agreed to give the interviews under the pretence of correcting reports that portrayed him as a fanatic. When Mao finally recounted his life, however, Snow soon realised "that

---

11    Ibid., 94.

12    Ibid., 90.

this was not only his story but an explanation of how communism grew—a variety of it real and indigenous to China—and why it had won adherence and support of thousands of young men and women."[13]

The communist movement had made significant gains in China before it was outlawed in 1927, after which it immediately rebuilt itself and began to establish Soviets and enact land reform. It then faced waves of attacks that culminated in the Fifth Campaign in 1934— initiating the Long March—where the Kuomintang boasted that 1,000,000 people had been killed or starved to death as whole areas were depopulated by forced migrations and mass executions.[14] It was a period of violent counterrevolution not just in China but globally. The "Permanent Revolution" in imperialist Europe had failed to come to fruition, the League of Nations had failed to halt Japan's expansion into Manchuria and Mussolini's conquest of the Horn of Africa, and the imperialist powers had refused to create an anti-fascist front with the USSR. Peasants and soldiers were keenly aware of what the failure of the revolution meant—the re-establishment of landlords, execution for communist sympathies, and a return to the cultivation of poppy that would lead to famine. The words that greeted Snow in a small village as he entered Red territory presented their demands:

> Down with the landlords who eat our flesh!
> Down with the militarists who drink our blood!

---

13   Ibid., 125.

14   Ibid., 188.

> Down with the traitors who sell China to Japan!
> Welcome the United Front with all anti-Japanese armies!
> Long live the Chinese Red Army![15]

## *Snow After China*

Like Reed, Snow faced censorship and repression both in America and abroad. Travelling through India, a secret service agent questioned him on a train to Calcutta about his alleged connection to the Comintern and, despite any assurances, this charge would surface again and again as Snow faced the threat of deportation. In America, the CIA produced and distributed publications specifically to counter the "sympathetic view of the emerging China as presented by Edgar Snow"[16] and the FBI's files on him ran to 555 pages as they attempted to determine his political beliefs and the extent of his support for Mao and the Communist Party of China. These files on Snow were regularly passed to McCarthy's House Committee on Un-American Activities in spite of his own protestations that it was "a lie to state or infer in any

---

15   Ibid., 64.

16   "For example, CIA records for 1967 state that certain books about China subsidised or even produced by the Agency 'circulate principally in the US as a prelude to later distribution abroad.' Several of these books on China were widely reviewed in the United States, often in juxtaposition to the sympathetic view of the emerging China as presented by Edgar Snow". "Foreign and Military Intelligence, Book 1: Final Report of the Select Committee to Study Governmental Operations with Respect to Intelligence Activities" (1975), 198.

way that I am or have ever been a communist."[17]

Snow also refused to make friends with communists in America. Following on from Mao's criticism of the Comintern, which insisted that the Party focus its efforts on the urban centres, Snow's work drew a scathing review from the Communist Party of America. In *The Communist,* the party's magazine of theory and practice, the book was dismissed as gossip and slander that led readers into the "quicksands of Trotskyism" for its criticism of the Comintern; yet Snow's stance was not borne out of any allegiance to Trotsky, but rather to the Chinese communists and to their struggle.

Snow had covered events on the ground in China some time before meeting Mao and entering Red territory. He interviewed the newly appointed Chinese governor of Manchukuo—occupied Manchuria—who protested that he had been put into that position against his will and hadn't even approved a budget because it was not translated into Chinese; reported the Japanese military's practice of herding Chinese peasants into bamboo thickets before setting it on fire and shooting if they came running out; and witnessed the first Japanese air raid on civilians, where he crawled over bomb craters to see whether the Kuomintang military had abandoned their posts.

> When you [have] been here as long as I have you would begin to see that this revolution is merely an expression of a historic need of the masses, too long suppressed, too long denied, and now become

---

17 Edgar Snow, "The Davies Case; Mr. Snow Takes Exception to Dispatch Published in *The Times*", *New York Times*, 1953.

volcanic and catastrophic in its manifestation. It is the people's thumbs down on the rulers of the realm.[18]

*Snow's Legacy in China (and Beyond)*

After Snow's death in 1972, he was memorialised in the Great Hall of the People in Tiananmen Square. It was the first such tribute to a foreigner there, and half of Snow's ashes were buried in Peking University with an inscription in English and Mandarin that reads, "an American friend of the Chinese people." *Red Star Over China* and Snow's journalism left an enduring reputation around the world[19] and in China, where the book became a primary source on the revolution when it was at its lowest ebb. And as China continues its successful "New Long March" against poverty,[20] Cao Wenxuan, a professor at Peking University, remarked that it is "to Snow's credit that we see how the revolution grew from the start".[21]

The book's importance extends beyond this, however. While it does present a detailed picture of the Red Army recovering from its lowest point, it doesn't just contribute

---

18   John Maxwell Hamilton, *Edgar Snow: A Biography* (Indiana University Press, 1988), 63.

19   In his autobiography *Long Walk to Freedom*, Nelson Mandela recalled "In Edgar Snow's brilliant *Red Star Over China* I saw that it was Mao's determination and non-traditional thinking that led him to victory".

20   "China sheds light on global poverty eradication", *Global Times*, 2021.

21   Cao Wenxuan quoted in Yamei's "80 years on, Edgar Snow's 'Red Star' keeps shining over China", *Xinhua Net*, 2018.

to the canon of revolutionary literature through recalling the strategy of the Communist Party of China; more fundamentally, it reiterates the necessity of communist revolution itself. It brings to mind Che Guevara's letter to Carlos Quijano, where he wrote that the revolution is not about "how many times a year someone can go to the beach", as contemporary proponents of Fully Automated Luxury Communism might well frame it,[22] or "how many pretty things from abroad you might be able to buy with present-day wages."[23] It is about liberation. Che remarks that at first it was those who fought in the Sierra Maestra who knew sacrifice, but soon everyone in Cuba came to know it, as increasing pressure mounted against its revolution and it fought off attacks and persevered under the US blockade. So too, in China, did the Communist Party, the Red Army and the peasantry know sacrifice—along with the communists in the Global South who have fought these same battles.

The question of moralism and suffering are endemic to discussions of communism in imperialist countries, as many on the left insist that any material sacrifice is at best superfluous and at worst disingenuous and cynical. This trend culminates in Mark Fisher's caricature of a "harsh Leninist Superego" which condemns everything that exists in the hope that one day they will be proven right and attain salvation draped in a red flag.[24] There

---

[22] Lewis Hodder, "Fully Automated Luxury Communism," *Ebb Magazine*, 2019.

[23] Che Guevara, "Socialism and Man" in *Che Guevara Speaks* (Pathfinder, 2016), 169.

[24] Mark Fisher, "Acid Communism", *Blackout*.

is a presupposition that capitalism in the imperial core has reached such a stage that, in spite of increasing casualisation, the working class will never know true struggle or even difficulty—that being without the most trivial consumer product is as alien to them as hunger. To introduce the question of struggle or sacrifice into this dialogue is seen as a futile attempt to pry them away from their consumer products and lecture them;[25] the only way to achieve revolution, so the argument goes, is to compete with capitalism and its culture industry to co-opt this desire for consumer products for positive ends.

Edgar Snow's book reminds us that, regardless of the working-class in the imperial core, this sacrifice has already been made. Regardless of whether they were able to complete a successful revolution, whether they were able to establish a dictatorship of the proletariat and defend those gains, countless communists around the world have already made this sacrifice—not out of feted moralism, but of necessity.

---

25  Ibid.

# The Cause of Anti-colonialism and Liberation is One: Fayez Sayegh's *Zionist Colonialism in Palestine*

Louis Allday

> Zionism is a form of racism and racial discrimination.
>
> United Nations General Assembly Resolution 3379, 10 November 1975

The Syrian-Palestinian academic and diplomat, Fayez Sayegh (1922-1980), a delegate of Kuwait's Mission to the UN in the mid-1970s, was the principal author of the landmark resolution quoted above. Much to the chagrin of the US, whose representative described it as a "great evil... loosed upon the world", the resolution was sponsored by the Arab states, and strongly supported by the Soviet Union and a large swathe of the newly independent states of the Global South.[1] Sixteen years later, Israel refused to participate in the Madrid Conference without its abrogation. With the opposing influence of

---

1   Daniel Patrick Moynihan, "Response to United Nations Resolution 3379", 10 November 1975.

the Soviet bloc gone, the US then exerted all its influence to ensure the resolution was repealed.[2] It remains the only UN General Assembly resolution to meet such a fate. Although short lived, it had served as global recognition of a position that Sayegh and his colleagues advocated for tirelessly over the preceding decades—one which had already been endorsed by a number of non-Western international organisations including the Non-Aligned Movement and the Organization of African Unity.

A vital institution in this effort was the PLO's Palestine Research Centre (PRC) in Beirut, as established by Sayegh in 1965. In its heyday, a who's who of Palestinian cultural and intellectual figures including Ghassan Kanafani, Mahmoud Darwish, Isma'il Shammout and Fayez's younger brother, Anis, worked for or contributed to the centre. Over almost two decades, it released more than four hundred publications about the Palestinian cause in multiple languages including Arabic, English, French, Spanish and even Esperanto.[3] This literature was distributed globally and was used in efforts to garner international support for Palestine. Organisations such as the Student Nonviolent Coordinating Committee (SNCC) released statements of solidarity with the

---

2 *The New York Times* reported that "United States embassies around the world were instructed to put maximum pressure to secure the repeal". It went on to state that the vote "reflected the shifting political currents of recent years, the Persian Gulf war in particular, which split the Arab and Islamic worlds, and the changes in the former Soviet bloc, fostered by the collapse of Communism". "U.N. Repeals Its '75 Resolution Equating Zionism With Racism", *New York Times*, 17 December 1991.

3 "'Palestine Liberation' Literature", *Patterns of Prejudice*, 1:6 (1967).

Palestinians that were informed directly by PRC publications.[4] The Centre's work was brought to a halt following Israel's invasion of Lebanon in 1982. During the subsequent occupation, its archive and library were looted by Israeli troops[5] and a bombing gutted its Beirut headquarters, killing twenty people and injuring dozens more—many of them staff members.[6] These attacks were part of a broader Israeli assault in which its forces "wiped out most of the Palestinian educational and cultural institutions they could get their hands on".[7]

The first monograph released by the PRC, Sayegh's *Zionist Colonialism in Palestine* in 1965, is a concise and powerful study of the origins, character and strategies of the Zionist movement. It epitomises the stirring and informative literature the Centre excelled at producing. Given the clarity of Sayegh's analysis and the prescience of his conclusions, the book remains strikingly relevant more than fifty years since it was written. Contrary to the liberal-Zionist myth that Zionism began as a noble cause,

---

4 Clayborne Carson, *In Struggle: SNCC and the Black Awakening of the 1960s* (Harvard University Press, 1981), 266-269.

5 Ihsan A. Hijazi, "Israelis Looted Archives of P.L.O Officials Say", *New York Times*, 1 October 1982.

6 Responsibility for the bombing was claimed by a group called the Front for the Liberation of Lebanon from Foreigners (FLLF) which was later revealed to be "a creation of Israel, a fictitious group used by senior officials to hide their country's hand in a deadly 'terrorist' campaign". Remi Brulin, "How the Israeli military censor killed a story about 'terrorist' bombing campaign in Lebanon in 1980s", *Mondoweiss*, 23 October 2019.

7 Munir Fasheh, "Graham-Brown, Education, Repression and Liberation", *Middle East Report*, 136/137 (October-December 1985).

but has been corrupted and dragged rightwards since 1967, Sayegh explains how Zionism was a colonialist and racist enterprise from its inception.[8] The present climate—in which there is an ongoing campaign by the US and Israeli governments (and affiliated Zionist pressure groups) to conflate anti-Zionism with anti-Semitism and, therefore, delegitimise opposition to Israel, makes the book's arguments all the more pertinent.

In his youth, Sayegh was a prominent member of the Syrian Social Nationalist Party but left after disagreements with its founder, Antoun Saadeh. He went on to complete a PhD on Existential Philosophy at Georgetown University, before holding a number of academic and diplomatic positions, mainly in the US. Surprisingly unfeted now, he was, at one time, one of the most prominent spokespersons of the Palestinian cause in the West and renowned as a master debater—a "calm and careful speaker [who] used language precisely".[9] Sayegh was also "famous for citing, by heart, paragraphs of given UN resolutions, dates of issuance, and books with page numbers".[10] His gift for communication is also evident in his writing, and *Zionist Colonialism in Palestine* is notable for the ease with which it translates complex historical developments into succinct, accessible language. Divided into four chapters—I) The Historical Setting of Zionist

---

[8] On this topic, see Steven Salaita, *Israel's Dead Soul* (Temple University Press, 2011).

[9] As'ad Abukhalil, "Before Edward Said: a tribute to Fayez Sayegh", *Al Akhbar English*, 9 December 2014.

[10] Anis F. Kassim (ed.), *The Palestine Yearbook of International Law, 1998-1999* (Brill/Nijhoff, 2000).

Colonialism, II) The Alliance of British Imperialism and Zionist Colonialism, III) The Character of the Zionist Settler State and IV) The Palestinians' Response: From Resistance to Liberation—the book's short length belies both its scope and importance.

When Sayegh was writing, the Palestinian cause did not enjoy the level of awareness or support it now does in progressive circles in the West, and Israel's reputation as an ostensibly "plucky" young state in an "unfriendly neighbourhood" had gained it widespread admiration, notably on the left. It was in this context that he approached the topic.

In the foreword, Sayegh points out the paradox that Israel was established when European colonisation had begun to retreat elsewhere. As such, the fate of Palestine was an anomaly, for at the very moment that others were beginning to enjoy their right to self-determination, the people of Palestine found "itself helpless to prevent the culmination of a process of systematic colonization".[11] This process led to them losing not only *political control* over their country, but *physical occupation* of it too—"deprived not only of its inalienable right to self-determination, but also of its elemental right to exist on its own land".[12]

*The Historical Setting of Zionist Colonialism*

Sayegh skilfully analyses the formation of the Zionist movement up until the outbreak of the First World War

---

11  Fayez Sayegh, *Zionist Colonialism in Palestine* (Palestine Research Center, 1965), v.

12  Ibid., vi.

in the book's opening chapter. He explains that, although it emerged in the context of late nineteenth century European nationalism and colonialism—and was thus heavily imbued with their ideological temper—Zionist colonization in Palestine was distinct from European colonization elsewhere in three crucial ways.

Firstly, unlike other European settlers, typically animated by economic or "politico-imperialist" motives, Zionist colonists "were driven to the colonization of Palestine by the desire to attain nationhood for themselves, and to establish a Jewish state".[13]

Secondly, while other European settlers tolerated the existence of indigenous populations, whom they commonly exploited as cheap labour, Zionism's aims—both territorial and political—could not be achieved so long as the Palestinians remained on their land. Therefore, unlike other European colonialist projects of the period, it "was essentially incompatible with the continued existence of the 'native population' in the coveted country".[14]

Finally, other European settlers could rely on the protection of their imperial sponsors to assist them settling in their chosen territory. By contrast, not only did the Zionist movement lack such support at this stage, it was likely to encounter resistance from the Ottomans.

Sayegh assesses the programme the Zionist movement adopted to counteract these obstacles along three lines: organisation, colonisation and negotiation. In so doing, he makes it clear that unlike many of their ideological

---

13   Ibid., 4-5.

14   Ibid.

heirs in the present day, Zionists of this formative era had no qualms acknowledging the explicitly colonial nature of their venture.

Organisationally, as the movement lacked "a state-structure in a home-base of its own to master-mind and supervise the process of overseas colonization" it needed to build a quasi-state structure in its place.[15] The World Zionist Organization, active to this day, was established in 1897 for that purpose. With regards to the process of colonisation itself, the haphazard, "mixed philanthropic-colonial venture" pursued previously with limited success was replaced with a more systematic approach.[16] This entailed the establishment of several institutions from 1897 onwards, all geared towards planning, financing and facilitating the arrival of Zionist colonisers in Palestine—these included The Jewish Colonial Trust, The Colonization Commission and The Jewish National Fund.

The third avenue, negotiation, entailed a diplomatic effort to try and foster the political conditions conducive to colonisation. This consisted primarily of an unsuccessful attempt to gain support from the Ottomans through financial and other incentives and, to a lesser extent, by making similar overtures to Germany and Britain. As summarised by Joseph Massad, "Zionism could only be realised through a colonial-settler project, which its founders understood was achievable only through an alliance with colonial powers".[17]

---

15   Ibid., 6.

16   Ibid., 2.

17   Joseph Massad, "Zionism, Anti-Semitism and Colonial-

Concluding the first chapter, Sayegh makes an important point: notwithstanding its growing organisation and militancy, up to the outbreak of the First World War, the Zionist movement's success had been limited. Its appeal remained narrow—Zionists constituted a tiny percentage of the Jewish population worldwide—and colonisation had proceeded so slowly that after thirty years, Jews still accounted for under 8 percent of the total population of Palestine and were in possession of no more than 2.5 percent of its land. Furthermore, the movement had not been able to gain the patronage of the Ottomans or any other imperial power. [18]

*The Alliance of British Imperialism and Zionist Colonialism*

A key turning point occurred during the First World War when the Zionist movement formed an alliance of convenience with Britain. It is this development and its implications that Sayegh analyses in the book's second chapter. Britain's pre-war policy towards the Ottoman Empire had been concerned with maintaining its territorial integrity in Asia. This approach changed once the Ottomans joined the Central Powers, leading Britain, France and Tsarist Russia to draw up plans for the anticipated division of the spoils.

Subsequently, Britain's desire to keep any rival European power away from the Suez Canal—crucial for securing the sea passage to India—led it to renege

---

ism", *Al Jazeera*, 24 December 2012.

18   Ibid., 8.

on an earlier agreement that would have seen the "internationalisation" of most of Palestine in the case of an Ottoman defeat. In its place, Britain began to lean towards the Zionist movement, realising that a "Jewish homeland" in Palestine could provide Britain with the pretext needed to place the territory east of Suez under its control—or what Ronald Storrs, the first British governor of Jerusalem, described as "a little loyal Jewish Ulster in a sea of potentially hostile Arabism".[19] As Sayegh puts it in characteristically succinct fashion, "[r]eciprocal interests had thus come to bind British Imperialism and Zionist Colonialism".[20]

It was in this context that Britain made the now infamous Balfour Declaration on 2 November 1917, proclaiming its support for the establishment of a Jewish "national home" in Palestine. This promise was then incorporated into the text of the Palestine Mandate, awarded to Britain by the League of Nations in the aftermath of the war. Once Britain established its rule, it wasted little time in fostering the conditions needed for Zionist colonisation to flourish.

Sayegh explains how the British authorities, ignoring Palestinian opposition, opened the country up to Zionist immigration and allowed the settler community to establish what by 1937 had become a "state within a state".[21] Britain permitted the Zionist community to run its own schools and maintain a military force, while at the same time denying the Palestinian community

---

19  Conn Hallinan, "Divide and Rule", *Irish Democrat*, 2004.

20  Sayegh, *Zionist Colonialism*, 12.

21  Ibid., 14 (quoting Britain's *Palestine Royal Commission*, 1937).

analogous facilities and suppressing their attempts at self-determination. After thirty years of Mandate rule, the Zionist settler-community had grown twelve times in size since 1917 and represented almost one third of the total population of Palestine.[22] Perhaps more importantly, under Britain's auspices, it had developed what Sayegh terms "its own quasi-government institutions and a sizeable military establishment".[23]

Britain had not entered into this partnership altruistically, so in order to justify its continued presence, whenever Zionism "sought to accelerate the processes of state-building… Britain pulled in the opposite direction to slow them down".[24] Sayegh details succinctly how this irresolvable tension ultimately caused the alliance to break down—violently so by the end of the Second World War. Britain's depleted condition and India's looming independence lessened its interest in maintaining its presence in Palestine, and the growing opposition of the newly-emerging independent Arab states forced Britain "to exercise some restraint in its formerly whole-hearted support for the Zionist cause".[25] Crucial too was the growing Arab nationalist movement from below and the protests, boycotts, general strikes and guerrilla attacks it carried out across the region.

The US, the triumphant and emerging global hegemonic power, offered Zionism the prospect of an alternative Western sponsor for what would prove a "new

---

22  Ibid., 15.
23  Ibid.
24  Ibid.
25  Ibid.

fateful phase of its capture of Palestine". Described by Sayegh as a "willing candidate" for such a role, the US then "led a European-American majority to overrule the opposition of an Afro-Asian minority" in the UN, and endorsed "the establishment of a colonial Zionist state in the Afro-Asian bridge, the Arab land of Palestine".[26]

Concluding this chapter, Sayegh explains that Israel's "vital and continuing association" with imperialism, its introduction of Western colonialism into Palestine and its "chosen pattern of racial exclusiveness and self-segregation renders it an alien society in the Middle East".[27] As its founding figure, David Ben-Gurion, himself proclaimed: "The State of Israel is a part of the Middle East only in geography".[28] It is the distinctive characteristics of this state that Sayegh assesses in the next chapter.

## *The Character of the Zionist Settler-State*

> The racist regime in occupied Palestine and the racist regimes in Zimbabwe and South Africa have a common imperialist origin... having the same

---

26 Ibid., 16. Two years after the release of Sayegh's book, and in language seemingly informed by it, the Afro-Asian Writers' Association condemned Israel as "an imperialist base and... tool used for aggressive purposes against Arab states in order to delay their progress... and as a bridge-head which neo-colonialism relies on in order to maintain its influence over African and Asian states". *Resolution on Palestine of the Third Afro-Asian Writers' Conference* (March 25-30, 1967, Beirut, Lebanon).

27 Ibid., 19.

28 David Ben-Gurion, *Rebirth and Destiny of Israel* (Philosophical Library, 1954), 489.

racist structure and being organically linked in their policy aimed at repression of the dignity and integrity of the human being.[29]

The three defining characteristics of the Zionist settler-state as defined by Sayegh are (1) its racial complexion and conduct; (2) its addiction to violence; and (3) its expansionist stance.[30]

As Sayegh maintains, racism "is not an acquired trait of the Zionist settler-state. Nor is it an accidental, passing feature of the Israeli scene. It is congenital, essential and permanent… inherent in the very ideology of Zionism".[31] Belief in the national oneness of all Jews—based on ostensibly common ancestry, not a religious or linguistic-based identity, is a central tenet of Zionism.[32] Sayegh identifies three corollaries this explicitly racial identification gives rise to: "racial self-segregation, racial exclusiveness, and racial supremacy".[33] It is these characteristics which made the forced removal of the indigenous population of Palestine central to the Zionist project.

Prior to the successful implementation of Plan Dalet and the resultant *Nakba* of 1948, the Zionist movement had contented itself with segregation from the Palestinians

---

29  Organization of African Unity, Resolution on Palestine, August 1975.

30  Sayegh, *Zionist Colonialism*, 21.

31  Ibid.

32  As Sayegh notes, at this time relatively few Zionists were "believing or practising Jews" and Hebrew "was resuscitated only after the birth of Zionism", Ibid.

33  Ibid.

through instituting a systematic boycott of their produce and labour. Contrary to liberal-Zionist journalist Owen Jones' claim that "[t]he collective communities of the *kibbutzim* seemed like incubators of a new socialist society",[34] a principle was established that "only Jewish labour would be employed in Zionist colonies".[35] The *Histadrut* or General Organization of Jewish Workers was established in 1920 specifically for this purpose, and as early as 1895, Theodor Herzl, the "spiritual father" of Israel, was planning to "spirit the penniless population [i.e. the Palestinians] across the frontier by denying it employment".[36] Indeed, organisations such as the Jewish National Fund "vigilantly ensured the observation of that fundamental principle".[37]

Sayegh, further demonstrating the racial exclusiveness inherent to the Zionist project, highlights the treatment that Palestinians who Zionist forces were unable to dislodge in 1948 have received since. He argues that through the systematic oppression of this internal population, Israel "has learned all the lessons which the various discriminatory regimes of white settler-states in Asia and Africa can teach it". Sayegh outlines the manifold official and unofficial oppressive measures these Palestinians faced—measures that have only grown more onerous and engrained since then—and remarks that, whereas "the Afrikaner apostles of *apartheid*… brazenly

---

34  As quoted in Oliver Eagleton, "Vicious, Horrible People", *New Left Review*, 127 (Jan/Feb 2021).

35  Sayegh, *Zionist Colonialism*, 25.

36  Ibid., 26.

37  Ibid., 25.

proclaim their sin, the Zionist practitioners of *apartheid* in Palestine beguilingly protest their innocence".[38]

Events since the publication of Sayegh's book offer grim confirmation of his assertion that Israel is addicted to violence. Since 1965, it has perpetuated an unbroken line of violent acts against the Palestinians too long to list here—both in and outside of Mandate territory. Echoing Sayegh's analysis, after Israeli snipers had massacred Palestinian protestors on the Gaza border in May 2018, Saree Makdisi commented, "[i]t is not possible for a settler-colonial regime to racially enable one people at the expense of another people without the use of violence".[39]

Furthermore, the target of this violence has not only been the Palestinians, Israel has also committed multiple aggressions against neighbouring states, including Lebanon, Syria and Egypt. It forcibly depopulated the Golan Heights in Syria and has illegally occupied this region since 1967. Israel has also played an integral role in the ongoing war against Syria, repeatedly launching air strikes against it in recent years. This trend underlines Sayegh's prescient observation that Israel is perpetually expansionist in nature, for not only has it consistently expanded the territory under its control, it has refused to ever declare its borders.

The fate that befell the PRC itself—subjected to multiple acts of violence by Israeli forces during its expansionist war against Lebanon in 1982—offers

---

38   Ibid., 27.

39   Saree Makdisi, "Kill and Kill and Kill", *Counterpunch*, 16 May 2018.

particularly direct evidence of Sayegh's tragically accurate foresight. As he wrote, expansion to the borders of so-called *Eretz Israel* "is the 'unfinished business' of Zionism. It cannot fail to be the main preoccupation of the Zionist movement, and of the Zionist state, in the future".[40]

*The Palestinians' Response: From Resistance to Liberation*

In the book's final chapter, Sayegh analyses the Palestinians' responses to Zionist colonisation. He divides this into five stages, beginning with the Palestinians' initially welcoming attitude to the early Jewish settlers,[41] moving through the various phases and avenues of resistance the Palestinian community put up against both the British authorities and Zionist forces up to 1964 with the formation of the PLO. In spite of this resistance, that reached its pinnacle in the Great Palestinian Revolt from 1936 until 1939, the bulk of the Palestinian population was forcibly dispossessed in 1948—their "unyielding resistance and their costly sacrifices had failed to avert national catastrophe".[42]

Sayegh stresses that these sacrifices were not made in vain, however, for "[r]ights undefended are rights surrendered. Unopposed and acquiesced in, usurpation is legitimised by default".[43] The Palestinians' unyielding

---

40  Sayegh, *Zionist Colonialism*, 38.

41  Sayegh notes that even Herzl himself commented on the "friendly attitude of the population", Ibid., 39.

42  Ibid., 46.

43  Ibid.

resistance and affirmation of their rights and heritage therefore ensured that Israel has "remained a usurper, lacking even the semblance of legitimacy".[44]

Though he stresses that liberation must be spearheaded by the Palestinians themselves, Sayegh contends that the "problem of Palestine… is not the concern of Palestinians alone". Israel's commitment to expansion is also a threat to the security and territorial integrity of the Arab states. Furthermore, as a colonial venture, "which anomalously came to bloom precisely when colonialism was beginning to fade away, it is in fact a challenge to all anti-colonial peoples…" "For, in the final analysis," Sayegh writes, "the cause of anti-colonialism and liberation is one and indivisible".[45]

He concludes that as a system "animated by doctrines of racial self-segregation, racial exclusiveness, and racial supremacy"—that then translates those doctrines into "ruthless practices of racial discrimination and oppression"—the political systems erected by Zionist colonialism in Palestine must be recognised as a menace to all those "dedicated to the safeguarding and enhancement of the dignity of man. For whenever and wherever the dignity of but one single human being is violated, in pursuance of the creed of racism, a heinous sin is committed against the dignity of all men, everywhere".[46]

At a time when solidarity with the Palestinians is increasingly under attack, slandered as anti-Semitic

---

44   Ibid.

45   Ibid., 51.

46   Ibid., 52.

or even criminalised, Sayegh's words serve as a timely reminder of why such solidarity has never been more important to express.

# A History of the Anonymous Masses: Rosemary Sayigh's *Palestinians: From Peasants to Revolutionaries*

Steven Salaita

Rosemary Sayigh calls her 1979 book, *Palestinians: From Peasants to Revolutionaries*, an ethno-history. The description is accurate. Sayigh does both ethnography and historiography. It's not certain whether the book rightly belongs to a single disciplinary category, though. It's an intimate study of a national community without any pretence of objectivity, which Sayigh rejects out of hand as a colonialist paradigm, professing instead a desire to highlight "the anonymous voices of the Palestinian masses".[1] She is interested in telling the story of Palestinians through their own voices and experiences. Even today, over four decades later, this straightforward methodology feels slightly heretical in relation to the restrictive norms of Middle East Studies.

For Sayigh, the book represents a long acculturation

---

1 Rosemary Sayigh, *Palestinians: From Peasants to Revolutionaries* (Zed Books, 1979), xxiii.

into a foreign culture. Born and raised in the United Kingdom, she married Palestinian economist Yusif Sayigh in 1953 and moved to Beirut, where she soon found herself involved in advocacy work for Palestinian refugees. Daily visits to refugee camps eventually became overnight stays and Sayigh cultivated deep relationships with the camps' rank-and-file. She earned an MA from the American University of Beirut and much later a PhD from York University in the UK. Despite the fact that *From Peasants to Revolutionaries* was well-received and would soon be considered a classic, Sayigh had difficulty in finding steady academic employment in Lebanon. Subsequent advocates of the Palestinian cause would face the same problem.

It isn't a stretch to say that the book became a classic precisely because it shuns conventional methodologies. Sayigh hints at a less traditional vision in the preface, noting that she wanted to produce a "people's history, not official history… concerned not with great events or leading figures, but with ordinary people's perceptions of these events, and with the ways they have transformed the lives of those classes of Palestinian—peasants, workers and the small bourgeoisie—who had no cushion between them and the Disaster of 1948".[2]

Palestinian society since 1948 has been scattered and sometimes isolated, with its various "branches" frequently unable to interact. The Palestinians of the Gaza Strip, for instance, are systemically disconnected from those of Lebanon, only a short distance up the Mediterranean coast. (Dozens of other such

---

2   Ibid., xxiv.

disconnections exist.) These divisions have created distinct economies and political cultures, which can result in tension among various segments of Palestinian society. Yet the divisions also deepen a sense of shared identity that's oriented around the homeland. Returning to Palestine is a collective aspiration.

Writing about the Palestinian nation can be a serious challenge because of this disaggregation. What is true of Palestinians in the Gulf States may not hold for Palestinians in North America. Sayigh, however, expertly delivers a narrative of post-Nakba Palestinian life that is both specific and universal. *From Peasants to Revolutionaries* speaks to a wide-ranging national identity by exploring the sensibilities of a particular diasporic community, Palestinian refugees in Lebanon. Sayigh achieved this because Palestine exists in the souls of its descendants as an inexorable lodestar, an always-present emblem of an unforgotten past and the endpoint of an imminent, hard-fought future. That's how her subjects present the nation—as a physical space, as a lost paradise, as a nostalgic geography—and she honours their words.

Oral histories pepper the book and offer powerful testimonies about the refugees' devotion to Palestine. Here, for example, Z.K., one of the refugees whose story Sayigh transcribes, reflects on the profound desire to return home:

> When we left the village [of al-Sha'b], my paternal and maternal grandfather was taken by the Jews and thrown out to Jordan, he and two of his sons. Two other of my uncles died on the way, near Jenin, but

> my grandfather, who was by now about 110 years old, went on to Aleppo where he had some relations with whom he stayed for a while, and then he joined us in Baalbeek [camp]. It was very cold in Baalback for an old man, so we returned to Tyre. There, he decided to go back to Palestine. My father tried to convince him that he's an old man, and that he can't make it. That was in 1950. But he insisted on going, and without telling anyone he bought a donkey and hired a guide, and he got back to Palestine and reached our village.[3]

The stories Sayigh gathered are filled with regret and longing, with some of the refugees proclaiming that if they could go back in time, they would choose to die rather than leave their villages. R.M. still suffers deep frustration:

> One of the political errors of our leadership was that they didn't prevent evacuation. We should have stayed. I had a rifle and a Sten gun. My father told me, "The Zionists are coming, you know what they do to girls, take your two sisters and go to Lebanon." I said, "I prefer to shoot my sisters, and shoot you all, and keep the last bullet for myself. This would be better than leaving".[4]

*Resistance Forms in Lebanon*

The Palestinians of Lebanon have had an enormous influence on Palestine's national liberation movement

---

3   Ibid., 89.
4   Ibid., 90.

(and also on Palestine's cultural accomplishments). In addition to hosting the PLO for many years, Lebanon was home to hundreds of notable poets, guerrillas, artists, and scholars. Despite their difficult circumstances—confinement to overcrowded camps, legalised employment discrimination, poverty, statelessness, racial acrimony—the Palestinians of Lebanon created a dynamic political and artistic culture. Proximity to the homeland informed their tenacity.

Sayigh conducted her research during the first stages of Lebanon's civil war (1975-1990), which added greater depth to the project. The war intensified the sense of foreignness Palestinians have been made to experience in the country (legally and socially). A recurring theme in the book is that while Palestinians will fight for better living conditions in Lebanon, residing there won't suffice as a long-term proposition. It's not Palestine. Returning home is the first and last priority. Home represents stability. Home is indivisible from personhood. Home is the precondition of existence. So-called host countries promise war and instability. Even in the better times, they cannot ameliorate the loneliness of exile. Such is the Zionist entity's terrible impact on the region. It is an ever-expanding repository of destruction. Having brought massive chaos and suffering to at least two continents, the Zionist entity isn't merely the material expression of the Palestinian's agony; it is the obverse of the Palestinian's primary aspiration.

Hence the basis for a dramatic history of resistance. Resistance comes in many forms, but Sayigh is concerned with the revolutionary variety. Her fieldwork isn't limited to interviews; she chronicles life embedded among Palestinian refugees. She also examines how Palestine, on the eve of the Zionist project (and throughout the first half of the 20th century) was a largely agrarian population—a "peasant society," in Sayigh's words—and how "in spite of Jewish immigration, and the growth of industry and urbanization, by 1948 two-thirds of Palestine's Arab population was still rural. There is thus good reason to regard Palestinian society as a peasant society, and its struggle for liberation a peasant-based struggle".[5]

Sayigh traces the development of Palestinians from a rural proletariat into urbanised communities engaged in a wide range of professions, teaching in particular. This development represents the story of Palestine's revolutionary sensibilities. The society evolved, but the peasant values survived. Palestinians in Lebanon would become a technocratic *fellaheen*, innovators of a vanguard playing on the imagination of every downtrodden community that took up arms against its oppressor.

Sayigh's notion of a peasant society is complex. She speaks of Palestinians across all economic strata, giving special attention to the descendants of the farmers and workers who ended up in Lebanon in large numbers (moneyed Palestinians and Christian Palestinians could often escape the camps). The ethnographic features of her analysis proffer a coherent framework for understanding a rapid, almost impossible societal transformation. The main conclusion is that Palestinian resistance didn't arise from urban centres in conditions of leisure or abundance.

---

5    Ibid., xxiv.

Peasantry, as Sayigh often reminds us, suggests intimacy with land. It's not possible to comprehend Palestinian resistance without a concomitant appreciation of the nation as a physical reality. The idea of Palestine derives life from the specific landbase on which the Zionist entity was established; Palestine cannot be replicated in any other geography

Sayigh develops her argument by focusing on individual villages, combining archival research with oral history to piece together a comprehensive narrative of Palestinian life in states of dispossession. She likewise gives a thorough overview of family structures and social conventions, which played a role in the Nakba and its aftermath. The guiding principle was communal self-sufficiency: "For Palestinian peasants, the city had never been economically indispensable. They looked to the cities for leadership, as the crisis generated by Zionist immigration intensified; but until their final 'cleaning' from their land in 1948, the villagers still produced the bulk of their foodstuffs".[6] Sayigh devotes a chapter to this "cleansing" and presents a damning indictment of Zionism, whose proponents committed massacres throughout the Palestinian countryside with the explicit aim of removing its inhabitants and taking their land.

This terror arose from a brutal strategic calculus: "An atrocity particularly calculated to horrify Arab peasants was the cutting open of the womb of a nine months' pregnant woman. This was the clearest of messages warning them that the Arab code of war, according to which women, children and old people were protected, no

---

6   Ibid., 24.

longer held good in Palestine".[7] The displaced populace had no choice but to become revolutionaries. Any other approach would have implicitly forfeited their claim to the land. As Sayigh's brother-in-law, Fayez, contended when extolling the virtues of Palestinian resistance, "[r]ights undefended are rights surrendered. Unopposed and acquiesced in, usurpation is legitimised by default".[8] Because of the geopolitical forces invested in the Zionist entity's existence, Palestinian nationalism is necessarily a revolutionary project. With great care and empathy, Sayigh traces its development from the countryside to the overcrowded camps of Beirut.

*The Situation Changes*

*From Peasants to Revolutionaries* isn't exactly a forgotten text, but it's closer to obscurity than it deserves. The second edition, which I am using for this review, was published in 2007 and sells for a price that suggests obsolescence. And yet, whatever the barriers to access, it should be read. (You can skip the two introductions by Noam Chomsky. He's only there for decoration.) The book is compact and lucid. Sayigh's theoretical rigor rarely leads to esoteric language. One would feel comfortable putting *From Peasants to Revolutionaries* into the hands of a high school student.

I try to rein in my nostalgia when it comes to classics

---

7   Ibid., 77.

8   Fayez Sayegh, *Zionist Colonialism in Palestine* (Palestine Research Centre, 1965), 46. See Louis Allday, "The Cause of Anti-colonialism and Liberation is One: Fayez Sayegh's *Zionist Colonialism in Palestine*" in this volume.

of scholarship and literature. There's always a whiff of sanctimony in ruminations beginning with some version of "back in my day," so I don't want to denigrate current writing about Palestine, which is often sharp and innovative. Yet the general sensibility of intellectual work feels different. I imagine that, with some notable exceptions, the change of sensibility has less to do with individual proclivities than with structural limitations. I don't know that people with professorial aspirations these days could afford to publish something like *From Peasants to Revolutionaries*—or even attempt a project with such a clear point of view. Not in English, anyway. It would be a sure path to tenure denial: not rigorous enough, subjective, polemical, dubious sourcing, published by a nonacademic press—everything, basically, that makes a history book pleasant to read, rather than formulaic deadweight calibrated to establishment sensibilities. Sayigh's own experience in academe validates any such timidity.

Perhaps the feeling of difference arises from the fact that conditions in Palestinian society have changed since Sayigh first started gathering research. Post-Oslo, the revolution was largely subsumed by diplomacy and the attendant shift of activism from armed struggle (or at least confrontation) to NGOs and cultural and religious organizations, many of dubious provenance. Revolutionary sentiment remains—the peasant values that Sayigh identifies—but it's no longer one of the defining features of Palestine's national movement. Major political parties have either embraced neocolonialism or wield little influence. The camps in Lebanon are impoverished and surrounded by the Lebanese military. A bloated class of mendacious functionaries interjects itself into everything, including (or especially) the public purse. In the United States, a new class of activist, invariably affiliated with the Democratic Party, barters Palestinian liberation for the cheapest possible return: individual clout. Arab states are lining up to normalise with the Zionist entity (while extracting no real concessions—the sole purpose is to further enrich the ruling class); the countries still supportive of Palestine suffer unending imperialist aggression. Palestine's civic sphere remains vibrant, but Basel al-Araj's fate portends a very difficult path for those who attach themselves to the revolutionary tradition.[9]

In turn, *From Peasants to Revolutionaries* is more important than ever. We need less accommodation to the logic of Western diplomacy, to the superficial comfort of white-collar decorum, and more focus on the peasant values that encompass an uncompromising vision of the homeland, intimate and indivisible. The book isn't merely an artifact of a bygone period, but a living document reminding today's activists and scholars that the struggle for Palestine's liberation is a spectacular phenomenon, relentless and unambiguous and often paid for in terrible acts of bloodletting.

We ought to keep the document alive, for the history Sayigh so vividly describes is only one arc in an uncompleted revolution. The text cannot be finished until

---

9   See Hazem Jamjoum, "Liberation, Wonder, and the 'Magic of the World': Basel al-Araj's *I Have Found My Answers*" contained in this volume.

Palestinians evolve from revolutionaries to repatriated citizens.

# Liberation, Wonder, and the "Magic of the World": Basel al-Araj's *I Have Found My Answers*

Hazem Jamjoum

> Basel did not call on us to be resistance fighters. Nor did he call on us to be revolutionaries. Basel told us to be true, that is all. If you are true, you will be revolutionaries and resistance fighters.
>
> Khaled Oudatallah in a eulogy for Basel al-Araj in al-Walajah, March 8 2017.[1]

It couldn't have been more than a few weeks after I had started a new role with a refugee rights organization in Bethlehem. It was the end of a workday when a friend and colleague, said to me "I have a cousin who is interested in political things like you. You should meet him… come, he's expecting us." Into his car we went, up the hill through Beit Jala and past the Israeli military base and checkpoint known as the "DCO" and into the village of al-Walajah. We drove to what looked like a

---

1   Basel al-Araj, *I Have Found My Answers* (Bisan, 2018), 388.

residential home, but when we entered I realised it had been transformed into a youth centre. Standing behind a desk in the middle of the entrance room was a thin man with thick glasses, somewhere in his mid-twenties. His name was Basel al-Araj.

Unlike most interactions between people meeting for the first time, this one involved almost no pleasantries. Somehow, both Basel and I realised that we could skip them, and that we preferred it that way. Within minutes he was talking me through the various maps and documents he'd prepared for my visit. An engaging story-teller, he was one of those people who are masters of communication, but for whom language felt like a curse—so much knowledge to share, so many stories, but you can only say one word at a time. Despite this, within what felt like no time at all, and illustrating each point with a document, Basel had shown me that al-Walajah is a microcosm of the Palestinian struggle.

On the eve of the Nakba, al-Walajah had a population of around 2,000 Palestinians living on over 20,000 fertile acres, dotted with fresh springs throughout the hills on both sides of the valley. The village itself was on the hilltop to the west of the valley—the Valley of the Giants in the Old Testament—where the Jaffa-Jerusalem railway was built in the 1890s. In October 1948, Zionist forces expelled all of the village's inhabitants, and took control of over 12,000 acres of the village's land. Most of the displaced villagers crossed over to the other side of the valley to the eastern hill of the village that came under Jordanian control after the 1949 armistice agreements—the valley itself becoming part of the armistice (or "Green") line between the West Bank and the new Zionist state.

The sun had begun to set in the middle of our conversation. Basel took me outside and pointed west. The colours were spectacular, but that wasn't all he wanted me to see—just below the resplendent reds and oranges was the silhouette of a Zionist settlement; amidst the shadows were some buildings with the iconic old stone that immediately identifies Palestinian buildings built before 1948. For all these decades, Walajees have been refugees on their own land, unable to see a sunset without looking at the remnants of their own village—now an Israeli settlement called Aminadav (which ironically translates as "a generous people")—their springs now waterholes along a network of hiking trails used by Israelis and tourists.

In 1967 Israel occupied the new site of al-Walajah, which had been a refugee camp in all but name since the Nakba. Soon thereafter, Israel's illegal settler colonies Gilo and Har Gilo, and the roads servicing them, were built on land that included 2,000 acres of what remained of al-Walajah. In 1980, the Israeli Knesset formally annexed Jerusalem, expanding its municipal borders to include parts of the new village but without extending Jerusalem residency rights to any of the inhabitants. Since then, Israeli police have harassed Walajees in those parts of the village, in some cases arresting them while in their own homes for being in Jerusalem without a permit.

Things only got worse after the Oslo accords, when what remained of the village's agricultural land was effectively annexed to Israel. Soon thereafter, the

Jerusalem Biblical Zoo was relocated to parts of al-Walajah's land, and construction began on the apartheid-annexation wall which now renders al-Walajah an enclave that is completely surrounded by settlements, walls and settler-only bypass roads, with effectively only one entrance in and out of the village. In the years before I met him, Basel and other villagers had banded together to try to pave the roads that kept them connected to Bethlehem, and the Israeli military would repeatedly destroy those roads and arrest the villagers who dared defy the transformation of al-Walajah into an open air prison. I visited the village every month or two after that, sometimes seeing Basel, but most often not. On every visit I would notice a subtle change—a road that had been paved now destroyed, the fence around Har Gilo settlement a few meters closer to the road, a house that once stood, now demolished.

Thanks to Basel, I met many of the community's leaders, as well as many of the older generation who remembered the revolutionary 1930s and the expulsion in 1948. I was collecting oral histories and interviews for television and radio to tell the story of what I had started describing as the "ongoing Nakba",[2] which al-Walajah exemplifies. Basel knew every one of them intimately, but didn't want to be interviewed himself. After 2008, Basel and I lost touch. He'd moved to the Shu'fat refugee camp in Jerusalem to take up his first real job as a pharmacist (he studied pharmacy in Egypt during the peak years of the Second Intifada).

---

2   "Palestine's Ongoing Nakba", *al-Majdal*, 39-40 (Autumn 2008/Winter 2009).

As the years passed, Basel became increasingly involved in the resistance movement as a regular at martyrs' funeral processions and political lectures. He began to translate his immense knowledge into writing, and around 2014 he joined the Popular University as an instructor to give classes on the resistance history of Palestine and design walking tours in which he'd take participants through the details of past resistance operations. He helped start the *Bab el-Wad* online magazine so he and others could share their historical research and political analysis and reconfigure the relationship of knowledge production to the liberation struggle.

In early April 2016, the Palestinian Authority (PA) police arrested Basel and two of his comrades outside of Ramallah, stating that the detention was to "protect" the young men from arrest by Israel. Three other arrests were later added to this group. The men were tortured, and Basel had to be given medical treatment often in the first few weeks of interrogation. Four months later, no charges were filed, and the six men went on hunger strike to demand their release, resulting in a public campaign calling for the PA to let them go, which it eventually did in early September. It has become routine for the PA to do Israel's dirty work of torturing Palestinians to attempt to extract information, then releasing them, handing over what they could discover to the Israelis, then facilitating re-arrest by the Israelis themselves. So it came as no surprise when Israeli soldiers began hunting down the six men after their release. All were hunted down in this way, but Basel evaded capture for six months.

On Monday March 6, 2017, Palestinians woke up to

the news. At dawn, a specialised tactical unit of Israel's Border Police had attempted to raid the house in al-Bireh where Basel was hiding. After a two-hour gunfight, the unit fired two rockets into the apartment, killing Basel al-Araj.

## *A History of Colonialism, A History of Resistance*

The Israelis held Basel's body for eleven days before giving it to his family for burial in al-Walajah. Those who went into his hideout after the battle found a stack of his unpublished writings. A year after his martyrdom, Bissan bookshop (well-known to book lovers who have been to the Hamra neighbourhood of Beirut) published a collation of these texts, together with some of his previously published work, as well as over one hundred pages of social media posts, and twelve obituaries and other texts written in remembrance of him, publishing them under the title *I Have Found My Answers: Thus Spoke Basel Al-Araj*.

The opening essay titled "The Wounded Memory of the Nakba",[3] begins with an abstract discussion of memory, but quickly becomes a retelling of the Nakba. It does not add much to existing histories of the Nakba empirically, but tackles it with an emphasis on the scale of the collective trauma, the use of massacres and rape; germ warfare, death marches and attacks on unarmed communities; lining villagers up against walls and shooting them down before getting their relatives to dig the mass unmarked graves they lie in to this day—all as

---

3   Al-Araj, *My Answers*, 17-34.

means of terrorizing Palestinians. As with most of his other essays, Basel isn't one for conclusions. Every essay leaves the reader to connect the introductory discussion with the nuts-and-bolts of the essay. In the case of his history of the Nakba, but unlike all the other essays, Basel's emphasis is not on Palestinian heroism and the culture of resistance. It is a story of pain and the egregiousness of the crimes that the forced expulsions of 1947-1949 had entailed. Reading it, despite the ample footnotes to scholarly historical work, I can't help but think of Basel hearing stories from his village elders, of the feeling of seeing their former homes silhouetted against every sunset. It is a reminder that the Nakba was a horror, lived in real time by our elders living and dead, not just a legal crime or a political event for which we seek redress. It is an exhortation to feel, over and above any invitation to think.

Among the only other pieces on the Nakba is also the only one where al-Walajah is at the centre. But what sets "Gharba: Where I was born and where I will not Die"[4] apart is that it is the only piece of historical fiction in the collection of essays. Here, Basel writes from the perspective of someone born into the al-Araj family in 1937. As the fruit of his many conversations with his family and elders, this piece is the story of the occupation, depopulation and destruction of al-Walajah in the Nakba. Almost every paragraph contains deep analysis of class, clan and gender disparities, and how they formed a backdrop to the forced removal of Palestinians from Palestine. It is an artful piece, mixing masterful standard

---

4   Ibid., 151-165.

Arabic prose, vernacular from the village, and even modified English words that had entered the lexicon.

One memorable example of Basel's descriptive subtlety, for instance, is his description of the failure of neighbouring Arab states to provide a modicum of protection for Palestinians in the face of the Zionist military onslaught: "Two weeks later, some Egyptian forces entered the village to help with its defense. Most were regulars, some were volunteers. The volunteers fought with ferocity, the regulars ate all the chickens in the village".[5] This short story is a rich imagination of village life at the moment when it was clear that, as the story ends, "we've become refugees, and the country is gone".[6]

Later in the collection, his essay on "The Armed Struggle in the Revolution of 1936"[7] is also empirical, but in a tone that characterises most of Basel's other writings; namely that Palestinian resistance history is one of immense and heroic accomplishment and a wellspring of lessons for the struggles ahead. He highlights the scale of the uprising, the thousands of operations, the high level of coordination and organization after August 1936 despite, and maybe because of, its decentralization, and systematically highlights the effectiveness of guerrilla warfare strategy in a situation of immense power asymmetry. He reminds us that "though it is largely a defensive strategy, its tactics are those of a war of attack" which enabled the revolutionaries to not only sabotage

---

5   Ibid., 159.

6   Ibid., 165.

7   Ibid., 77-84.

British occupation communications infrastructure, but to liberate and hold vast tracts of the country, including the cities of Nablus, Bir al-Sabe' (Beersheva) and Jerusalem for months at a time in 1938.[8]

Other essays include valuable historiographical interventions that relate to Palestinian resistance. In an article on the Black Hand group ("Al-Kaf al-Aswad"),[9] a name made popular by the Serbian group that assassinated the Austrian crown prince in 1914, Basel begins by stating that he could find little well researched pieces of writing on this secret organization, and that what he found was often conflicting. Taking it upon himself to put one together, he finds that the main Black Hand group was a resistance organization that worked in secret in the 1930s, mostly focused on tracking and taking down Palestinians who collaborated with the British occupation, including spies and those facilitating land sales to Zionist organizations. The group was characterised by its horizontal organization, structured in such a way that no member knew any more than three or four others.[10] Women were significantly active, especially in hiding weapons and in carrying out secure communications, including delivering ultimatums and demands. Basel then surveys other mentions of the Black Hand in Palestine (as well as Egypt, Libya and Syria), arguing that this was a name used by many different and unrelated groups from the 1920s until the mid-1950s. This effectively solves a particular source of

---

8   Ibid., 81.

9   Ibid., 47-52.

10  Ibid., 47.

historiographical confusion for histories of Palestinian resistance during the Mandate period.

Basel's perspective on resistance history does not cast it only in the light of armed struggle, pitch battles and underground guerrilla cells. His essay on "Art in Palestine"[11] resuscitates a mostly forgotten history of Palestinian cultural production in the mandate period that focuses primarily on poetry, song and theatre, with some mention of other fine arts. Though by no means comprehensive, the essay effectively points to a Palestinian cultural efflorescence, thoroughly tied to the broader region, and particularly Egypt from which many musicians and theatre troupes visited Palestine, and where many of the painters and sculptors studied at the then-recently established art academies.

His discussion of poetry and song provides in-depth discussions of many less renowned poets and popular singers The piece focuses on the role such figures played in marking historic events related to the struggle against British occupation and Zionist colonization as part of mass mobilization "using the poems as if they were militant communiqués and a means of spreading military knowledge and culture, a loud voice publicizing the strategies and orders of the leaders to the populace".[12] In a particularly memorable passage, Basel discusses the tactical use of songs, such as those women would sing outside prisons and in the hills where Palestinian commandos hid to deliver communications through

---

11   Ibid., 85-101.

12   Ibid., 90.

coded language, and a version of the popular *dal'ona*[13] that would signal to the resistance that they were being used as human shields by British occupation troops and communicate their position.[14]

*Revolutionary Biography*

The attentiveness to revolutionary biography, as is evident in his "Art in Palestine", takes center stage in two other essays: "Abdelqadir Continues to Return to Jerusalem" (on Abdelqadir al-Husseini)[15] and "Fawzi al-Qutb: For the Love of Gunpowder"[16] in which Basel deepens his project of recoding well-known historical figures (al-Husseini is well established within the Palestinian pantheon of leaders and martyrs), and—as with the Black Hand group and the forgotten resistance singers and poets mentioned above—of shedding light on forgotten moments and figures whose stories are both instructive and deserving of membership in that pantheon.[17]

---

13   A rural genre used when villagers would join together to help put up a roof to a fellow villager's house.

14   Al-Araj, *My Answers*, 91.

15   Ibid., 102-118.

16   Ibid., 127-136.

17   Fawzi al-Qutb was a Damascus-born explosives expert who participated in the 1936 revolution, after which he was sent to Germany for further explosives training. When the Nazi army attempted to deploy him as a soldier, he refused saying "this is not my war," (Ibid., 131.) after which he was sent to the Wroclaw concentration camp, the tattoo from which he bore for the rest of his life. After the camp was liberated, he was detained by US forces, and upon his release he returned to Palestine and partici-

He gives revolutionary biography particular attention as a genre in his essay "Out of the Law and into the Revolution",[18] which he introduces by reminding us that exceptional revolutionary figures are often cast either as bandits or heroes. After a foray into the literature on bandit-revolutionaries that brings together renowned pre-Islamic bandits in the Arabian peninsula, Frantz Fanon, Izz al-Din al-Qassam and Eric Hobsbawm, Basel settles on an analysis of the law as "a tool of normalised hegemony in the hands of authority," which the state uses to give itself the monopoly on determining right and wrong. By doing so, it places both secret revolutionary organizations and the underworld of "criminality" in the same "outlaw" status and incentivizing them to dig into the same pool of strategies and tactics to challenge power and evade capture.

With this introduction in place, Basel discusses a number of outlaws, starting with Ibrahim Hekimoğlu, an anti-feudal bandit from Ottoman folklore with a story almost identical (as Basel points out) to that of Robin Hood, William Wallace, and Henry Martini, the Iraqi revolutionary hero Suwaiheb al-Fallah (immortalised in the poetry of Muthaffar al-Nuwwab) and the Egyptian, Adham al-Sharqawi (the focal point of many a popular song). In all of these cases, Basel is attentive to how these symbols are then co-opted by state narratives to domesticate them for popular consumption, while attempting to derive legitimacy for state power through this co-option. The essay culminates with an extended

---

pated in the resistance in the 1948 Nakba.

18   Ibid., 137-143.

discussion of Malcolm X and Ali La Pointe, both of whom began their outlaw careers as thieves and honed their skills for what would become historic leading roles in the Black and Algerian liberation struggles of the mid-twentieth century.

*Cultural Intervention*

Here a key thrust of Basel's approach to his revolutionary scholarship is made clear: it isn't historical analysis as academic exercise or to fill a gap in the literature. And though it may be instructive on an organizational level, its real value is in its potential to transform the way we look at, and interpret, the world around us. Whether it's through reinterpreting the past or through juxtaposing our own lives to those in the biographical accounts, Basel pushes us to rethink our relationship to such things as authority, the permissible, and the possible. His history of the "*'awna*"[19] makes his project of cultural transformation explicit. *'Awna* is a mainly rural Palestinian concept akin to mutual aid, which came into Arabic usage from 1994 onwards as Western-backed NGOs worked to find concepts homologous to their own, and settled on this one as the analogue to "volunteerism."

In its neoliberal variant, NGOs distorted 'awna into a glorified version of volunteerism, a way for NGOs to extract free labour while somehow arguing that this was part of "local culture." Basel saw the danger in this, and sought to fight back by providing an actual history of *'awna* by distinguishing it from lofty notions of altruism

---

19   Ibid., 35-46.

that are so central to volunteerism, and by showing that it was part of a set of concepts (like *faz'a*)[20] that emerged from the political economic contexts of rural communities banding together in the face of scarcity brought on by greedy landlords and tax farmers. He goes on to show how gender equality and anti-hierarchical organization are central to the notion, and that it is, at its core, about survival rather than lofty humanitarianism. He substantiates his arguments with a stunning breadth of sources that range from etymological texts, popular proverbs, songs and oral histories.

In an even more far reaching essay on "The Palestinian Couch Faction",[21] he makes a scathing intervention criticizing cynical Palestinian pronouncements on the 2011 Egyptian uprising, which he juxtaposes to the increasing levels of Palestinian inaction in the face of accelerating settler-colonial theft and violence, which he directly connects to the increasing influence of the Palestinian Authority, neoliberal transformation of the Palestinian economy and the breaking of the community into atomised and self-serving economic units as a result

---

20  *Faz'a*, Basel shows, is the broader concept, of jumping to aid someone in need of help. It was commonly evoked in the Nakba by people rushing to aid people and communities coming under Zionist attacks and expulsions. In making sense of the Nakba after 1948, writers blamed the spontaneity of *faz'a* for the failure to defend Palestinian communities against Zionist aggression, and the term took on a negative connotation of being outdated, unfit and equating to disorganization. In Basel's analysis, this is why *'awna* rather than *faz'a* was the term deployed by the NGO sector in their effort to invent a local tradition of altruistic volunteerism.

21  Ibid., 176-185.

of Israel's apartheid infrastructure.

*Lessons of the Past, Fuel for the Future*

In "The Economy in the Intifada",[22] Basel describes resistance as having three parts: direct action (protest, sabotage, etc), popular mobilization and organization and economic self-sufficiency and development. The essay, as its title suggests, focuses on the third pillar in the context of the First Intifada, but emphasises that each of the three pillars are thoroughly imbricated in, and are necessary for, the success of the others and the overall movement. As with his essays on *'awna* and the Black Hand, Basel is attentive to the merits of non or even anti-hierarchical organization, emphasizing that decentralization and non-hierarchy do not entail the absence of organization.

Basel extends this valorisation of decentralised organization down to the immediate tactical level in his discussion of the first intifada. He reminds readers that the street battles between largely unarmed Palestinians and the armed-to-the-teeth Israeli soldiers were not coordinated from a particular centre, but were by no means spontaneous, disorganised or without a clear goal. On the contrary, fighters in Jabaliya, Balata, Dheisheh, and Nusayrat refugee camps and elsewhere acquired and held on to basic weaponry and used it in their confrontations with the Israeli military. The militants managed to surround the occupation forces in particular streets and neighbourhoods, where they could attack

---

22  Ibid., 53-76.

them from all sides. Very often individual occupation soldiers found themselves alone in refugee camp alleyways after being steered there by stone throwers, while the Palestinian strike forces strategically placed themselves on rooftops to either support a particular defensive attack on the invading troops or to break the encirclement by such troops on a particular group of Palestinian militants. Citing Israeli military reports, he shows that the occupation forces would often find themselves under intensive coordinated attack, "hounded from street to street" by stone and Molotov cocktail throwers, just as they had declared an area "safe".[23] This highly decentralised level of tactical organization made a mockery of Israel's undeniable military superiority.

Basel offers some historical background to what he characterises as organised spontaneity. He shows how over the course of the 1970s, annual commemorations, such as the Balfour Declaration or Nakba anniversaries, and martyr funeral processions that became occasions for large rallies. Over time, the resistance tactics then expanded to include special operations (*'amaliyat naw'iyyah*) in which the more agile and daring youth developed tactics to obstruct Israeli military patrols and raids. With time, these militants could count on schoolchildren to hinder soldiers' visibility by burning tires at the end of each school-day.[24] Meanwhile, the engaged population developed the mass tactic of large rallies into city and country-wide sector strikes and

---

23   Ibid., 57.

24   Hazem Jamjoum, "Ramallah commemorates the ongoing Nakba", *Electronic Intifada*, 28 May 2008.

general strikes, culminating in the memorable tax, labour, rent, commercial strikes and the refusal to pay fines and penalties that were a key weapon of the first intifada. The corollary of this non-cooperation, which emphasised the boycott of everything relating to the occupation (which parallels the strategy of ungovernability in the South African liberation struggle) was the emphasis placed on domestic economy in the form of growing food and raising animals at home, and the proliferation of retail, craft, agriculture, community hygiene, public health and educational cooperatives.

With his immense range of reading and knowledge, one of the striking facets of Basel's writing is its accessibility. In one of his quirkier essays he interweaves the scientific literature on porcupines and mosquitos with stories and memories of villagers' interactions with these creatures and quotes from Mao Tse Tung and Friedrich Engels to deliver a moral, as if from a fable: "Live as a Porcupine, Fight like a Mosquito".[25] He was able to bring the most specialised scientific writing into everyday language, and always for the purpose of saying something meaningful. In another, titled "No Love for the Oppressed"[26] he cites no writings whatsoever, but reflects on lessons he had learned from a former lover to come to his own understanding of the ways settler-colonial oppression disfigures Palestinian masculinity into a narcissism that renders women "either prostitutes or tools for the reproduction of little slaves".[27] (In another essay on

---

25    Al-Araj, *My Answers*, 166-169.

26    Ibid., 170-172.

27    Ibid., 172.

gendered power relations in the collection, "Don't side with the Occupation against Palestinian Women",[28] Basel draws on psychoanalysis to argue that Palestinian men take out the frustrations of their own emasculation on Palestinian women who fight back, but struggles with how to address this without alienating "broader society").

Other essays and social media posts contained in the book draw on lessons from other liberation struggles such as the Vietnam and Black liberation movements in the USA and intervenes in the protest movements of the early 2010s that targeted the PA and offers detailed histories of Palestinian resistance operations. Others offer commentary on various topics, ranging from child marriage and forgotten heroes, to how to reckon with Israel's use of triple action pepper spray. Though variable in length and style, each one has a lesson to teach, each is as engaging as it is carefully thought out and presented, and most leave one with awe at a mind that took seriously the questions "how do we get free?", "how do we surmount the seemingly-insurmountable power of one of the most powerful militaries in the world that enjoys complete impunity?", and "how do we become free as people without falling into yet another postcolonial authoritarian patriarchal society?" Basel argues that knowledge, critical analysis and action are all essential to finding the answers, and his writings reveal the depth and commitment he brought to this task.

---

28   Ibid., 191-196.

*Towards the Re-enchantment of the World*

Of the pieces Basel wrote in his last days—found together with his other writings in the apartment in al-Bireh where he fought off the Israeli soldiers—two in particular stand out. One was a piece titled "Why do we go to War?".[29] His answer to the question is surprising coming from someone who knows more than most about the crimes of colonialism in Palestine and almost everywhere else. His answer: *al-romansiyyah,* or romanticism. arguing that the romance of war is by far the most enticing. He supports his answer with examples from Hollywood and Bollywood films to great narratives of struggle from the world over. "All other attempts at explanation are not answers, they are attempts to evade an answer; rationalizations of romanticization".[30] Basel surrounded himself with militant intellectuals, and this was his last word to those who would ground everything in Reason, who insisted that any romanticizing of heroism, martyrdom and glory was at best a childish motive, one unworthy of Palestinians' struggle. Basel's last words on this:

> You, the academically inclined, set your sights on disenchanting all things by defining and explaining, reckoning that it will land you on the truth. In these overcast days I tell you I need no explanatory framework for rainfall - whether it is Thor's hammer or God's mercy or meteorologists' consensus. I want none of it. What I want is my unabating wonder and

---

29   Ibid., 326-335.

30   Ibid., 329.

my silly smile whenever the rain falls. Every time as if the first time, a child bewitched and the magic of the world.

The second is a letter Basel wrote as his final testament when he was sure the Israelis hunting him would kill him. It is from the last passage of this testament that the book is titled, a passage that says everything about where he had arrived in his question-riven romantic quest.[31]

Greetings of Arab nationalism, homeland, and liberation,

If you are reading this, it means I have died and my soul has ascended to its creator. I pray to God that I will meet him with a guiltless heart, willingly, and never reluctantly, and free of any whit of hypocrisy. How difficult it is to write your own final testament; for years I have contemplated such texts by martyrs, and been bewildered by them. Succinct, and without eloquence, they do not sate our burning desire for answers about martyrdom.

Now I walk to my fate, satisfied that I have found my answers. How stupid I am; is there anything more eloquent than the actions of a martyr? I should have written this months ago, but what kept me was that this question is for you, the living. Why should I answer for you? You should search for it. As for us, the people of the graves, we seek nothing else but God's mercy.

---

31  Ibid., 345.

# Ireland's Struggle for Self-determination: Robbie McVeigh and Bill Rolston's *Ireland, Colonialism and the Unfinished Revolution*

Chris Beausang

Robbie McVeigh and Bill Rolston's *Anois ar theacht an tSamhraidh: Ireland, Colonialism and the Unfinished Revolution* is one of the finest works of Irish and anti-imperialist historiography written to date.[1] Published in June 2021 by Beyond the Pale books, it fills an enormous gap in Irish political discourse, which has tended to overlook the influence of imperialism on the particularities of Irish capitalism. McVeigh and Rolston frame these issues within a *longue-durée* perspective, reaching as far back into the past as ancient Celtic society and as far forward as the COVID-19 pandemic. Their scholarly apparatus is hugely impressive and McVeigh and Rolston offer an enormous number of examples drawn from world history. Despite this, the book has not received the attention it deserves

---

1 '*Anois ar theacht an tSamhraidh*' a line from the traditional Irish song, *Óró sé do bheatha abhaile*, translates as 'Now that summer's coming'.

Ireland's Struggle for Self-determination 163

and has not yet been reviewed in any major publication. What follows intends to rectify this state of affairs.

McVeigh and Rolston position their work as emerging from a post-2008 moment, a point at which the global capitalist system was brought to the brink of collapse as the extent of the fictitiousness of global bank balance sheets and property investment portfolios became clear. Out of this came the collapse of the twenty-six county state's "Celtic Tiger" economy, the discrediting of an economic model that provides special tax arrangements for multinationals to secure investment, the collapse of the Good Friday Agreement (GFA) and the United Kingdom leaving the European Union.[2] All these events

---

2  The Anglo-Irish Treaty of 1921 imposed a border on the island of Ireland, separating six counties in the island's north-eastern corner—Antrim, Armagh, Derry, Down, Fermanagh and Tyrone—from the other twenty-six counties. This was undertaken in order to secure British imperialism on the island as well as to bolster the unionist dispensation within this synthetic construction. As this border violates the terms of the Irish Republic, declared as an all-Ireland state in 1916, the titles one uses in order to refer to either of these entities are highly politicised as they ascribe legitimacy, either to the Republic locating itself in a broader history of anti-imperialist struggle, or the border imposed on the island which overturned the will of the Irish people, as expressed in the election of 1918. A Fine Gael-Labour coalition government declared the twenty-six county state to be the Republic of Ireland in 1949, but for many Republicans this affords a legitimacy to the idea that two separate states exist on the island and that the Republic possesses no territorial claims on the six counties. For those who accept the legitimacy of partition, the six-county state in the north is referred to as 'Northern Ireland', while Republicans opt for 'the six counties', 'the northern statelet' or 'the occupied territories'. While those who accept the legitimacy of the twenty-six county state would refer to it as 'The Republic of Ireland' or 'the Republic', Republicans would refer to it as

have taken place in and around the one hundred year anniversary of a protracted period of social struggle in Ireland and have underlined the long-standing legacies of imperialism and placed new emphasis on the importance of self-determination.

McVeigh and Rolston demonstrate how resources from Ireland's past can inform developments currently underway in radical politics. More traditional models of industrial worker power in the west, expressed in mass action or general strikes, have come under severe pressure over the past half-century, through bureaucratisation as well as more direct attacks on trade unions, casualisation of labour contracts, containerisation and de-industrialisation. As such, working-class unrest increasingly expresses itself more spontaneously and among sections of the working class often referred to as forming part of the systematically under-employed "reserve army of labour"; we might think of the 2011 London riots or the 2014 Ferguson uprising in this context. Through counter-insurgency consisting of armed operations undertaken by state forces and media co-option, the concessions the capitalist state metes out in response to these challenges are often highly regressive. Despite the electoral endorsement given to women's reproductive rights in a 2018 referendum, reproductive rights in the twenty-six counties remain in many respects conditional. In answer to demands for specific police units to be disbanded in the US, additional

---

'the twenty-six counties', 'the south' or 'The Free State'. For the purposes of this review I use the terms 'the twenty-six counties' and 'the six counties'.

funding is provided. Calls for reparations for the victims of the British Empire are used by the ruling class to stoke culture wars, which are themselves largely veneers for criminalising opposition, as can be seen in the content of the Conservative party's Higher Education (Freedom of Speech) Bill.

That McVeigh and Rolston are mindful of these developments is obvious. They make the effort to touch upon topics that have inflamed enormous amounts of online debate in recent years, such as Irish slavery, as well as the degree to which the Irish people have a case to answer as foot-soldiers of the Empire. The idea that the Irish have not been victims of Empire has developed currency firstly among well-intentioned people seeking to challenge cynical fascist usage of indentured servitude,[3] and secondly among anti-Republican revisionist historians, who have received ample space to spread their apologia for genocide in Irish newspapers. One of the many statistics McVeigh and Rolston draw our attention to are mortality rates for indigenous children separated from their parents and installed in residential schools in the Americas, which matched or exceeded those of the Nazi concentration camps.[4] Mass murder has therefore always been a crucial part of colonialism, which is why attempts to rehabilitate British, French, Dutch or Belgian imperialism, are undertaken only by the most reactionary blocs of the ruling class. McVeigh and Rolston however, shift the emphasis to historical actuality; the ambivalences

---

3   McVeigh and Rolston, *Ireland, Colonialism and the Unfinished Revolution* (Beyond the Pale, 2021), 69.

4   Ibid., 51.

as well as the very real solidarities that existed between the Irish and other colonised peoples, taking us from the idea that anti-imperialist politics should involve ascribing the correct amount of guilt to both sides.

McVeigh and Rolston divide the history of imperialism into stages. The first was initiated by Spain and Portugal who divided the world in the 1494 Treaty of Tordesillas, making large territorial acquisitions and vassals of the peoples they encountered. With the emergence of the Dutch Empire more recognisably modern economic relations can be identified, with private commercial concerns, shipping routes and mercantilism. The Dutch East India Company established the first capital market, opening the benefits of imperialism to a broader stratum of society beyond the aristocracy. France and England then launched similar ventures and furthermore imposed restrictions to prevent their settlements from trading with any other country; thereby become enormously wealthy. In the nineteenth century, the European powers divided Africa and Asia until "by the start of World War I, nearly all the world outside Europe… had been formally colonised at some point by at least one European state".

As Vladimir Lenin argued, World War I was a natural outgrowth of the world the imperial powers had created. With no markets left to expand into, they had no choice but to turn against themselves. The old European colonial system entered into terminal decline from the end of World War II, but not without having shaped the new global order. Large parts of the globe had been systematically underdeveloped, meaning that strict limits were imposed on decolonisation as an economic as well as a political project. The failure or inability of South Africa's ANC to transfer back to its original owners as it set out to do is just one of many examples. Sections considering this history are excellent, dense with information about the concrete operation of colonialism, the selective apportioning of voting rights, citizenship being denied indigenous peoples and racial hierarchies within the supposedly independent states.[5]

McVeigh and Rolston also demonstrate that Ireland has not in any sense been decolonised and that imperialism has shaped the structure of the two statelets on the island. McVeigh and Rolston argue this has been an oversight in the works of the canonical theorists of the state, such as Jürgen Habermas, Michel Foucault, Ralph Miliband and Nicos Poulantzas. These theorists have all, to greater or lesser extents, developed abstract models of nation states in the imperial core, which are not subject to the same dynamics of underdevelopment, unequal exchange or militarisation of state forces that prevail in former and current, colonies. Our understanding of the social dynamics surrounding class, religion, and gender in an Irish context would therefore all be very poorly served by adopting these theories uncritically.

What is widely understood to be the first moment in the Irish state's inception was the declaration of the Republic declared in Easter 1916 and ratified by the Irish people in an election in 1918. This was the first and only stage in Irish history in which we have seen the will of the Irish people express itself in an election, with the exception of younger women who were not afforded the franchise.

---

5   Ibid., 314-26.

The Irish people's struggle to extricate themselves from Empire; British, American or European, remains ongoing. It would not be uncommon for individuals or organisations on the Irish left to ridicule the invocation of the Republic in the present moment. The Official IRA/Worker's Party often wrote off Republican struggle as the expression of lumpen elements within the working class, often valuing their connections with loyalist paramilitaries armed and assisted by British Intelligence, such as the Ulster Volunteer Force and the Ulster Defence Association, over and above the nationalist working class. McVeigh and Rolston demonstrate that since the forced exile of the Celtic aristocracy, the struggle for national self-determination has by necessity fallen to the Irish peasantry and the most immiserated sections of the working class. Furthermore, "a state built on inequality finds the demand for equality metaphysically threatening… the demand often has side effects long before the ultimate point is reached". A full inquiry into the psychology of the ruling class in the twenty-six county state is too broad a subject for the purposes of this review, but the palpable discomfort the political establishment exhibit around the decade of centenaries, the eagerness with which they have proposed initiatives such as a state celebration of colonial police, joining a monarchical trading bloc or guaranteeing cabinet seats to unionists, will serve well enough for our purposes for the moment.

Descendants of the original Norman colonists of the twelfth century largely assimilated into the Irish population, began to speak Irish, marry Irish people and take on Irish customs.⁶ The colonisation of Ireland proper began with Poynings' Law in 1494, which gave the English Crown claims on the Irish Kingdom. This was consolidated with the Plantations of the sixteenth and seventeenth centuries, during which English planters were granted lands in southern and eastern parts of the country. These ventures initially failed, both due to administrative incompetence as well as native resistance. Discontent reached a climax with the 1641 uprising, which prompted Oliver Cromwell, the Lord Protector of the newly-declared English Republic, to invade and crush the nascent Irish Confederate government. That this Confederacy was more progressive than it is often given credit for and planned to institute measures of religious toleration, has not received nearly enough attention in the historical discourse, which tends to uncritically repeat British propaganda framing 1641 as a sectarian eruption of Catholic barbarism in which thousands of Protestants were massacred in uniquely brutal and inhumane ways. Cromwell granted poor-quality land to Catholics who could demonstrate they had no part in the rebellion in western parts of the country and many prisoners were sent as settlers or workers to the Americas and the Caribbean.

English identity proper begins with these exercises in subjugation and the clear distinction which arises between the conquerors and the conquered. The Irish are held to be idle, lazy and uncivilised Catholics versus the industrious and civilised Protestant English. This idea of England and a racialised conception of Englishness

---

6   Ibid., 67-70.

wields immense ideological power throughout the history of the British Empire, but was never concretised in any state formation outside of it; rather it is merely not-Wales and not-Scotland. In order for the plantations to remain viable it was necessary that Irish resistance be crushed. Massacres, forced deportations and clearances were undertaken as a first step and then a system of apartheid was enforced. Land grants became conditional on restricting the number of servants or tenants drawn from the native population. Vivid descriptions of the human cost and aftermath documented by perpetrators, victims and onlookers abound and it is easy to see echoes of Christoper Columbus' butchery in the Americas.[7] The British response to each instance of native resistance became an opportunity for imposing draconian legislation. The Penal Laws, introduced towards the end of the seventeenth century prevented Catholics from obtaining positions in the state bureaucracy, the professions or the judiciary. They could not handle firearms, intermarriages were outlawed and any orphan had to be parented by a Protestant.

Ireland's containment within the 1801 Act of Union, afforded some expansion of the vote to Irish men who owned or rented property worth more than 40 shillings. This measure was never granted to peoples in England's other colonies and led to figures within the Irish middle-class seeing the opportunity to receive some share of the Empire's dividends. It is within this tradition that figures such as Daniel O'Connell, Isaac Butt and Arthur Griffith, each of whom were involved in various parliamentary

---

[7] Ibid., 294-95.

ventures through the nineteenth and early twentieth centuries, are best understood. To the extent that the Irish were admitted into Empire, they were definitively junior partners; both due to its unpopularity—merchants in Belfast and Galway seeking to establish slave-trading companies are documented as having had their meeting interrupted by the future United Irishman Thomas McCabe who declared, "May God eternally damn the soul of the man who subscribes the first guinea"—as well as the British seeking to maintain their monopolies. British manufacturers succeeded in ending the woollen trade and ensuring the Irish peasantry could not diversify their agriculture, leaving them uniquely vulnerable to the catastrophe of *An Gorta Mór*, during which Irish grain was continually exported to feed the British working class.[8] There are of course a surfeit of examples of individual Irish people who entered into armed service on the Empire's behalf and were involved in subduing native peoples in Africa, Asia and the Americas, even if we might feel as though figures such as Michael O'Dwyer are over-represented by *The Irish Times* as if they represented some sort of norm. It is important to recall as well that Irish Catholics were foot-soldiers and that their officers were drawn from the ranks of the English and Anglo-Irish.

McVeigh and Rolston square this circle through the idea of dominion, the ways in which the limitations of

---

8  *An Gorta Mór*, or in English, 'The Great Hunger' is the term used by Irish Republicans and socialists in order to underline the role of British imperialism in the event and not a mere consequence of a blight on the potato crop.

post-colonial statehood have been radically proscribed by imperialist powers. One of the most striking examples is the inability these supposedly post-colonial states have to rid themselves of borders drawn up by the imperialists, due to imperial self-interest or on the basis of arbitrary distinctions between racial, ethnic or religious groups. Democracy therefore becomes a gift the imperial state bestows upon their subjects, retrospectively casting all historic resistance as illegitimate. The British partition of Ireland in 1922 can be understood in this context. The six-county statelet did not align with the historic province of Ulster.

Many will already be familiar with the central argument of Noel Ignatiev's *How the Irish Became White* (1995) in which it is argued that Irish labourers sought to assimilate themselves with the interests of the white and Anglo-Saxon Protestant establishment in the US rather than making common cause with freed slaves and their descendants. From McVeigh and Rolston's perspective, Ireland did not become the anti-imperialist and revolutionary state on which the Republic was declared because of partition. The Anglo-Irish Treaty merely tinkered with some aspects of the relationship of the Irish nation to Empire; both statelets remained within it. This can be seen by the power the British continued to wield over the twenty-six counties; the Irish currency was linked with the British sterling until 1978, the British considered the twenty-six county state a member of the British commonwealth until 1949 and representatives even attended imperial conferences in London. The Free State also continued to compensate British landlords who had acquired their lands through colonisation. When Republicans opposed to the Treaty established a garrison in the Four Courts in Dublin, a building in which Ireland's higher courts have been housed since the eighteenth century, British Prime Minister Lloyd George ordered the Minister for Finance in the Free State government Michael Collins, to engage them and Winston Churchill even planned to do so himself. The Republicans were unable to secure a foothold in the cities and therefore retreated into the countryside to wage guerrilla warfare. W.T. Cosgrave, Chairman of the Free State Government after Collins was assassinated by Republicans in West Cork, passed a "public safety bill" which empowered the armed forces of the Free State government to execute Republican combatants. In this way the twenty-six county state comes into existence, as Karl Marx described the birth of capitalism, "dripping from head to toe, from every pore, with blood and dirt".

Fianna Fáil, elements of the Republican movement which accommodated themselves to the Free State became its natural party of government and only symbolically committed themselves to re-unification as a long-term goal. Despite rhetoric from more populist figures in Fianna Fáil, the twenty-six county state never defended the Catholic population from British forces, was always eager to shed Irish claims on territory and never sought to hold the British state responsible for the murder of its own citizens in the Dublin and Monaghan bombings, the worst atrocities committed in the whole of the Troubles. After a brief period spent pursuing economic and political autarky, the state began to pursue an economic model based on securing investment from overseas and joining the European Economic Community (EEC). Charles De Gaulle vetoed the twenty-six county state's entry, regarding the twenty-six counties as a vassal of the UK. Sure enough, the Free State government did not regard entering the trading bloc independent of the UK as a viable option. In this way accession to the EEC further solidified the twenty-six county state's neo-colonial status.

The democratic deficits that have followed will be familiar to anyone who has looked into the EU's peripheries; the effective abrogation of sovereignty and an increasing tendency towards militarisation and so-called peacekeeping activities overseas.[9] While McVeigh and Rolston emphasise that whatever dividends can be ascribed to the twenty-six county state's tax haven status amount to state propaganda, these initiatives frequently enter into contradiction with EU membership. Without it, McVeigh and Rolston speculate, the twenty-six county state would probably look more like the Isle of Man or the Virgin Islands.

Once the economy of the twenty-six county state entered into a protracted boom period from 1995 until 2007, it experienced significant amounts of inward migration for the first time in its history. This prompted the imposition of new regulations of the Free State's labour markets, and the emergence of a new blood-and-soil rhetoric around twenty-six county nationality.

---

9   See Samuel Parry, "Entrenching Inequality: The European Dependency School's *Underdeveloped Europe*" contained in this volume.

McVeigh and Rolston identify this as a turning point, indicating that the conditions which formerly existed for the extension of Irish identity to people of colour no longer exist and are unlikely to re-emerge as Ireland remains within the EU/UK dominion.

During the War of Independence the IRA in the northern parts of the country faced a very different prospect than in the south. State forces waged far more determined armed resistance and more extensive pogroms and assassinations of Catholic civilians. Sectarianism was encoded into the very structure of the six-county statelet that arose out of partition which McVeigh and Rolston convincingly describe as a proto-fascist *Herrenvolk* democracy.[10] Native capitalists who were also often ministers in the partitionist parliament would only hire Protestant workers. All-Ireland campaigns for the liberation of the north were largely desultory. Northern Protestants were successfully recruited in the early stages of The Republican Congress' campaign, although these elements left after a confrontation with IRA members at a commemoration in Bodenstown. This state proved in the long-term to be non-viable. Indigenous industries were bought out by foreign capital after the global slump in the 1930s and heads of industry became mere intermediaries. The social actors foregrounded in other accounts of the Troubles at this stage in the work recede in favour of a focus on economic relations, capital ownership and differences in employment figures across the Catholic and Protestant population.

---

10   McVeigh and Rolston, *Ireland, Colonialism and the Unfinished Revolution*, 212.

McVeigh and Rolston are unstinting in their criticism of the six-county state that has emerged in the wake of the GFA, seeing it as yet another example of a failed instance to fully escape imperialist dominion by enlisting a broader set of political parties north and south of the border in order to prop up a failed economic and political entity. The GFA was not, as John Hume sought to argue, an instance of self-determination by the Irish people. The votes were not aggregated and it therefore remained firmly within the two nations paradigm. The essential basis of the agreement was that Republicans would stop using violence against the statelet so sectarianism and clientelism could be dismantled. This winding up of the excesses of the wartime security regime, which employed 10% of Protestant men, as well as de-industrialisation has led to a state of affairs in which the twenty-six county state has an economy four times larger with a workforce only 2.5 times the size. Sectarianism has not been broken with, but rather encoded into the "reformed state" such that the increasing migrant population have limited space for political representation, despite representing 10% more of the working population than Protestants. Community funding are apportioned within areas in which particular political parties have a larger vote share and the latent genocidal tendencies in the unionist community are pandered to. Post-2008 these issues have only come into sharper focus; the six counties cannot offer Protestant supremacy, but nor can it provide parity to the Catholic population, who remain more likely to be long-term unemployed. 158 political killings have occurred since the agreement was passed and state forces remain complicit in killing of Catholic civilians.

The final sections of the book consider the history of the broader anti-imperialist movement, outlining how the UK, the US and Israel have successfully put the breaks on decolonisation by exercising their vetoes in the United Nations, as well as imposed sanctions, blockades or conducting assassinations of prominent leaders. The footnote in which the death toll we can lay at the feet of the CIA, Mossad as well as various British and French intelligence agencies is long, non-exhaustive and very depressing.

Despite the Free State's incorporation within UK and EU dominion, there are moments in which the twenty-six county state, under consistent popular pressure, expressed support for Algerian, Chinese and Palestinian independence struggles. It is here that McVeigh and Rolston demonstrate the ways in which Irish history has always been a site of struggle between nationalism and Republicanism. While the Young Irelander John Mitchel, transported to Australia in 1848 for his agitation against landlords and the export of Irish grain to Britain may have been an apologist for slavery, at a mass meeting addressed by Charles Stewart Parnell held in Navan in 1879, 30,000 Irish people chanted the name of the Zulu king Cetshwayo, at that point waging a war of resistance against the British.[11] The Irish Republican Brotherhood (IRB), a clandestine organisation founded in 1858 devoted to the establishment of the Irish Republic even attempted to send $20,000 and military strategists to assist the Zulus. Among the many colonised peoples who

---

11   Ibid., 298.

sought direct inspiration from the Irish independence struggle include Indian nationalists, freed slaves in the US and Marcus Garvey who named the headquarters of the UNIA in New York Liberty Hall in reference to James Connolly.

In assigning a central position to the history of struggle for self-determination in Ireland, McVeigh and Rolston demonstrate how intersectionality may be bolstered within an Irish context by having its demands relate themselves to calls for social equality which have historically been made by the Republican movement. This is to be undergirded by the concept of *mestizaje*, which acknowledges the hybrid nature of the colonial state and transcend categorisations which might otherwise function in sectarian ways. Though the progressive tendencies of, for example, the Republic declared in 1867 should not be forgotten, the rebellion organised by the United Irishmen in 1798 is of course the key example and deserves to be understood, along with the Haitian Revolution, as among the first modern anti-colonial uprisings, inspired by the universal politics of the French Revolution but moving beyond self-determination for colonists to a radical vision of postcolonial self-determination.

It is only towards the end of the work that McVeigh and Rolston discuss political strategy directly. In many respects their programme is significantly more radical than one would expect from a scholarly work; McVeigh and Rolston argue that we are living in a revolutionary moment in which the Union, the British state and the six counties are in a state of collapse. Though this may be the case, their claim that this current state of affairs offer a clear "'reformist' route to liberation" requires further interrogation.¹² The model that McVeigh and Rolston cite, is that of the Parnellite popular front of the 1880s, when Charles Stewart Parnell led the Irish Parliamentary Party bringing together "insurrectionary movements, mass mobilisations and representative parliamentary intervention". What exactly is meant by "insurrectionary movements" is hedged here. McVeigh and Rolston posit that the "the republican movement ditched insurrection as a core principle" which would obviously preclude "dissident" Republican groups from being considered, although the word "dissident" is also put in quotation marks. This is probably the most pragmatic line to take, I do not see the sense in being proscriptive as to what the revolution will look like.

McVeigh and Rolston's idea that this moment opens up "a whole new continuum of broader Republican thinking from Fintan O'Toole to the politics of the 'dissidents'"[13] is generous, given O'Toole has had a lifetime to do more than pay lip service to what he calls "classical Republicanism," a term that can only be interpreted as anything other than actually-existing Republicanism, and has not done so. Dan Finn's survey of O'Toole's career underlines that he is a model of a vacillating intellectual, whose default position is to cosy up to the Labour Party, whose historic function is and will continue to be to betray the working class and to provide Fine Gael with a working majority.[14] This is all

---

12   Ibid., 402.

13   Ibid., 405.

14   Daniel Finn, "Rethinking the Republic: Fintan O'Toole

without getting into his post-Brexit output, the only word for which is "embarrassing". Marriage equality and Repeal certainly offer encouraging signs of a mass base for a socialist and anti-imperialist movement, as younger and more working class elements in the population circle Sinn Féin as a likely parliamentary vehicle for the delivery of some approximation of social democracy. This has already led Fianna Fáil and Fine Gael to advocate unionist positions due to the electoral calculus of a United Ireland. I do not think a revolution in Ireland backed by the EU or partitionist parliaments is likely to be democratic, nor do I think the counter-revolutionary tendencies of a decaying Union should be understated.

Had this excellent book been longer it might also have provided McVeigh and Rolston space to consider in greater depth where we are now and where we have to get to. What lessons can anti-imperialist movements of the future take from the previous century? What are the prospects for organising worker power? In what way do we need to adjust the classic model of industrial worker organising in the context of low-wage service economies? It would be possible to argue that providing conclusive answers to these questions are a matter of practice and we should not expect conclusive answers to them within the confines of a single work. And so we should not. A political discourse that would take this work as a starting point would be a far better one than the one we have now and in overall terms, these small oversights should not distract from the central point; McVeigh and Rolston must be applauded for the contribution they have made

---

and the Irish Crisis", *New Left Review* 90, Nov/Dec 2014.

in bringing one of the greatest works that has ever been written on the subject of imperialism into the world and everyone should read it.

# The Capitalist Roots of Anti-Indigenous Racism in Canada: Howard Adams' *Prison of Grass*

Owen Schalk

> We need to liberate ourselves from the courts, ballot boxes, school system, church, and all other agencies that command us to stay in our "colonised place." This oppression of the native people is so deeply rooted in the capitalist system that it cannot be completely eliminated without eliminating capitalism itself.[1]

In 1975, the Métis intellectual Howard Adams (1921-2001) published *Prison of Grass: Canada from a Native Point of View*.[2] While it was reprinted several times in subsequent decades, the book remains largely

---

1   Howard Adams, *Prison of Grass: Canada from a Native Point of View* (Fifth House Publishers, 1989), 176-177.

2   Métis refers to peoples of mixed Indigenous and European (usually French) ancestry. The Métis are a unique cultural group within Canada, and they have historically faced considerable oppression at the hands of white settlers and their institutions.

inaccessible to modern readers, and used copies sell for upwards of US$100 online. This unavailability has meant that the book is largely underappreciated outside academic circles and privileged readerships with access to diverse libraries of Canadian historiography. This is an unfortunate reality, because *Prison of Grass* is a remarkable book that combines autobiographical reflections with an elaborate and illuminating analysis, rooted in historical materialism, of the origins and perpetuation of anti-Indigenous racism in Canada.

Over the course of 190 pages, Adams applies a framework of Marxist analysis to the processes of capitalist expansionism and extractivism that are commonly obfuscated in state-sanctioned histories of Canadian colonialism. His areas of focus include the Red River Resistance of 1869-1870, the Northwest Resistance of 1885, the co-constitutive ideological networks of Canadian schooling, media, and academia which perpetuate nationalist myths, and episodes from Adams' own life as a Métis man in the white supremacist society of early twentieth-century Canada. What results is a dynamic, multi-faceted, interdisciplinary polemic against dominant bourgeois histories and the prevailing structures of Canadian racism which expose their authoritarian machinery to this day in ongoing examples such as the Wet'suwet'en resistance,[3] the struggle against old-growth logging at Fairy Creek,[4] and the ongoing

---

3   Pam Palmater, "RCMP invasion of Wet'suwet'en Nation territory breaches Canada's 'rule of law'", *Canadian Dimension*, 2019.

4   Karin Larsen, "Fairy Creek protest on Vancouver Island

political persecution of land defenders such as Skyler Williams.[5]

*Background and Reception*

Howard Adams was born on September 8, 1921, in St. Louis, Saskatchewan, a village founded by Métis settlers in the late 1800s. His mother was French-Cree and his father English-Cree. His experience of racism in the rural prairie town affected him deeply, although he laments in *Prison of Grass* that the sense of inferiority hammered into him by encounters with police, religious institutions, and the schooling system forged an intense self-loathing that manifested as hatred of his own family and heritage. After completing high school, he enrolled in the University of California-Berkeley and acquired a doctorate in 1966. He was the first Canadian Métis person to obtain a PhD.

As a student at Berkeley, Adams attended a speech by Malcolm X. After hearing Malcolm speak, he began to make transnational connections between the struggles of the Canadian Indigenous and Métis, the black population of the US, and liberation movements in colonised Africa. Most importantly, he came to recognise capitalism as the common oppressor of these geographically disparate groups. He returned to Canada in the late 1960s and briefly served as the president of the Métis Society of Saskatchewan. Later, he worked as a

---

now considered largest act of civil disobedience in Canadian history", *CBC*, 2021.

5   Megan Ross, "Skyler Williams is a Political Prisoner", *Canadian Dimension*, 2021.

professor of Native Studies, a position through which he "instructed hundreds of Aboriginal people to be proud of their heritage and history and provided them with the intellectual framework to decolonise themselves."[6]

In his writing and teaching, Adams espoused a constructive, socially conscious worldview rooted in internationalism and historical materialism. He urged his students and readers to view racism in Canada not as an unalterable fact of nature but as the product of the same historical processes that drove European settlers to colonise the continent in the first place: capitalism. He wrote three books in his lifetime—*The Education of Canadians, 1800-1867: The Roots of Separatism* (1968), *Prison of Grass* (1975), and *Tortured People: The Politics of Colonization* (1999)—but his middle work caused the largest stir upon its release.

Initial reception for *Prison of Grass* was largely negative within academia. A 1977 review by Jean Friesen, a history professor at the University of Manitoba, called the book a "weak history" and accused Adams of oversimplifying the attitudes of colonisers, arguing that some colonists "saw in the aborigines of North America the finest examples of human nature." She also took issue with Adams' materialist analysis of racism in Canada and asserted that "white society is more complex and ambivalent in its attitudes than Adams suggests."[7]

---

6   Metis Museum, "Howard Adams Image Collection", *Metis Museum*.

7   Jean Friesen, "Adams, "Prison of Grass: Canada from the Native Point of View" (Book Review)", *Canadian Ethnic Studies/ Etudes Ethniques au Canada*, 9:2, (Jan 1, 1977), 128.

Friesen's views were shared by many critics, including D. Paul Lumsden of York University, who described Adams' book as "overly rhetorical" and "sweeping in its assertions."[8]

In spite of these criticisms (which result in both Friesen and Lumsden arguing that settler society was not *entirely* racist and therefore the colonization of Canada was not *entirely* immoral), *Prison of Grass* remains an indelible addition to the woefully meagre catalogue of leftist histories of Canada. Whether or not one believes Adams' historical conclusions to be overly general, his perspective still provides a necessary disruption of the colonial myths that continue to pervade Canadian society.

*The Capitalist Roots of Anti-Indigenous Racism*

In *Prison of Grass*, Adams synthesises concepts from a variety of revolutionary Global South thinkers, ultimately resolving that Canada's Indigenous and Métis populations have far more in common with colonised peoples in Africa and Asia than with white society in Canada itself. In analysing the base of this historical reality, he draws from dependency theory (including the notion of "psychological dependency") and concepts of underdevelopment, while his analysis of Canada's ideological state apparatuses borrows heavily from both Ivan Illich and Paulo Freire.

Adams begins *Prison of Grass* by describing the

---

8  D. Paul Lumsden. "Prison of Grass: Canada from the Native Point of View", Howard Adams Trent Native Series No. 1. *New Press*, 1975, xi, 238. *Canadian Journal of Political Science*, 10:1, 176-177.

conditions on his "halfbreed [Métis] ghetto" in St. Louis. He describes his difficulty finding work from white employers, the demoralizing employment conditions, and the frequent occurrence of being cheated out of his wages with zero recourse, because, in his own words, "I knew how police regard halfbreeds and Indians and how they support white bosses."[9] After locating himself in the text, he expands to a broader historical view, writing that "the racism that native people encounter today had its origins in the rise of western imperialism during the 1600s."[10]

Adams describes pre-colonial American cultures as largely classless societies with decentralised power structures, lacking the systemic coercions that one might associate with modern capitalist economies. European colonists brought racializing processes which were rooted in the capitalist drive for cheap labour to service the metropole. Adams writes: "Racial stereotypes and prejudices then developed from the realization that Indians provided potentially cheap labour for trapping furs and for whatever jobs had to be done… So European scholars and clergymen began creating racial theories which showed that the native people… were primitives, innately inferior and subhuman."[11] Therefore, in the Canadian context, Adams asserts that anti-Indigenous racism developed out of superstructural justifications for the invasion and exploitation of the American material base, similar to European-led racialization processes

---

9   Adams, *Prison of Grass*, 10.

10  Ibid., 11.

11  Ibid., 12.

which occurred across Africa and Asia during the initial stages of colonization.

Adams recounts how the introduction of a settler fur-trading enterprise resulted in the collapse of traditional economies. In his account, Indigenous labour was increasingly subjugated to European consumer demands for fur, meaning that these communities needed to spend more time trapping animals in order to receive the short-term benefits of settler trade. This resulted in the imposition of colonial labour specialization. This specialization eroded the traditional administrative structure of Indigenous society by "forc[ing them] into dependency on commercial trapping," for which the Europeans provided various forms of payment.[12] The introduction of the profit motive to these communalist society was catastrophic, fostering hostilities between different tribes as they contended with one another in the competitive fur trade.

Alongside the erosion of communalism, Adams examines the common colonial practice of empires selecting proxies from the local population and elevating them to privileged positions in which they are meant to serve the metropole's interests. Adams describes how, in the Canadian context, colonisers often elevated individual chiefs to positions of great power, isolating them from their communities and creating an authoritarian top-down system of rule that he connects directly to "neo-colonial" management by a more privileged class of chiefs in the 1970s, many of whom receive grants

---

12    Ibid., 26.

directly from the government.[13]

*Material and Psychological Underdevelopment*

Adams laments what he calls the "ossification" of Indigenous societies brought about by colonialist and neo-colonialist capitalism—in other words, a perpetual state of underdevelopment that he explicitly compares to apartheid. He writes that the "grinding paternalism" of a class of settler businessmen, government bureaucrats, and religious authorities has destroyed formerly equitable and self-sustaining systems of living and created both a material and psychological dependency in many communities, which he used to feel himself.[14] While writing about the shame that he once harboured for his own family, he bemoans the fact that "[the system] had replaced the beauty and love of my Indianness with disgust and contempt. But at that time I still did not understand how cultural genocide systematically operated to colonise me."[15] His eventual awareness of the role of white supremacy in shaping his mindset imbued him with an "obligation to work toward the destruction of such a system."[16]

The inculcation of self-loathing and a hatred for Indigenous cultures in Indigenous peoples was a clearly stated policy of the Canadian government. The residential school system was the core of this strategy.

---

13  Ibid., 161.
14  Ibid., 37.
15  Ibid., 125.
16  Ibid.

During the late nineteenth and twentieth centuries, tens of thousands of Indigenous children were forcibly separated from their parents and placed in "schooling" institutions, often run by churches, whose explicit goal was to destroy Indigenous languages and cultural practices and "assimilate" the children into settler culture. Duncan Campbell Scott, who oversaw the program from 1913 to 1932, stated its goals openly: "I want to get rid of the Indian problem… Our objective is to continue until there is not a single Indian in Canada that has not been absorbed into the body politic."[17] Sexual abuse was rampant in these institutions, and a combination of poor nutritional regimens, a lack of building maintenance, and direly underfunded healthcare infrastructure contributed to the deaths of thousands of children, many of whom were buried in unmarked graves on the school grounds. The system continued for longer than most Canadians are aware: the last residential school closed in 1997.

Adams' analysis of the ideological state structures (schools, media, academia) that infuse settler society with pride and Indigenous societies with shame is cutting and precise. One of the principal issues he identifies with Canadian historiography is its capitalist nature, which means that it "represent[s] only the forces contending for power and their power relationships," which in the Canadian context means that history is primarily made by the Hudson's Bay Company and its

---

17  Facing History and Ourselves, "Until There Is Not a Single Indian in Canada", In *Stolen Lives: The Indigenous Peoples of Canada and The Indian Residential Schools,* Facing History and Ourselves, 2018.

benefactors. This model of history-making excises the experiences of common people, and especially racialised communities, because "in capitalism the masses are not a ruling force."[18] His disdain is palpable and affecting. He describes histories that whitewash the racist origins of the RCMP as "sweetheart myths written by 'WASP's who have never experienced insults, beatings, and bullets from a Mountie."[19] He describes the CBC, Canada's foremost public broadcaster, as "the epitome of snobbish middle-class culture [which is] not even remotely connected with native society."[20] Ultimately, the fact that the colonisers have total control of communications media and the schooling system means that settlers are continuously indoctrinated into nationalist myths at the expense of a people's history rooted in the masses, and the Indigenous and Métis masses in particular. Specifically, Adams emphasises the central role of communications media to the assertion of colonial power while describing the John A. MacDonald government's response to the Northwest Resistance of 1885.

The Northwest Resistance occurred when a diverse range of Indigenous, Métis, and white settler groups, enduring near-starvation conditions in areas of modern-day Saskatchewan and Alberta, united to push for greater material concessions from the more industrialised eastern provinces, where the Canadian seat of government is located. The resistance embodied a great challenge to the continental expansion of industrial capitalism, as

---

18   Adams, *Prison of Grass*, 18.

19   Ibid., 78.

20   Ibid., 158.

represented by the threat it posed to the completion of the cross-continental Canadian Pacific Railway. Fearful that a revolutionary movement would cause profits to the eastern provinces to dwindle, Prime Minister MacDonald quickly took over the *Times* newspaper in Prince Albert and used it to spew racist propaganda and sow division amongst the resistors, which Adams says was "partly successful in alienating some white support from the Indians and Métis."[21] A short time later, MacDonald sent troops into the Northwest and put a violent end to the resistance movement.

In short, Adams identifies the ideological hand of a racist colonial system in media, schooling, and academia, all of which serve to placate the minds of an impressionable settler society for the continuing benefit of the forces of capitalism. The purpose of this communications network is thus, in his words, to "develop [public] attitudes that harmonise well with apartheidism."[22]

*Radical Nationalism and Revolution*

In thinking of ways to remove prevailing structures of white supremacy, Adams can find no alternative but to strive for a new socialist society. He rejects the legitimacy of government-aligned groups, even those led by Indigenous or Métis people. He rejects electoral politics, writing that the Liberals, Conservatives, and New Democrats are "equally a part of the capitalist

---

21   Ibid., 82.

22   Ibid., 43.

system and therefore unable to bring about any real and basic changes in society." [23] Any resistance that does not target capitalist labour relations is ultimately, in his opinion, nothing but "image betterment."[24] He declares that "native people did not create these [racist] images," and if they were destroyed, "[capitalist] society would simply create new racist images for us to work at." [25]

Adams argues that the only way to craft an equitable future is through an organizational strategy he calls "radical nationalism." Radical nationalism is similar in character to the revolutionary nationalism of independence movements in the Global South which were beginning to enter the postcolonial period at the time of his writing—however, he stops short of calling his strategy "revolutionary" due to the impracticality of such an ambition within Canada. This does not mean that Adams is not a revolutionary thinker; rather, he is simply realistic that, among the Canadian working class, there is no revolutionary potential of the type adopted by the Cuban or Vietnamese people in their struggles against imperialism.

His model of radical nationalism is a bottom-up, community-centred form of Indigenous resistance which seeks to unite with white workers and inaugurate a broader class struggle. This process necessarily involves building local social organizations of the type that the resistors would like to see implemented on a national scale, such as community-run educational institutions. The end-goal

---

23   Ibid., 162.

24   Ibid., 147.

25   Ibid.

of this process is the toppling of the capitalist system, and thereby the removal of the economic system which generates anti-Indigenous racism in Canada.

Adams admits that this constitutes a significant challenge, especially because white workers often align themselves with the state that ostensibly represents them against the demands of Indigenous and Métis class allies. But despite the shortcomings that Adams finds in his own theory of radical nationalism—namely, the tendency of the white lumpenproletariat to sympathise with the settler-colonial state apparatus—Adams nevertheless offers a clear blueprint for anti-colonial struggle. Since racism in Canada was founded by capitalist imperialism, the only way to truly eradicate racism and create social institutions capable of generating new anti-colonial consciousness is the removal of the productive modes that imperialism implanted in Canada and the recreation of society along socialist lines. While the pervasive influence of the state's ideological apparatuses on Canada's majority white polity causes Adams to doubt the possibility of such a transformation, it remains necessary for those seeking to enact a more just future to seek out instructive, nourishing texts like *Prison of Grass* and apply their lessons to one's own social and political activities.

# Independence with Blood: The Decolonial Vision of the Malayan Conscious Youth Movement's *Political Testament*

Fadiah Nadwa Fikri

The present is where we get lost—if we forget our past and have no vision of the future.

Ayi Kwei Armah[1]

The Political Testament of API[2] drafted by Ahmad Boestamam, one of the founders of the *Angkatan Pemuda Insaf* (API, Conscious Youth Movement) in December 1946 embodies a profound commitment to anticolonialism. API was the youth wing of the *Partai Kebangsaan Melayu Malaya* (PKMM, Malay Nationalist Party of Malaya), a radical left-wing nationalist party established in December 1945 to fight for Malayan independence. API was formed in February 1946 during a rally organised by the PKMM to celebrate Indonesia's

---

1  Ayi Kwei Armah, *The Healers* (Heinemann Educational Books, 1979), 176.
2  Ahmad Boestamam, *Testament Politik API* (1946).

six month independence.

After the Second World War, the British colonial government returned to Malaya and felt the urgent need to release itself from the cumbersome three-fold system of administration which consisted of the Federated Malay States, the Unfederated Malay States, and the Straits Settlements. To effectuate this new change, the British decided to put forward a constitutional scheme that would embody a unified system of administration under a strong central government—a scheme known as the "Malayan Union".

The Malayan Union, which sought to transfer full power and jurisdiction in all Malay states to the British colonial government, attracted strong opposition from the Malays. As a result, the United Malay National Organisation (UMNO), a right-wing nationalist organisation was formed by Malay aristocrats in May 1946 to oppose the scheme. It is important to note that the PKMM and API, which at first worked with UMNO to oppose this scheme, decided to withdraw all cooperation as UMNO was only interested in protecting the interests of the aristocrats and the monarchs rather than fighting for the complete independence of Malaya.

To achieve their goal, the PKMM and API proceeded to join hands with various political parties, trade unions, youth organisations, and women's associations comprising members of all races. API, in particular, played a significant role in carrying out a Malaya-wide campaign to raise consciousness amongst the masses. API unequivocally averred that the attainment of freedom was contingent upon genuine independence which sought to liberate oppressed and colonised people not only politically, but also socially and economically. The Political Testament of API, whose spirit carries immense potential to turn unfreedom on its head and breathe life into freedom, however, has been removed from Malaysia's national consciousness.

It is worth noting that the historical silences around radical opposition to British colonialism like API's are also evident in the historical writing about "British Malaya" whose concerns centre around the development and execution of British colonial policy. Anthony Milner has described the way in which the history of "British Malaya" has been written as "colonial" where the British are portrayed as "the principal actors in the period, the initiators of action."[3]

One of the many functions of unfreedom is to limit our imagination. It tells us that another world where we can be free is impossible. To dream of a world where possibilities abound and speak about those possibilities would inevitably attract a barrage of condemnation and ridicule. It can be immobilising and alienating to be punished for having the courage to dream and be told that the act of dreaming of something radically different is futile, purist, unrealistic, and should be abandoned and never be spoken of.

The shaming that often befalls someone who dares to imagine differently is illustrative of what Paulo Freire described as the "fear of freedom".[4] The fear of freedom,

---

3   Anthony Milner, "Colonial Records History: British Malaya" *Modern Asian Studies*, 21:4 (1987), 774.

4   Paulo Freire, *Pedagogy of the Oppressed* (Herder and Herder, 1970), 36.

which carries doubts and misgivings, emanates from the oppression inflicted by the oppressor and internalised by the oppressed. Not only does this fear relegate the oppressed to the wretched position assigned by the oppressor, but it also instils in the hearts and minds of the oppressed that the oppressor's dehumanising way is the only way that should inform the terms of the oppressed's existence and how they interact with the world they live in.

As a result, we become detached from the very essence of our existence—our dignity as human beings. Dehumanisation becomes something we not only tolerate but believe in. Unfreedom consequently becomes inscribed into our minds; deference to power becomes the norm that is often weaponised against dissenting dreamers. Unfreedom poses a great danger to our humanity. It occludes our ability to tell the difference between crumbs and the whole loaf of bread and understand that the slightly loosened shackles wrapped around our necks are still the same shackles that are preventing us from flying. Unfreedom clouds us from seeing that evil takes many forms and can never be hierarchised; it clouds us from seeing that lesser evilism is an illusion created to obstruct people from working to eradicate evil in all its forms. How did we get here? Why is freedom—which essentially means the absence of all forms of oppression and violence, and that nobody in our society goes hungry, without a home, education, healthcare—viewed with such disdain?

The systematic silencing and erasure of what we were and what the world could have been throughout history plays an enormous role in reinforcing this fear of freedom. How can we possibly know ourselves and our present, and change the miserable conditions we find ourselves in without learning about what came before us and how it defines what we are today? To continue turning our backs on history and insist on its death will inevitably be the death of us. Given this imminence, we cannot afford to treat history as a matter of the past. In emphasising the importance of critically examining one's existence vis-à-vis history, Antonio Gramsci observed:

> The starting-point of critical elaboration is the consciousness of what one really is, and is "knowing thy-self" as a product of the historical process to date which has deposited in you an infinity of traces, without leaving an inventory.[5]

History, in particular the history of colonialism, is replete with fierce opposition to and denial of freedom. But it is crucial to be reminded that history also constitutes a reservoir of the yearning of the oppressed to break free from the state of unfreedom—a reservoir that has been long buried by the oppressor. To uncover what history entails and critically examine its silences, erasures, and distortions means to consciously resist forgetting and dispel the dehumanising colonial myth that colonised subjects were, as Amílcar Cabral put it, "peoples without history".[6] Only by doing so can we break down the walls

---

5  Antonio Gramsci, *Selections from the Prison Notebooks of Antonio Gramsci* (Lawrence & Wishart, 1971), 324.

6  Amílcar Cabral, "The Weapons of Theory," in *Unity and Struggle: Speeches and Writings* (Monthly Review Press, 1979), 125.

that have long imprisoned our ability to imagine and act.

## Independence with Blood

The Political Testament of API illustrates one of the manifestations of the yearning of the colonised to liberate themselves from the yoke of oppression—a yearning that has long been silenced. The Testament, which starts and ends with the slogan *"Merdeka dengan Darah"* (Independence with Blood), pays tribute to the anticolonial movements led by the youth around the world, in particular the anticolonial movement in Indonesia. Citing the Russian Revolution as one of its inspirations, API was committed to achieving unconditional liberation with all its might, even if it meant death. The Testament affirms:

> There is not a single nation on this earth that was once colonised that gained genuine, total independence because it was handed to them, but because it was fought for with blood.
>
> Given the immense responsibility carried on its shoulders, API is committed to achieving total liberation of the nation and homeland by any means necessary.[7]

The Testament makes it clear that armed struggle which involves the use of violence is necessary to counter the violence unleashed by colonialism. This aspect of resistance requires closer examination given how

---

[7] All translations from the text are by the author of this review.

contentious the question of violence is today. It dispels the pervasive ruling idea that Malayan independence was achieved solely by peaceful means; rebellion was never part of the national culture, and therefore should be unequivocally condemned. It is important to note that this idea underplays the fact that UMNO—to which API was ideologically opposed—colluded with the British to suppress the left-wing anticolonial movement through the imposition of the so-called Emergency which lasted from 1948 to 1960. As Azmi Arifin highlights in his study of the historiography of Malay nationalism from 1945 to 1957: "Realising that the rightist Malay leaders were not entirely anti-British, the British approached these leaders to seek a deal that would diminish the influence of the leftist movement".[8]

The idea that non-violence has been the only defining feature of the national culture continued to be reinforced by the UMNO ruling elite (and internalised by the people) after independence. The perpetuation of this idea serves two purposes. First, it erases the fact that colonialism and other interlocking systems of oppression—racism, capitalism, feudalism, patriarchy, imperialism—were forms of violence. This erasure is necessary for maintaining these systems and their different manifestations whose implications continue to deny people their full humanisation today. Second, it

---

8   Azmi Arifin, "Local Historians and the Historiography of Malay Nationalism 1945-57: The British, The United Malay National Organization (UMNO) and the Malay Left", *Kajian Malaysia*, 32:1 (2014), 14.

equates the violence used by the oppressed to liberate themselves from oppression with the violence unleashed by such oppression.

Not only does this false equation mask the enormity of the violence inflicted by the oppressor, but it also serves to delegitimise radical opposition to it. It conceals the fact that the oppression inflicted by the oppressor on the oppressed thrives on asymmetrical power relations. When carried out without intervention, this function further entrenches the state of unfreedom which continues to rob people of their dignity and humanity. Freire's observation of the question of violence is noteworthy:

Never in history has violence been initiated by the oppressed. How could they be the initiators, if they themselves are the result of violence? How could they be the sponsors of something whose objective inauguration called forth their existence as oppressed? There would be no oppressed had there been no prior situation of violence to establish their subjugation.

It is important to note that API's commitment to translating its emancipatory imagination into action became a cause for concern. API's growing influence amongst the masses posed a serious threat to British colonial rule. To alleviate their fear, the British banned API in July 1947, making it the first organisation to be outlawed in Malaya. API's leader Boestamam was put on trial for sedition. Tim Harper's observation concerning colonial repression of resistance in Malaya is worth recalling: "It was API, and not the Chinese left, that provoked the British government into passing legislation to narrow the parameters of political activity".[9]

*Redistribution of wealth*

It is noteworthy that the Testament also avers that total freedom can only be achieved when people are politically, economically, and socially free. It explains the principles upon which the doctrine concerning redistribution of wealth and reorganisation of society ought to be based. To achieve political sovereignty, the text emphasises the urgent need for an independent nation to uphold a democracy that is genuine—a democracy that seeks to embed people's sovereignty in its heart.

The essence of this democracy, according to the Testament, is that all power emanates from the people who constitute the vast majority of the population. This power is to be exercised solely to ensure that their collective interests are unconditionally safeguarded and upheld:

> API seeks to build an independent nation that upholds a democracy that is genuine; a government of the people, by the people, a government that is run by the people's representatives for the benefit, welfare, and security of the people.

As regards economic sovereignty, the Testament states that the responsibility lies with the state to implement economic programmes aimed at redistributing the nation's wealth to the masses. These economic programmes

---

9 Tim Harper, *The End of Empire and the Making of Malaya* (Cambridge University Press, 1999), 119.

ought to be designed to lift the people out of poverty and enhance their living standards. They should incorporate the right to free education, the right to mother tongue education, the right to freedom of association, the right to free healthcare, the right to decent and safe housing, and agrarian reform.

The Testament emphasises the need for reorganisation of society to resolve the antagonisms between the capitalist classes and the proletariat, plus the marhaeans. "Marhaen" was the term used by Soekarno in 1924 to refer to farmers who owned and worked on small farms but were destitute. This reorganisation requires the abolition of classes whose function is to enable the upper classes to subjugate, exploit, and impoverish people of the lower classes. In stressing that only by eliminating classes can society be liberated socially, the Testament states:

> The unequal economic system that is currently in place creates two classes, the capitalist class and the Marhaen (proletariat). These two classes are in conflict due to the irreconcilability of their different interests—where the former oppresses and exploits the latter. API believes that in order to obtain social justice, the class conflict must be eliminated.

## Radical Change vs. Reform

To achieve total liberation, the Testament unequivocally opts for a radical overthrow of the systems of oppression built, controlled, and run by the capitalist ruling classes instead of reform. It emphasises that only by overthrowing these oppressive systems can meaningful change be brought about in totality and without delay. In short, it vows to never compromise with the oppressor. This method requires that the masses be conscientised and organised to utilise their labour to realise their goal.

Reform, on the other hand, relies solely on compromise and *air liur* (empty words devoid of meaningful action)—in other words, performativity. The Testament avers that opting for reform as a method also puts people in a position to beg for what is rightfully theirs: the first method requires struggle, labour, property, and blood; the second method rests solely on empty words.

Reform, the Testament warns, would inevitably hamper the total change that is desperately needed to put an end to all systems of oppression that fortify the state of unfreedom. It understands with immense clarity that the oppressor's house that was never built to accommodate the oppressed needs to be demolished and replaced, not repaired.

## *API's Decolonial Vision*

By centring class antagonisms and their irreconcilability, the Testament makes explicit how the class system creates the division that empowers the upper classes to continually subject the lower classes to subjugation, domination, and exploitation. After laying bare the cause of the mass suffering, the Testament emphasises that it is the masses' responsibility to resist and put an end to the systems of oppression that are responsible for their suffering. To achieve this, the Testament calls for the abolition of classes which necessitates a revolutionary struggle organised and led solely by the might of the people, followed by a total reorganisation of society through redistribution of wealth.

API's commitment to mass organisation was evident in its ballooning membership which grew from 2,560 members in the year it was established to between 10,000 and 15,000 members in mid-1947. It is noteworthy that API was also instrumental in organising the masses to participate in the Malaya-wide *hartal* (general strike) in October 1947 which the Indian Daily Mail described as "the greatest country-wide political strike in the history of Malaya".[10] The strike was carried out to protest the British colonial government's decision to reject the 1947 People's Constitution. API had notably undertaken the crucial task of elevating critical consciousness amongst the masses—consciousness that had moved and empowered them to act collectively to reclaim their sovereignty and be in charge of their own destiny.

What makes the text a vital instrument of liberation and a rarity is its incorporation of what Freire described as "dialogics"—the word that embodies reflection and action; the word that is capable of transforming reality, awakening critical consciousness, and moving people to act. The radicalism and clarity of the terms and principles which inform API's struggle for the full humanisation of the oppressed and colonised echo Frantz Fanon's observation concerning the importance of building national consciousness—the kind that seeks to uphold humanism:

---

10   *Indian Daily Mail*, 14 November 1947.

> The living expression of the nation is the moving consciousness of the whole of the people; it is the coherent, enlightened action of men and women. The collective building up of a destiny is the assumption of responsibility on the historical scale.[11]

API's undivided commitment to freedom, reflected both in its revolutionary decolonial and anticolonial theory and praxis, ought not to be forgotten. It is worth remembering that the silencing of this part of history is not fortuitous. It is deliberately and systematically perpetuated to prevent the awakening of critical consciousness—meant to propel people to act to restore their lost humanity—while leaving the various systems of oppression unchallenged. In light of this, the Political Testament of API undoubtedly serves as an important frame of reference for reminding us that to imagine another world and act to achieve it is not only possible but also imperative.

---

11  Frantz Fanon, *The Wretched of the Earth* (Grove Press, 1963), 204.

# Walter Rodney's Lost Book: *One Hundred Years of Development in Africa*

Leo Zeilig

One of the most astonishing books that Walter Rodney—the Guyanese revolutionary and historian—ever wrote was published several years after he was assassinated on 13 June 1980. The story of this book and how it came to be published is almost as remarkable as the life of the revolutionary himself. In 1978, Rodney was working as a full-time activist of the Working People's Alliance (WPA) in Georgetown, the capital of Guyana. The WPA was a revolutionary organisation seeking to unite the African and Indian working class in the highly divided country, then run by the brutal Forbes Burnham. Rodney was the group's principal organiser and intellectual, and to support himself and his family, and to fundraise for the WPA, he travelled overseas to teach and work.

One trip to Germany in 1978 shows us how his last book came to be. Rodney travelled from Guyana to Hamburg in April of that year. He was already the celebrated and outspoken author of *How Europe Underdeveloped Africa*, and his arrival was eagerly anticipated. He had been invited by the radical German scholar, Rainer Tetzlaff, to teach a course on the history of African development at the University of Hamburg.

The lecture course Rodney was employed to teach was titled, "African Development, 1878-1978", and comprised, according to the one-page programme, "(i) a brief introduction to development concepts; (ii) a survey of African colonial economies with special reference to East and West Africa; and (iii) an examination of post-colonial developments in Kenya and Tanzania." According to the brief programme there were going to be twelve lectures, comprising, "The debate on development concepts in Africa' and 'Post-colonial development strategies".[1]

The book—still unknown by most people familiar with Rodney's work—was published from these lectures, which were recorded on audio cassettes, and transcribed in 1984 (and included the question-and-answer sessions with his students). The entire course was then compiled and turned into a small, photocopied book entitled, *A Tribute to Walter Rodney: One Hundred Years of Development in Africa*.[2] The book was placed in the library at the University of Hamburg and distributed to a number of comrades and students. Copies also ended up in Peter Lock's private collection, a colleague and comrade of

---

1    *TransAfrican Journal of History* (Roberts, Andrew) 1960-1987, Series E, Box 4, Folder 45, Walter Rodney Papers, Archives Research Papers.

2    Walter Rodney, *A Tribute to Walter Rodney—One Hundred Years of Development in Africa* (InstitutfürPolitischeWissenschaft der Universität Hamburg, 1984).

Rodney and Tetzlaff at the University of Hamburg, who had helped organise the lectures.

## *A Revolutionary Course*

The lectures and resultant book are perhaps the best example of the dizzying breadth of Rodney's scholarship, reading and activism, synthesised into a single document. The course also showcased Rodney's astonishing ability to communicate. His capacity for clarity and description—a rare and vital ability among scholars and activists—which had been developed from his work "grounding"— literally meaning to sit on the ground, listen and discuss among the poor in Jamaica in 1968 from which his first book, *The Groundings with my Brothers*, emerged. Speaking to students at the university is one thing, but Rodney was also working as a political organiser among sugar, rice, timber, and coconut workers.

Working across disciplines, and addressing different audiences including students, workers *and* children, Rodney developed a rare ability to effectively communicate complex ideas. The course, Tetzlaff and Lock explained in 1984—in the preface to the book—was "an entirely new enriching experience when the students of the Institute for Political Science and the Seminar of History at the University of Hamburg were offered an intellectual discourse with an authentic representative of the Third World".[3]

Rodney opens the lectures by challenging two distinct views of African history. One represented by Hugh

---

3   Ibid., 1.

Trevor Roper—an establishment British historian and racist, who saw pre-colonial African history as primitive and basic. The second view, Rodney explained, sees the colonial period as "insignificant, almost irrelevant." These historians arrive at this position by "saying that African history and African development must be seen in a totality, that African history is almost ageless…"[4]

Unsurprisingly Rodney rejects both positions. The second view which sees colonialism as insignificant, a "flea-bite", argued that Africa had already "moved away from the colonial heritage". These were arguments made by both academics and politicians, who saw Europeans as simply 'visitors' and now that they had formally left the continent, Africa could re-establish its "authenticity".

By the late 1970s, the idea of "authenticity"—the return to a "real" and "proper" African culture and history—had been taken-up and established as official government discourse in different parts of the continent, justifying often draconian and dictatorial policies. Congo's President, Mobutu Sese Seko, used to his own advantage the so-called "recourse to authenticity" in 1971, renaming the Democratic Republic of the Congo, Zaire that year. His own change of name and title, and the names of towns and streets reflected this ostensible "authenticity".[5] While the official proclamation of

---

4   Tape 2B, typescript, 1978, Series H, Box 19, Folder 1, Walter Rodney Papers, Archives Research Centre.

5   Speaking of this development, the Beninese philosopher, Paulin J. Hountondji wrote that "hypertrophy of cultural nationalism generally serves to compensate for the hypotrophy of political nationalism". Paulin J. Hountondji, *African Philosophy: Myth and Reality* (2nd Ed.). Translated by Henri Evans with the Collaboration

Patrice Lumumba as a national hero, a man Mobutu had been involved in murdering, was all part of an attempt to forge a new African national identity true to its glorious historical past. These efforts were part of an endeavour to increase the resources available to the state and drive out "foreigners" through use of "nationalist" slogans. The class of state bureaucrats and businessman were the chief beneficiaries of this policy—a process Rodney discussed in devastating detail.[6]

The second stage of these state-led reforms in the Congo was the institutional and economic consolidation of "Zaïrianisation", which was initiated with the "take over" of the bureaucracy and the "nationalisation" of sectors of the economy previously in private or corporate (Belgian), hands into either private Zaïrean ownership or state ownership. This change tended to encourage the development of two different, and conflicting, social formations. The process saw small and medium businesses, mainly in the transport and service sectors, transfer from expatriate private ownership to Zaïrean private ownership. One of the major forces behind this process was a concern to gain greater control for the political elite over the resources of the Zaïrean economy, so that the profits generated could more easily be appropriated; another was to extend the range of resources under nominal state control, and to increase the profits available to a "bureaucratic elite". This was the reality of the second type of history Rodney had

---

of Jonathan Rée. (Indiana University Press, 1996), 159.

6  Tape 4A and B, typescript, 1978, Series H, Box 19, Folder 5, Walter Rodney Papers, Archives Research Centre.

identified - the "return to an ageless African history". As he explained explicitly, "I feel that the talk of authenticity has generally been associated with this desire to suggest [that] ... colonialism really did not make much of an impact".

Rodney moves onto his "third framework of analysis", which sees colonialism not as a minor moment in the continent's history, but a "major intervention" on Africa's politics and societies. As he describes to the students, "colonialism in spite of being in Africa for a mere 70, 80 or 100 years, made a tremendous impact and that impact is visible and will continue to be visible on the African continent…"

Rodney's own work on the continent's history is most closely aligned to this third approach. In Rodney's words in Hamburg, "colonialism reinforced tendencies that had already begun with the trade in slaves ... for those sections of the African continent which were involved in the trading of slaves, it represented their first major involvement in the world economy and that with the coming of colonialism that involvement was going to be intensified in very many ways".

*Understanding African History*

Rodney's fluency when surveying the five centuries-long history of Africa in these lectures is remarkable. Though never lost in the details, he examines the movements of resistance within a Marxist framework—for example, the decades it took the Portuguese to pacify resistance in Guinea—to imperial competition for African territory that led to the Berlin conference in 1884 and the colonial scramble on the continent.

Rapidly he moves quickly on to examine the solidarity between colonial liberation movements and the "labour movements and left-wing movements of the colonialising powers themselves." While this solidarity did exist, it was highly uneven, so "one notes … that the French communist party was the largest communist party in Western Europe … was itself ideologically tied to its own bourgeois state apparatus with regard to colonial rule…"[7]

What gives Rodney's lectures such a dynamic and living energy is that he was often interrupted by the audience with questions and queries. On Algeria, for example, one student, asked: "There are opinions many of which go back to the writings of Frantz Fanon which say that the use of violence or the armed struggle is a necessary pre-condition for a real independence, and you have already indicated that there are other ways of struggle…"

Rodney responds, "I think Fanon himself of course was aware of the different possibilities of access to Independence… But what we have to take as the premise is this: African people as such, did not make the decision about armed struggle or no armed struggle; that decision was really dictated by the character of colonial rule…" Rodney was not simply a teacher in Hamburg but a militant whose own activism in Guyana at the time would raise the possibility of armed struggle. He was

---

7   Tape 5A and B, typescript, 1978, Series H, Box 19, Folder 7, Walter Rodney Papers, Archives Research Centre.

responding—and lecturing—as a scholar *and* militant involved in the *on-going* post-independence struggle for liberation in the Caribbean.

*To Tanzania*

One of the most significant parts of Rodney's course were his lectures on Tanzania—an important focus for this review. Tanzania at the time was led by the socialist Julius Nyerere, and the country represented for many an alternative and radical path to socialist development in the Third World. Partly autobiographical, he starts by telling his students, "My own experience with those who have really loved Nyerere's words or read descriptions or discussions of Tanzanian socialism is normally when they come to Tanzania … they experienced a certain amount of shock." In Hamburg he was speaking about a large community of fraternal scholars, and fellow travellers who came to the country with a romantic notion of "Nyerere's words … [and] Tanzanian socialism." Rodney had worked with his family in Tanzania from 1966 to 1974, he knew the country and its politics intimately.[8]

Yet what these foreign socialists experienced, and saw for themselves when they arrived, was shocking. Rodney continues, "they had already begun to imagine the society transforming itself into a socialist society of plenty,

---

8  In the late 1960s and 1970s, Rodney had a complicated relationship with Nyerere. At some point Rodney sided with African Marxist critics of Nyerere which led to tensions between him and the Tanzanian government. On this topic, see Zeyad el Nabolsy's review, "African Socialism in Retrospect: Karim Hirji's *The Travails of a Tanzanian Teacher"* that is contained in this volume.

when in fact, we are dealing with an underdeveloped society where poverty and destitution is as much the common run as you would find in any one of the African territories which may not necessarily be claiming to be moving towards socialism." Moving quickly on to consider Tanzania's history and political economy, Rodney explains to his listeners that the real explanation of this "underdevelopment" was caused by the fact that Tanzania "began at the rear."

Rodney then proceeds to provide a detailed analysis of independence and dependency in the country—while continuing to engage with the audience, "That is another thing you have to learn when you are looking at third world countries, when you see companies and firms that begin with Tanganyika this, or Sudan this or Nigeria this, don't entertain any illusions that they belong to Tanzania or Sudan or Nigeria, in fact that is precisely the moment when you have to become suspicious because foreign firms like to decorate their companies with the names of these national countries…" He illustrates his point with a vivid example, the Tanganyika Development Finance Company—that sounds "home grown," a national financing company, but it is in fact "partly owned by the Netherlands Government…"

With his exceptional power of explanation, Rodney provides the simplest description of what happens to a newly independent African country as it reaches for economic development. Foreign governments and companies, Rodney explains, say

> to African governments and other third world

countries, "we are going to set up a manufacturing centre in your country. This is in line with your development strategy, you are becoming industrialised. Now if we are going to help you to be industrialised then obviously you must include the conditions under which this industry would succeed. You must provide tariff protection against other exports from Europe and Asia" ... Never mind that the domestic industry is owned lock, stock and barrel in many instances by foreign firms, it's still called domestic, it is still seen as local industry.

Returning his focus directly to Tanzania, Rodney explains, that from the country's low economic level, colonial era dependence and the failure to build a genuine autonomous basis for independence, meant that Nyerere's socialism, pioneered as "*Ujamaa*"—a programme for socialist economic development—was doomed to fail. *Ujamaa* was celebrated widely around the world by left-wing radicals but by 1978 Rodney was extraordinarily sober in his analysis, "So Ujamaa" he explained to the class, "has not increased production in Tanzania. It has not transformed technology... It has not transformed social relations in the countryside as it aimed at... It has strengthened the bureaucracy. It has failed to cut the dependency links... And at the ideological level it has created confusion in so far as it has sought to negate the concept of class struggle and class responsibilities." We should note here that Rodney came to this realisation in part through being pushed by Marxist students on campus at Dar es Salaam (most notable of these was the brilliant young Marxist and for a time, Rodney's PhD student, Issa Shivji,[9] but also Karim Hirji).

## A Fork-in-the-Road

Yet it is when Rodney examines the agency and activism of working people on the course that the excitement becomes tangible. In the final section of his lectures in Hamburg, Rodney moved on to discuss class struggle in Tanzania. In this part of the course, Rodney's teaching is a giddying, exciting roller-coaster. He tells his class that, "The idea of class struggle does not suit a bureaucratic bourgeoisie or any sector of the petit-bourgeois because it's an idea that speaks about the negation of their own existence over time". At times, Nyerere suggested that there were no real social classes in Tanzania and that consequently, it did not make any sense to adopt a theory that emphasises the role of class struggle in bringing about social transformation.[10]

Rodney argued the "petit bourgeoise ... were trying to disseminate the idea that workers exploit the countryside." This was a self-serving point that could be used against wages claims and demands "for a larger share of the surplus which they produce." These were

---

9   See Paul O'Connell's review "Critiquing Human Rights Like It Matters: Issa Shivji's *The Concept of Human Rights in Africa*" contained in this volume.

10  See Julius K. Nyerere, "Education for Self-Reliance: March 1967." In *Freedom and Socialism [Uhuru na Ujamaa]: A Selection from Writings and Speeches, 1965-1967* (Oxford University Press, 1968), 267-290.

not abstract arguments in an academic discussion, but justifications made directly by the Tanzanian state (and "socialist" and "capitalist" states across the continent). Nyerere, the radical president of Tanzania, was fond of making such claims himself, Rodney explained, "if the workers ask for more, the bureaucratic bourgeoise would reply, 'You are getting that at the expense of the peasants.'"

On the role of the state in Tanzania, his attitude had become much more critical. In the strikes and occupations reported by Issa Shivji in his 1976 book, *Class Struggles in Tanzania*, and noted by Rodney in his lectures, there was a new politics in formation.[11] Reporting on the working class action in the factory occupations in the early 1970s, in Hamburg he described, "We as workers are capable of running this enterprise more efficiently than the economic bureaucracy." In directly challenging the management of companies, workers were "making arguments that went beyond their own immediate material interests. They were carrying the class ... to even higher levels by in fact

---

11   Rodney has been aware of the struggles of workers, specifically the reaction to *mwongozo*, considerably earlier. In a lecture he delivered on 'Class Contradictions in Tanzania' in 1975 at North-Western University he discusses the contradictions and class tensions in the country after the implementation of the *mzongozo* guidelines. He writes, 'The workers used to move around with a very small version of the guidelines, a document printed up into a very tiny booklet, which could be stuffed into a top pocket or any pocket. Workers had a habit of moving around with the *Mwongozo* and taking it out ... and opening it to the appropriate page, and confronting bureaucrats...', "Class Contradictions in Tanzania" in Haroub Othman (ed), *The State in Tanzania: A Selection of Articles* (Dar es Salaam University Press, 1980).

posing the question who should control production…"

## Omissions and Inclusions

During these last years of his life, Rodney was at the height of his powers. He had a capacity for work which was extraordinary. Increasingly, Rodney's efforts were focused resolutely on the struggles from below and on the agency and capacity of working people to change society. There are invaluable signs of this shift, this new orientation, in the lecture course he presented in Hamburg and that was then published in the photocopied, limited-edition book in 1984.

The book, and lectures that comprise it, give a powerful impression of an activist and thinker engaged with challenging and wide-ranging issues such as the continent's history, slavery, independence, and projects of radical socialist development. Frequently interrupted by students to clarify a point, or justify a statement, Rodney deals with complex issues of history, political economy and Marxist theory with sophistication and clarity, never losing patience, or his narrative thread. The transcripts and recordings of the lectures held in the Walter Rodney Papers in Atlanta also give a sense of Rodney's own political development, reflecting on his activism, and his work with the working class in Guyana.

One of the most impressive aspects of the course is Rodney's criticism of Tanzania's socialist efforts. He is uncompromising, there was, he said to the "large group of students", simply nothing socialist about the reforms. He points to the strikes and working-class activity in a wave of action from 1973 as the centre of a genuine movement for socialist change—which saw a shift in the consciousness of those involved in struggle, Rodney explains. This is where we need to look for change, he asserts. This critical reappraisal, made in front of his class in 1978, was still, to me—reading the transcripts of the lectures in the windowless reading room of to the Robert W. Woodruff Library of the Atlanta University Center—in 2018, a tremendously exciting experience.

Understanding this wave of working-class action required that Rodney undertake a detailed reading of what had taken place. Nyerere was not a socialist in the way Rodney now understood the term, and he had crushed the strikes and occupations of workers, when these workers had dared to take matters into their own hands.[12] Yet as I scanned the 1984 book of these lectures, I realised that this significant part of the course, Rodney's account of the strikes and the "wild-cat" action in Tanzania had been excluded—this vital story had simply disappeared from this 1984 publication of the lectures.

What could be the reason for leaving out this still scintillating account of Nyerere and Tanzania and the role of the post-colonial working class? I can only imagine that even in 1984—when Nyerere had resigned as president—it was still considered too critical. Whatever the reasons, the book—only a few copies now

---

12   Rodney was in favour of Nyerere's attempt at independent national development and supported these efforts while he was in Tanzania. Nyerere was a committed African nationalist, who fought hard for real independence and development, and his politics and approach were clearly distinct from other figures who proclaimed socialism on the continent.

available anywhere in the world, including in the library in Hamburg—remains an astonishing tour de force of modern African history up to 1978, and evidence of Rodney's mastery and application of Marxism and radical political economy.

*The author would like to thank Louis Allday and Zeyad el Nabolsy for their comments and suggestions on an earlier draft of this review.*

# African Socialism in Retrospect: Karim Hirji's *The Travails of a Tanzanian Teacher*

Zeyad el Nabolsy

Tanzania in the 1960s and 1970s was a beacon of progressive politics on the African continent. The country served as a base for Southern African liberation movements as a key "front-line state", and assumed the mantle of Pan-African leadership in the aftermath of the coup against President Nkrumah of Ghana in 1966. As such, it attracted radical scholars and activists from all across the African diaspora, including Walter Rodney, Malcolm X, and Kwame Ture.[1]

Under its first president, Julius K. Nyerere, it embarked on a program of development guided by the ideology of "African socialism". Nyerere argued that traditionally Africans had "lived as families, with individuals supporting each other and helping each other on terms of equality" based on communal ownership of

---

1 Seth M. Markle, *A Motorcycle on Hell Run: Tanzania, Black Power, and the Uncertain Future of Pan-Africanism, 1964-1974* (Michigan State University Press, 2017), 48.

land.[2] Thus, "traditional African society was a socialist society".[3] At times, Nyerere seemed to imply that there were no classes in Tanzania and consequently; it did not make sense to adopt a theory that emphasised the role of class struggle in bringing about social transformations.[4] To this extent, African socialism was advanced by its proponents as an indigenous version of socialism that was more suitable for African conditions than Marxism-Leninism.

A fascinating first-hand account of how Tanzanian Marxists interpreted and criticised economic, social, cultural, and political developments in the country during this period is provided by Karim F. Hirji's memoir, *The Travails of a Tanzanian Teacher* (2018).[5] Hirji was involved in Marxist political organizations in Dar Es Salaam, and even though his Marxist orientation eventually led to his internal exile, he remained active as a Marxist scholar and activist in Tanzania, and he still contributes articles to progressive outlets on the African continent such as

---

2   Julius K. Nyerere, "Principles and Development: June 1966" In *Freedom and Socialism [Uhuru na Ujamaa]: A Selection from Writings and Speeches, 1965-1967* (Oxford University Press, 1968), 198-99.

3   Ibid.

4   Nyerere, "Education for Self-Reliance: March 1967." In *Freedom and Socialism* (1968), 276.

5   This constitutes the third volume of Hirji's memoirs. This first volume, *Growing Up with Tanzania: Memory, Musings and Maths* (2014) dealt with his childhood in Tanzania. The second volume, *Cheche: Reminiscences of a Radical Magazine* (2010), which was edited by Hirji and included contributions by others, provided an account of radical student movements at the University of Dar es Salaam (UDSM) during the 1960s and 1970s.

Pambazuka News.

Hirji's book, somewhat overlooked since its release, offers a compelling analysis of the history and sociology of the sciences in Tanzania, with a focus on Hirji's own field of statistics, from the post-independence period through to the 2010s. The first chapter provides an overview of Hirji's career as a teacher. The second presents an account of Hirji's experiences as a teacher under training, especially in light of the Arusha Declaration of 1967 and the turn towards building socialism in Tanzania, and the philosophy of education for self-reliance that Nyerere attempted to institutionalise. The next four chapters provide a detailed account of Hirji's years as a teacher at the University of Dar Es Salaam (UDSM) from 1971 until his dismissal and internal-exile in 1974.

Of particular interest is chapter five, which provides a detailed account of the confrontation known as the "Akivaga Crisis," which took place in July 1971.[6] This incident saw progressive students and faculty, in alliance with campus workers, face off with the UDSM's governing body. Hirji also provides a critical literature review of what has been written on these events (Appendix B: Akivaga Crisis in History), which is an invaluable source for anyone who wants to acquire an understanding of their importance. The events in question derive their significance from the fact that they can be interpreted as

---

6   It is so-called in reference to the student leader Symonds Akivaga whose dismissal and deportation to his home country of Kenya became a key issue in the struggle between the students and the university's governing body.

showing the limits of TANU's progressive politics.[7] In a confrontation between the party's appointed university administration on the one hand (which by all accounts was not tremendously competent) and progressive students, faculty, and campus workers on the other hand, the party employed the coercive apparatus of the state to back its appointed men. Even when it appeared that the people whom the party was backing were further away from the ideals of African Socialism than the students whom they were confronting.

Hirji criticises the exaggerated role which has been attributed to Walter Rodney by other socialist scholars, such as Haroub Othman and Issa Shivji.[8] Hirji asserts that, contrary to what is sometimes claimed, "Rodney kept a low profile during the crisis".[9] Hirji thus provides a much-needed corrective to the one-sided accounts of intellectual and political life at UDSM during the early 1970s which tend to centre on Rodney.[10]

---

7   TANU or Tanganyika African National Union was the ruling political party headed by Nyerere.

8   Karim F. Hirji, *The Travails of a Tanzanian Teacher* (Daraja Press, 2018), 194-198.

9   Ibid., 197.

10   To be clear, Hirji does not aim to undermine Rodney's significance as a scholar and activist. Hirji was a member of the University Students' African Revolutionary Front (USARF), a student Marxist group which was active on campus and formulated criticisms of Nyerere's policies from a Marxist perspective. It was as a member of USARF that Hirji first met Rodney at UDSM in 1969, after a lecture he delivered entitled The Cuban Revolution and its Relevance to Africa. Hirji then developed strong personal and working ties with him. In fact, Rodney's attitude towards students, whom he considered his peers and comrades,

Hirji's tenure as assistant lecturer, during which time he was actively involved in attempts to develop courses that would breakdown disciplinary boundaries, is detailed in chapter six of the book. This involved the introduction of two new courses: East African Society and Environment (required for all social sciences students) and Development Studies (required for all non-social sciences students). The seventh chapter of the book discusses Hirji's 18-month stint as a bureaucrat following his dismissal from UDSM in 1974. The reason for his dismissal was his critical stance towards some of Nyerere's policies –specifically, his critique of the policy of "education for self-reliance" published in 1973. Hirji argued that the requirement for manual labour was imposed on teachers without any planning. This meant that most teachers were unenthusiastic about it. He also pointed out that despite "the idealistic rhetoric, white collar jobs paid much more than manual work" and it was unpopular with many African students who

---

is evidenced by the fact he asked Hirji, still an undergraduate at the time, to provide feedback on the manuscript of How Europe Underdeveloped Africa. This assistance is acknowledged by Rodney in the preface of his seminal work: "special thanks must go to comrades Karim Hirji and Henry Mapolu of the University of Dar es Salaam, who read the manuscript in a spirit of constructive criticism". Hirji has also recently defended Rodney against some common criticisms in his 2017 work, *The Enduring Relevance of Rodney's How Europe Underdeveloped Africa*. Hence, his criticism of the inflated role assigned to Rodney in other accounts of the Crisis is not motivated by any hostility towards him. Hirji clarifies that Rodney kept a low profile—not because he was afraid—but rather because he did not want to do anything that would feed into the university administration's narrative of "foreign interference" as the cause of the Crisis.

associated manual work with colonial education.[11] In Hirji's view, the kind of political education which would have made it clear to students that manual labour, as mandated by the policy of education for self-reliance, was different from what took place under colonialism was altogether absent. Instead, students were only taught political education in an "insipid, sloganeering style".[12] For his trouble, Hirji was dismissed from UDSM and appointed as a bureaucrat in the Regional Planning Office of Rukwa region, with a posting in Sumbawanga, the regional capital. Sumbawanga was previously used by the British as a place of internal exile and Hirji clearly understood his appointment in such terms.

Hirji's experiences as a cog in the machine of the Tanzanian bureaucracy were decidedly negative. No real work was done by his office, and his boss was simply not interested in deploying Hirji's statistical knowledge (a planning office that does not care much for statistics does not inspire much confidence!). In fact, Hirji notes that he was not really expected to produce much, and that he could get away with spending the workday reading newspapers and other materials in the office, so long as he pretended to be doing something. It is noteworthy that Hirji's appointment took place just two years after the Tanzanian government had unveiled its new regional administration system, which was purportedly aimed at increasing popular political participation through decentralization. Hirji notes that for all of Nyerere's exhortation of self-reliance, this decentralization project

---

11   Hirji, *Tanzanian Teacher*, 86.

12   Ibid., 87.

"had been constructed for Tanzania with the expertise of the McKinsey Corporation, a global American consultancy firm that facilitates the smooth operations of the international capitalist order".[13]

In general, Hirji is rather harsh in his assessment of Tanzania's development programs under Nyerere. He points out that despite the rhetoric of self-reliance; Tanzania was dependent on foreign donors, who drove the country's educational policies even during the 1960s and 1970s.[14] Moreover, while TANU deployed the rhetoric of "African socialism", workers had no say in how the nationalised public-owned companies were managed.[15] Hirji is especially critical of the forced villagization program which was launched in the 1970s. While the aim of the villagization program was to concentrate rural inhabitants in villages so that services could be more easily provided, inadequate planning meant that farmers who were forced to move to the new villages often had to wait a year or more in order to get deep wells dug in them.[16] Hirji's criticisms of the Ujamaa period are not directed at undermining the significance of the achievements of the independence struggle, but rather to take aim at excessively nostalgic treatments of the period.[17]

---

13   Ibid., 89.

14   Ibid., 29.

15   Ibid., 133.

16   Ibid., 106.

17   Such as Godfrey Mwakikagile, *Tanzania Under Mwalimu Nyerere: Reflections on an African Statesman* (New Africa Press, 2006).

One striking feature of the book is Hirji's sociologically self-conscious account of his role as an individual teacher and of teaching in general. During his time as a bureaucrat, he recounts his founding of a mathematics club at the local secondary school. Hirji did not separate his role as a teacher of mathematics from his role as a Marxist educator. He gave lectures to the students on mathematics, but also incorporated a Marxist account of the history of mathematics into his lectures: "the students are fascinated by the diversity of ways in which mathematics developed in ancient Babylon, India, China, Egypt, and Greece. I venture into the general history of those societies as well, and relate mathematics to the level of economic development".[18] This approach seems to have been pedagogically successful, since it allowed students to understand mathematics as a fundamentally human practice whose abstractions can, in the final analysis, be historically traced to human social activities.

Hirji's sensitivity to sociological questions pertaining to science and mathematics education and research in Tanzania is evident throughout the book. One example points to the costs of what Paulin Hountondji describes as "extraversion" in scientific research and training on the African continent, i.e., externally oriented and directed practices of research and teaching.[19] Due to donor dependence, an approach to the teaching of mathematics that was shortly to be abandoned in the US was imported into Tanzania during the late 1960s with funding support

---

18   Ibid., 99-100.

19   Paulin J. Hountondji, "Scientific Dependence in Africa Today", *Research in African Literatures*, 21.3 (1990), 5-15.

from USAID. The approach in question, "Modern Maths" centred on a set of pedagogical techniques developed in the US in an attempt to catch up with Soviet advances in science and technology. It aimed to modernise the teaching of mathematics in the country by placing an emphasis on the introduction of general and abstract concepts at the beginning of instruction before moving onto concrete exercises. Students would begin by considering such questions as "'What is a number?' 'What is a variable function?' 'What is an equation?'"[20] This approach to teaching mathematics was in place in the US from the late 1950s to the early 1970s. However, by the mid-1970s, it had clearly failed due to its over-emphasis on abstract elements. This makes it all the more remarkable that it was adopted as the primary teaching approach to mathematics in Tanzania in the late 1960s and 1970s.[21] What this means is that Tanzanian students were subjected to a second-hand, cast-off curriculum that was on the way to being abandoned by its donors in their home country. A more devastating example of the long-term consequences of scientific dependency and extraversion at the level of both teaching and research would be hard to find.

Chapter eight provides an account of Hirji's role as a teacher at the National Transport Institute, while the last three chapters of the book provide an assessment of the state of universities in Tanzania today—as well as Hirji's own teaching philosophy. Hirji paints a grim

---

20   UICSM Project Staff, "The University of Illinois School Mathematics Program", *The School Review*, 65.1 (1957), 457-465.

21   Hirji, *Tanzanian Teacher*, 28-29.

image of the present condition of Tanzanian universities, especially since he situates his account within the context of the imposition of structural adjustment programs on Tanzania—Nyerere was eventually forced to enter into negotiations with the IMF between 1981 and 1985.[22] The salaries of professors were cut dramatically as part of the austerity program. Universities are now run on a business model with students occupying the role of customers. Naturally this places pressure on faculty to pass failing students and to lower academic standards.[23] Moreover, because many academic institutions depend on foreign funding, their academic programs are sometimes guided by foreign academics and administrators who often do not know what they are talking about, but are tolerated because they provide funding.[24]

However, Hirji is careful to point to internal problems as well. Hirji himself refuses to lay all the blame at the feet of international financial institutions. After all, it was TANU's failure to restructure the Tanzanian economy that provided the opening for international financial institutions to swoop in. For example, while Hirji recognises the significance of the expansion of university education under Nyerere—in 1971 Tanzania had one university with less than 3,000 students, by 2017 it had fifty universities with around 200,000 students—he also notes that there was a decline in the quality of

---

[22] Mwakikagile, *Tanzania Under Mwalimu Nyerere: Reflections on an African Statesman*, 78-79.

[23] Hirji, *Tanzanian Teacher*, 162.

[24] Ibid., 160-161.

the education that was provided.[25] In the 1970s, degrees obtained at UDSM were recognised by other universities (e.g., in the United Kingdom), but this is no longer the case today.[26] Understaffing is a serious problem with professors lacking adequate numbers of teaching assistants. In fact, Hirji had no teaching assistants during his time as a professor at Muhimili University of Health and Allied Sciences, MUHAS.[27] The situation in Tanzanian universities became so dire that, in 2017, 19 universities were ordered not to enrol new students and a further 22 were prohibited from enrolling new students in 75 programs.[28] Clearly this is a recipe for the perpetuation of dependency on foreign "experts" with all the connected negative consequences. Hirji provides us with an important account of the different factors which have contributed to the crisis of the university in Tanzania. Yet, he does not explicitly provide answers to the question, *what is to be done?* Nevertheless, readers who are interested in a Marxist account of the historical origins of the current plight of universities in Tanzania will find this book of tremendous use.

Overall, Hirji's book is an excellent account of the dilemmas that Marxists faced during the Bandung-era. In countries like Tanzania, where a progressive nationalist government was in power, Marxists had to make difficult decisions in relation to the extent to which they should support their governments in their struggle against

---

25  Ibid., 152.

26  Ibid., 156.

27  Ibid., 154.

28  Ibid., 176.

imperialism (the "national question") while also pushing for the recognition of the importance of internal social transformations (the "social question"). Perhaps the primary failing in this respect is that Marxists in Tanzania (and in other places where similar conditions prevailed) were unable to convince those in power that an adequate resolution to the national question required internal social and economic transformations. This book shows how, absent the requisite internal structural transformations, the rhetoric of self-reliance can lead to a path that terminates in the most humiliating forms of dependency.

# Critiquing Human Rights Like It Matters: Issa Shivji's *The Concept of Human Rights in Africa*

Paul O'Connell

Human rights language is ubiquitous today. Starting with the Universal Declaration of Human Rights in 1948, we have since seen the proliferation of international and regional treaties and monitoring bodies. This gained pace, in particular, with the end of the Cold War and Fukuyama's putative end of history—with human rights emerging as the "post-ideological" common sense of the late 20$^{th}$ and early 21$^{st}$ centuries.[1] Precisely because of the very hegemony of human rights talk in the contemporary world, critiques of human rights abound; ranging from the friendly critiques which seek to perfect an otherwise laudable idea and system, to more radical dismissals of human rights as the avatars of neoliberal capitalism and inequality.

---

[1] Stefan-Ludwig Hoffmann, "Introduction: Genealogies of Human Rights" in Hoffmann (ed.), *Human Rights in the Twentieth Century* (Cambridge University Press, 2011), 1.

There is much value in some of these recent critiques of human rights. It is noteworthy, however, that in a short book written in the late 1980s, the Tanzanian author and academic, Issa Shivji, articulated a critique of human rights that both anticipated many of these more recent critiques and, crucially, remains more incisive and politically relevant than most of them. Although in certain respects it is a work of its time, Shivji's critique of human rights remains relevant for both a research agenda on human rights and radical politics in the 21st century. This review sets out the key elements of Shivji's account of rights, and the continuing relevance of his work and this book for today.

Shivji begins the book by stating clearly that human rights, or at least what he terms the dominant/liberal conception of human rights, "constitutes one of the main elements in the ideological armoury of imperialism".[2] As such, Shivji sets out to engage "the subject of human rights so as to avoid the pitfalls of a liberal perspective".[3] In contrast to the claimed neutrality of the dominant discourse, Shivji's explicit "point of departure and reference are the interests of the broad masses of the African people",– thus from the outset, Shivji's account of human rights is both critical and partisan.[4]

Importantly, unlike "petty bourgeois radical" accounts of human rights, which are just another variation on the liberal tradition in the way in which they "absolutise the

---

2   Issa Shivji, *The Concept of Human Rights in Africa* (CODIS-ERA, 1989), vii.

3   Ibid.

4   Ibid.

human rights question", it is not Shivji's aim or intention to "throw away ... human rights talk", but instead to "reconstruct ... human rights ideology to legitimise and mobilise people's struggles".[5] In this latter endeavour we find one of Shivji's most distinctive contributions: the attempt to articulate what he calls a revolutionary conception of human rights.

## *The Dominant Account*

Shivji's work then sets out an account of the dominant discourse of human rights in Africa, so that he can then critique it and from that critique begin to articulate an alternate account of human rights. Shivji notes that, in real terms, one "can hardly talk of the African philosophy of human rights",[6] instead the "dominant argument ... propounded by most of the African and Africanist lawyers and jurists" has proceeded on the basis of an uncritical acceptance of Western liberal conceptions of human rights.

As such, notwithstanding some variations, these dominant accounts suffer from five key deficiencies: (i) they abstract from social history and concrete material conditions; (ii) they divorce the history of human rights from the history of the class struggles that were crucial in shaping them (with natural rights as the sword advancing the class interests of the rising European bourgeois and positively enacted rights as their shield once in power); (iii) they elide the "ideologically and politically charged"

---

5  Ibid., vii-viii.

6  Ibid., 15.

nature of debates over the priority of rights (civil and political v social and economic etc.); (iv) "the prevailing human rights discourse on Africa has been singularly 'deficient' in contextualising the human rights ideology within the imperialist domination of Africa"; and (v) the individualist and ahistorical approach to human rights allows for a focus on discrete episodes or human rights violations, while remaining blind to the structural causes of human rights abuse and denial.[7]

Taken together, the effect of all of these characteristics and deficiencies of the dominant discourse contributes to "the production and reproduction of a human rights ideology which objectively buttresses the imperialist oppression of Africa on the one hand, and the authoritarian/military domination of its people on the other".[8] As such, Shivji argues that human rights and human rights discourse, in their dominant rendering, are a barrier to the nascent democratic revolution necessary for the fundamental transformation of Africa.

*Human Rights and Struggle*

Shivji, however, does not stop with critique—cognisant of the important role human rights (in their natural rights rendering)[9] played in mobilising the earlier bourgeois

---

7   Ibid., 50-53.

8   Ibid., 53.

9   The argument Shivji rehearses is that from Hobbes and Locke onwards a particular conception of the natural rights of the atomised, utility maximising individual formed a central tenet of revolutionary bourgeois ideology; an ideology which was mobilised to help disrupt and overthrow the old feudal orders of

revolutions of the 18th and 19th centuries, and the ideological cachet of human rights in the present, Shivji insists that "there is a need to build a new perspective of human rights in Africa".[10] At this point, Shivji shows an acute awareness of the need to connect theory with practice, noting that "this reconceptualisation is obviously a process involving constant interaction between the struggles of the African people and activists".[11]

So, while it is not possible to articulate a full blown reconceptualisation of human rights "at a stroke", the preceding critique of the dominant discourse "provides some elements or building blocks for beginning to erect a new perspective".[12] Central to Shivji's critique of the dominant human rights discourse is that it divorces human rights from concrete history, the role of imperialism and from the masses of African people as active subjects in their own life and history.

The central elements for Shivji's rethinking of human rights flow directly from this—as such he identifies three key elements that must inform a revolutionary reconceptualisation of human rights in Africa. The first is that any account or theory must be "historically situated" and grounded in a concrete analysis of the conjuncture, in the context of Africa this must emphasise that "imperialist domination of Africa, from colonial to neocolonial forms, constitutes the main point

---

Europe. Ibid., 45-50; and see Eugene Genovese, *Roll, Jordan, Roll* (Vintage Book, 1976), 44-47.

10  Shivji, *The Concept of Human Rights*, 69.

11  Ibid.

12  Ibid.

of departure for understanding the conditions of the African masses". A new theory of human rights must "be thoroughly anti-imperialist, thoroughly democratic and unreservedly in the interest of the 'people'" (understood here as the mass of workers and peasants).[13]

The second key element of such a theory is that it must stress the centrality of class struggle in shaping and conceptualising human rights, as Shivji puts it:

> the human rights ideology has to be appropriated in the interest of the people to play a mobilising role in their struggle against imperialism and compradorial classes and their state. Therefore, the new perspective must distance itself openly from imperialist ideology of human rights at the international level and cultural-chauvinist/developmentalist ideology of the compradorial classes, at the national level. This is the second element or building block in the new perspective.[14]

This latter point is crucial to Shivji's account, as he understands that the contradictory role that human rights and human rights talk has played in the past (both subverting and legitimating the status quo) is the product not of unresolved intellectual abstraction, but the concrete product of class struggles.

The third element of Shivji's reconceptualisation of human rights is an insistence that "new conceptualisation must clearly break from both the metaphysics of natural law as well as the logical formalism and legalism of

---

13  Ibid., 69-70.

14  Ibid., 70.

positive law. It must be rooted in the perspective of class struggle". This implies that rights, rooted in struggle and a revolutionary perspective, would not be primarily conceived as individual rights, but as collective rights of peoples; rights are not primarily conceived as legal entitlements, but "as a means of struggle, 'right' is therefore not a standard granted as charity from above but a standard-bearer around which people rally for struggle from below"; all of this, in turn, transforms the vocabulary of human rights so that

> one does not simply sympathise with the "victims" of human rights violations and beg the "violators" to mend their ways in numerous catalogued episodes of violations; rather one joins the oppressed/exploited/ dominated or ruled against the oppressors/exploiters/ dominant and ruling to expose and resist, with a view ultimately to overcome, the situation which generates human rights violations.[15]

In line with Marx's view of the role of critique being to find the kernel of the new in the old,[16] Shivji's reconceptualisation of human rights does not 'begin from a clean slate', but instead begins to sketch the elements of the new from his critique of the old.[17]

---

15   Ibid., 70-71.

16   Karl Marx, 'Letters From the *Deutsch-Französische Jahrbücher*' in *Marx-Engels Collected Works: Vol. 3* (Lawrence & Wishart, 2010) 133, 142.

17   Shivji, *The Concept of Human Rights*, 72.

## Another Way

Importantly, Shivji also illustrates that this theoretical difference is present in concrete terms in the contrast between the African Charter on Human and Peoples Rights, which for Shivji suffers from all of the maladies of the dominant account, with its "neo-colonialist statist disposition", developmentalism and obeisance to a fictive international cooperation.[18] In stark contrast, Shivji invokes the Universal Declaration of the Rights of Peoples (or Algiers Declaration) of 1976, a document which is avowedly anti-imperialist and centred on the collective rights of oppressed peoples.

The Preamble to the Algiers Declaration, which Shivji quotes approvingly, recognises from the outset the "new forms of imperialism" that have evolved to oppress and subjugate the peoples of the world, thus fundamentally undermining human rights. It sets itself against imperialism in all its forms, and provides support for "all those who, throughout the world, are fighting the great battle, at times through armed struggle, for the freedom of all peoples", with the hope that people will "find in this Declaration the assurance of the legitimacy of their struggle".[19]

Whereas the African Charter provides firm protection to private property, and in this way undercuts many of the other rights proclaimed in it as well as legitimating imperial relations of exploitation, the Algiers Declaration

---

18  Ibid., 97.

19  "Universal Declaration of the Rights of Peoples (Algiers Declaration)" 1976, Preamble.

provides no such protection. This is crucially important, as Shivji notes, because a "careful reading of its provisions shows that it is clearly aware that private property, in this case particularly imperialist property, lies behind the system of underdevelopment and domination in the Third World".[20]

In its explicit anti-imperialism, its rejection of the centrality of private property (the fundamental right *par excellence* of the bourgeoisie) and its foregrounding of the rights of collectives in struggle, the Algiers Declaration provides a concrete illustration of Shivji's revolutionary and struggle centred reconceptualisation of human rights. As Shivji notes, the subsequent neglect of the Declaration speaks to the persistent ideological biases of human rights discourse rooted in the hegemony of imperialist ideology.[21] In the more than thirty years since Shivji produced this book the Algiers Declaration has remained a more or less forgotten moment in the history of anti-imperialist and radical critiques of imperialism and human rights, whereas the African Charter system has consolidated itself.[22]

20   Issa Shivji, *The Concept of Human Rights*, 103.

21   Ibid., 106.

22   The Charter was adopted through intergovernmental negotiations under the auspices of the Organisation of African Unity (now the African Union), as such it has greater official/formal status from the outset, along with an increasingly robust enforcement mechanism—at present 53 African states have signed up to the Charter. In contrast the Declaration was adopted by activists and revolutionaries brought together by the Lelio Basso Foundation, in consequence it never enjoyed the same formal/binding character of the Charter—coupled with its radical political content this informality, along with the course of historical

## Shivji's Critique Today

As noted at the outset, critiques of human rights are commonplace today. Few, however, have the incisiveness or political relevance of the critique Shivji outlined in 1989. With a very few exceptions, the most notable being Radha D'Souza's excellent recent book,[23] few critiques of human rights seriously understand or attempt to engage with imperialism in any meaningful sense. Others are wrapped up in the critique of human rights as an idea, traversing the interesting terrain of intellectual history, but ending in political immobilisation and quietism.

In contrast, Shivji's account foregrounds class antagonisms and class struggle in both how we understand the development and place of human rights in the world today, and how we might engage with human rights in movements for fundamental change. Imperialism remains the defining feature of our world system,[24] so when thinking about human rights it is crucial to avoid the pitfalls of abstraction, in its various forms, and foreground the role of contemporary imperialism in both reproducing human rights ideology, and structurally undermining the possibility of human rights protection—Shivji's work provides an important lodestar and entry point in this regard.

Much like the Algiers Declaration, Shivji's work has not received the attention that it merits. This is no doubt

---

development in Africa and elsewhere over the last 40 years, has ensured the neglect of the Declaration to date.

23   Radha D'Souza, *What's Wrong With Rights?* (Pluto, 2018).

24   Utsa Patnaik and Prabhat Patnaik, *A Theory of Imperialism* (Columbia University Press, 2017).

in part due to the very relationships of imperial and neo-colonial hierarchy that Shivji himself identified, but it is also because Shivji's critique of human rights and attempt to reconceptualise human rights in the service of revolutionary struggles, is far less palatable than the petty bourgeois and pseudo radical critiques that leave the essence of imperialism and class struggle untouched.

His critique of human rights remains incisive and relevant, both in the context of the continued imperial plundering of Africa[25] and in light of the various social movements, such as Abahlali baseMjondolo in South Africa,[26] that are engaging with human rights in subversive and imaginative ways. But its relevance goes far beyond Africa, and in an era of persistent capitalist crises and imperialist barbarism, Shivji's work provides us with a starting point for thinking about and engaging with human rights without "mindlessly reproducing imperialist and neo-colonial ideological domination".[27] A way of critiquing and engaging with human rights as if they really matter.

---

25  Lee Wengraf, *Extracting Profit* (Haymarket 2018).

26  Nigel Gibson, *Fanonian Practices in South Africa* (Palgrave Macmillan, 2011), 144-180.

27  Issa Shivji, *The Concept of Human Rights*, 110.

# Insurgent Theory in Times of Crisis: Dani Wadada Nabudere's *The Political Economy of Imperialism*

Corinna Mullin

Dani Wadada Nabudere (1932-2011) was a prolific Marxist-Leninist, Pan-Africanist, anti-imperialist scholar, freedom fighter, lawyer and politician whose knowledge production was firmly rooted in his extensive and diverse political experience. It is remarkable that he is not more renowned worldwide given his stature. It is hard to make sense of a figure like Nabudere in today's academic context that is dominated by professionalism or claims to political purity on the one hand, and institutional policing and a capitalist-imperialist driven political economy of publishing on the other. His unapologetic materialist analysis and clear writing are refreshing given the obscurity of so many contemporary scholarly texts. Nabudere took real material as well as physical risks, and seemed driven by Mao's maxim that "all genuine knowledge originates in direct experience" and the only way to know the "theory and methods of revolution" is to take part in making it, even if that means making mistakes.[1]

In addition to his scholarly writings and academic positions across the African continent, including at the University of Dar es Salaam (Tanzania), University of Zimbabwe, and the Marcus Garvey Pan-African Institute (Uganda), which he founded, Nabudere had a long and complicated history as an activist, from student organizing to armed insurrection and institutionalised politics. For this alone, Nabudere's scholarly works should be revisited as they are informed directly by praxis. Nabudere's empirically and theoretically rich body of work should also be studied for what it can tell us about contemporary manifestations of imperialism— particularly in Africa—and how to resist them.

*A Political Biography*

Nabudere first became involved in politics as a student in London in 1961, where he was a member of the Executive Committee of the anti-colonial United Kingdom Uganda Students Association (UGASA) together with Yash Tandon and other prominent Ugandan Marxists and Pan-Africanists. Nabudere returned to Uganda in 1964 and was involved with the nationalist Uganda People's Congress (UPC), although his Marxist ideology clashed with that of the leadership and resulted in his marginalization and eventual expulsion in 1965. He went on to engage in more grassroots forms of organizing,

1  *Selected Works of Mao Tse-tung*, "On the Relation Between Knowledge and Practice, Between Knowing and Doing", July 1937

helping to establish the Uganda Vietnam Solidarity Committee "to oppose the American war of aggression against the Vietnamese people," as well as the first Maoist party in Uganda.[2]

Nabudere's relationship with Idi Amin's government followed a similar trajectory, with initially good relations turning sour after he protested Amin's brutality.[3] He eventually resigned from the government and moved to Tanzania, where he co-founded the Uganda National Liberation Front (UNLF) and even engaged in armed struggle for a short period. With significant support from the Tanzanian army, the UNLF eventually brought down the Amin government. This was also the period, as Tandon details, when Nabudere's Pan-Africanism and internationalism were further forged, as he and the UNLF "made far-reaching contacts" with other revolutionary movements in Africa, the Middle East and Asia.[4]

He participated in the "first turbulent year" of the UNLF government, although it was not long before Nabudere was in exile again, as the UNLF government was overthrown in a military coup in May 1980.[5] Together with other compatriots he went to Nairobi, and eventually moved to Denmark, where he would spend several years as a high school teacher. He returned to Uganda in 1993

---

2   Yash Tandon, "Nabudere: An uncompromising revolutionary", *Pambazuka News*, 12 July 2012.

3   He was appointed Chairman of the Board of Directors of the East African Railways.

4   Yash Tandon, "Nabudere: An uncompromising revolutionary".

5   Victoria Brittain, "After Amin", *London Review of Books*, 3:17, 17 September 1981.

and briefly joined the US-backed Museveni government, although that position was short-lived, after which he became an outspoken critic of the government. Tandon, his long-time friend and comrade, recalls that "Nabudere was a Marxist scholar and practitioner to his bones" and "was not dogmatic in political tactics."

Despite his political activity, Nabudere still found time to research and publish. He has an impressive list of publications, many of which intersect with ongoing critical themes in economics and development studies, including *The Rise and Fall of Money Capital* (1990), *Essays on the Theory and Practice of Imperialism* (1979), *Imperialism in East Africa* (1980), and the subject of this review: *The Political Economy of Imperialism* (1977). Through these works, Nabudere contributed to the development of a political economic analysis of "African social formations" not only empirically, but also theoretically, as Zeyad el Nabolsy argues, to "the refinement and… development of Marxism-Leninism."[6]

Nabudere was central to a generation of radical scholars who would challenge the epistemological and pedagogical underpinnings of the colonial African university, and who participated in the famous "University of Dar es Salaam debates' on 'socialism, social emancipation, underdevelopment and imperialism," in the late 1960s and throughout the 1970s.[7] His contributions were

6   Zeyad el Nabolsy, "The Leninist Legacy in East Africa: Abdul Rahman Mohammed Babu and Dan Wadada Nabudere" (Unpublished Chapter, 2019), 22.

7   Horace Campbell, "The Impact of Walter Rodney and Progressive Scholars on the Dar Es Salaam School", *Social and Economic Studies*, 40:2 (June 1991).

particularly critical to contesting the Eurocentrism of the social sciences, demanding instead a disciplinary approach that would "reflect the African context and conditions." Although the Dar es Salaam scholars were for the most part much more at ease with the Marxist-Leninist analytical framework than their contemporaries from the "decolonial school", their work nevertheless prefigured the methodological and epistemological concerns that are central to the latter, as they stressed the importance of "interpret[ing] African history from an African viewpoint and epistemology rather than from the viewpoint of the colonisers".[8]

The creation of the African Association of Political Science (AAPS) in 1973 emerged out of this formation, with Nabudere as one of its earliest presidents. The AAPS included other Pan-African luminaries such as Okwudiba Nnoli, Emmanuel Hansen, Mahmood Mamdani, Yash Tandon and Helmi Sharawi. As Tandon explained, Nabudere was a foremost proponent of AAPS's pan-Africanist orientation who "showed how the social sciences as ideological expressions of dominant classes faced a crisis of relevance in Africa, and how these needed to be challenged."[9] Influenced by Paolo Friere, Nabudere's later work was much more concerned with "emancipatory and liberatory pedagogy". He sought to "connect institutions of higher learning to

---

8   Dani Wadada Nabudere, "Research, Activism, and Knowledge Production", In Eds. Charles R. Hale and Craig Calhoun, *Engaging Contradictions: Theory, Politics, and Methods of Activist Scholarship* (University of California Press, 2008), 68.

9   Yash Tandon, "Nabudere: An uncompromising revolutionary".

the knowledge generated in communities" as part of the "struggle for self-determination" and a "bottom-up", participatory model of knowledge production. His work in establishing the Marcus Garvey Pan-Afrikan Institute in Mbale in Uganda was an institutional expression of this insurgent pedagogy, as it aimed to "highlight African indigenous knowledge as a source of valuable human achievement by mainstreaming it through rediscovery, research, and recognition."[10]

*Knowledge in the Service of Liberation*

Although *The Political Economy of Imperialism* is less concerned with questions of pedagogy, it shared with Nabudere's other projects a theoretical commitment to liberation. Written at the dawn of neo-colonial structural adjustment, the book is impressive not only for the breadth and depth of its historical assessment and the sharpness of its analysis, but for its foresight as well. Wedded to a stadial analysis, the book begins with the dissolution of the Roman Empire and transition from production based on (pre-modern) slavery to feudalism, and from mercantilist imperialism to competitive capitalism. Nabudere employs a Marxist interpretation of crisis to explain the transitions within capitalism, initially to monopoly and finance imperialism and finally to what he describes as "multilateral imperialism".

It was the transition to monopoly and finance imperialism, as Nabudere described it, that resonates most with the current moment as it engendered the

---

10 Nabudere, "Research, Activism, and Knowledge Production", 83.

rise of fascism in Germany and Italy following WWI. Nabudere's insight is that "fascism came into assist monopoly capitalism by smashing all the bourgeois individual democratic rights and institutions in order to protect the bourgeoisie as a class against the possibilities of socialist revolution"; it is helpful for explaining the rise of blatantly fascist heads of state like Trump, Bolsanaro and Modi.[11] However, his historical materialist analysis helps us to move beyond liberal ideology's emphasis on individuals and instead shed light on the structural causes of the crisis and capital's response.

Nabudere's analysis also encourages us to think about how fascism already exists under the imperialist system, and that it requires consistent state violence to maintain racialised exploitation and value extraction in both the centre and periphery. The racist police and carceral state work to maintain social order in the former, whereas in the latter, there are the "puppet armies… trained and equipped with modern NATO weapons and maintained on US and other imperialist official aid" and are "held up by the petty-bourgeois regimes" to prevent the emergence of "revolutionary forces of national liberation and socialist construction". Despite the enormous depth and reach of imperialist tentacles, Nabudere's dialectical approach to history combined with a revolutionary praxis demonstrate a profound belief in the possibility of radical transformation.

---

11  Dani Wadada Nabudere, *The Political Economy of Imperialism: Its theoretical and polemical treatment from mercantilist to multilateral imperialism* (Zed Press, 1978), 37.

## Contributions to Understanding and Resisting Late-Stage Imperialism

Nadubere's most important empirical and theoretical contributions emerge from his analysis of crisis. In Marxist fashion, he holds that crises are at the heart of the major transitions within the global capitalist economy. The first such transition was in 1870, at a time when the consolidation of the "liberal state" and significant population growth were taking place, and when the capitalist system experienced a historical fall in the rate of profit. This was partly a result of industrial development, which required an expansion of foreign markets. As el Nabolsy points out, what distinguishes Nabudere's analysis from much Marxist-Leninist political economy is the importance it ascribes to Marx's "basic law of motion of capitalism" (or "the tendency of the rate of profit to fall") to explain the economic imperative behind imperialism. This process "could only be reversed by increased supplies of cheap raw and auxiliary materials, expanding markets, and lower wages, which implied an intensification of the exploitation of labour."[12] Together with the domination of finance capital, which was the result of a merger of industrial and bank capital, these changes birthed "modern imperialism".

The new financial oligarchy that emerged from this transition went on to divide "the remaining uncolonised world among monopoly concerns and big imperialist states." As a result, the capitalists were able to restore the high rate of surplus-value and hence high rate of profit,

---

12   Ibid., 77.

as well as finish the process of linking all countries of the world in one economy. Yet in dialectical tradition, Nabudere analyses how the horizons of monopoly imperialism were soon "narrowed... by the emergence of the socialist system that was marked by the October Revolution."[13]

The next major capitalist crisis resulted in World War II and exacerbated the contradictions between the imperialist countries, "leading to a devastating destruction of the productive forces among vanquished and victors alike."[14] This crisis served as a cypher for the consolidation of US imperial power under the guise of "free trade" and "multilateralism". The US's "new imperialist policy of redivision"—i.e., the "Open Door" strategy—was intended to solve the problem of liberalised trade and the mobilisation of capital for "reconstruction".[15] This could not be done with the "closed markets, closed sources of raw materials and closed outlets for capital exports that existed in the inter-war years." The US subsumption of British and French colonial possessions based on "closed markets, closed sources of raw materials" was achieved by a multi-pronged approach; "namely by creating trade, monetary, financial and political institutions" under the domination of US imperialism.[16]

Nabudere grasped very early on the central role of international financial institutions in providing a cover for imperialist interests and providing transnational

---

13 Ibid., vii.

14 Ibid.

15 Ibid., vii, 147.

16 Ibid., 147.

corporations with the illusion of diffuse power through a discourse of global value chains—while continuing to enable imperialist modes of accumulation based on the transfer of value from the periphery to the imperialist core. Under "multilateral imperialism", what appears as "transactions between nations and separate national enterprises" was in actuality "transactions between units of the same monopolies."[17] Rather than the diffusion of power and wealth, what this era actually witnessed was "the increasing concentration of production and capital, which is the sole means by which a transnational corporation can maintain its profitability amidst the intensified competition in the world market by monopolies"—with US-owned multinational corporations as the greatest beneficiaries.[18]

Nabudere goes on to explain the central role of the IMF in maintaining imperialism "as a financial arm of the multilateral arrangement that has wielded the real big stick, enforcing monetary and financial discipline according to the dictates of monopoly capitalism."[19] As a result of imperialist domination, "any 'advice' rendered by the IMF to the neo-colony represents monopoly interests."[20] Crucial from the perspective of current discussions of medical imperialism is Nabudere's analysis of the role of patents, intellectual property law and unequal sovereignty. He explains how the neo-colonies are forced, "upon the attainment of their formal political independence"

---

17  Ibid., 38.

18  Ibid., vii.

19  Ibid., 260.

20  Ibid.

and as part of their "new international status", to "subscribe to the objectives of the International Union for the Protection of Industrial Property under whose convention they are obliged to protect the patent rights of foreign monopolies"—meaning they are, "of course, monopoly 'rights'." As such, they are an imperialist rent that facilitates accumulation in the centre.[21]

Rather than approaching neo-colonial states as independent entities engaged in negotiations with imperialist institutions and multinational corporations (a perspective that obscures profoundly unequal power relations), this political economy of imperialism demystifies what is in fact monopoly domination. Referencing agreements like the Lomé Convention of 1975, Nabudere contends that "the national bourgeoisie and petty bourgeoisie pride themselves that they are engaged in 'bargaining' with the monopolies in order to advance 'national development,'" while in "actual fact no such nation exists nor does any 'development' take place."[22] On this point, Mamdani and Bhagat charge Nabudere with underestimating the agency of the Global South in achieving improved terms of trade for African producers, for example, which can potentially pose as a serious challenge to imperialist domination and achieve a "victory for the Third World."[23]

---

21   Ibid., 250.

22   Ibid.

23   M. Mamdani and H. Bhagat, "Comments on the Political Economy of Imperialism", 43 in *Debate on Class, State & Imperialism* (Tanzania Publishing House, 1982).

## Anti-Imperialism and the Global Struggle for Socialism

For Nabudere, the only way to upend to this global system of accumulation through dispossession is through worldwide socialist revolution. Yet, his conceptualization of the revolutionary trajectory in the imperialist centre is limited. It is unclear, for example, how "the internationalisation of the class struggle" will materialise given the gross inequalities in global labour and living standards and the often reactionary role played by the trade unions of the Global North as they seek to defend their privileges.[24] Or, how the "subjective conditions" of a proletarian vanguard will come about in the belly of the beast without centring the experiences, needs, leadership and "freedom dreams" of those most oppressed, exploited and dispossessed by racial capitalism and settler colonialism. This reality has been exposed and exacerbated by the health crisis of the coronavirus pandemic, which has disproportionately impacted working class Black, Indigenous and other people of colour.

Nabudere's analysis of the prospects for revolution in the "colonial, semi-colonial and neocolonial" countries is more compelling. Although he explained that each context requires "class analysis as well as the study of the [specific] concrete material conditions", as a general rule he insists that revolution in the periphery required that the "national question [must be] linked up with the socialist revolution".[25] Employing Mao's

---

24  Nabudere, *The Political Economy of Imperialism*, 271.
25  Ibid., 215.

conceptualization of revolution as a two-phase struggle, Nabudere explains that national democratic revolution on the "basis of new democracy" must be immediately followed by a transformation "into a socialist revolution under the leadership of the proletariat" in order to be successful.[26] His own ideological commitments as well as personal experience with political struggle guide him to conclude that this revolution would be bound to fail in the absence of a clear break with imperialist forces: "a revolt against imperialism becomes the only basis… for the national democratic revolution."[27]

*Engaging Nabudere's Critics*

There are shortcomings in Nabudere's analysis. Most notably, Nabudere failed to centre the role of slavery in his history of capitalism—unlike "racial capitalism", which connects capital accumulation and the history of slavery to the "mutually constitutive entanglements of racialised and colonial exploitation".[28] Absent a racial capitalist framework, Nabudere fails to grasp the full extent of super-exploitation, or the "gross markup on labour costs… both in the relative sense of above-average rates of exploitation and also, frequently, in the absolute sense of workers paid less than the cost of the reproduction of their labour power", as a feature of neo-colonial accumulation in the Global South (and among

---

26  Ibid., vii.

27  Ibid., 263.

28  Zophia Edwards, "Racial Capitalism and COVID-19", *Monthly Review*, 1 March 2021.

racialised and oppressed communities within the Global North).[29] As a result, Nabudere fails to situate either workers in the periphery, or Black, Indigenous and other racialised workers in the imperialist core as the "main force" of potential revolutionary action, despite the fact that past protagonists of such action have emanated from these communities.

Nabudere's position on World System and Dependency theory is curious. He criticises what he calls "the neo-Marxist centre-periphery ideology" as "ahistorical and hence unscientific".[30] He particularly disagrees with Arghiri Emmanuel's concept of "unequal exchange" in global trade, which renders primitive accumulation an ongoing rather than an historical phenomenon for the Global South, which, for Nabudere, "smack[s] of economistic explanations". For Nabudere, Emmanuel's stance that the Global South is "exploited through the imperialism of trade and not through the imperialism of finance capital," is at odds with the correct application of a Marxist-Leninist framework.[31] Instead, Nabudere argues that unequal exchange must be understood as a temporally specific concept, and applied to the early era of primitive accumulation (including slavery and colonial rule), when "trade of commodities between Europe and the undeveloped areas of the world [was conducted]… between two different modes

---

29   Intan Suwandi, R. Jamil Jonna and John Bellamy Foster, "Global Commodity Chains and the New Imperialism", Monthly Review, 1 March 2019.

30   Nabudere, *The Political Economy of Imperialism*, vii.

31   Ibid., 225.

of production".[32] For Nabudere, unequal exchange was also not only geo-politically limited to trade with the colonies, but also relations between developed and underdeveloped European states, as exemplified by a series of British-Portuguese treaties in the seventeenth century, which situated Britain as a net importer of food and primary products and net exporter of textiles, ensuring "Portuguese dependence on England and... destroy[ing] her potential to industrialise."[33]

Yet Nabudere's critique is firmly rooted in an anti-imperialist perspective shared by the World Systems theorists whom he castigates, specifically acknowledging systematic surplus drain from the Global South and naming the "perpetrators of neo-colonialism" as "the US, the European and the Japanese imperialists"—or what Samir Amin described as the "collective imperialism of the triad."[34] Thus, Nabudere clearly identifies the Global North to be where imperialism is centred. Although Nabudere does not see the North-South relationship through the lens of unequal exchange, he acknowledges that the historical record clearly shows that multilateral imperialism has intensified the exploitation of the neo-colonial world through increased capital exports, and thereby increased the political subordination of these countries to the financial oligarchies of the imperialist countries.[35]

---

32　Ibid., vi.

33　Ibid., 79.

34　Ibid., 216; Samir Amin, Contemporary Imperialism, *Monthly Review*, 1 July 2015.

35　Nabudere, *The Political Economy of Imperialism*, viii.

What is interesting is that this does not translate into an analysis of the super-exploitation of workers in the periphery. Fundamentally, he sees the global working class as an unvariegated whole, "dominated by capital and subjected to capitalist exploitation," a position shared by many Second Internationalists.[36] Connected to this was his understanding of the bourgeoisie in the neo-colony as being completely subordinated to capital in the imperialist core. Mahmood Mamdani and Harku Bhagat question whether Nabudere believed a national bourgeoisie existed at all. They claim that its sparse treatment in the book, as well as the use of "inverted commas" when discussing it, demonstrated a failure to grasp what is distinct about this class, even if comprising only a "tiny fraction" of the peripheral bourgeoisie— namely that it derives its wealth from a production based on "national resources and the national market," and which therefore finds its "interests threatened by the imperialist export of capital and commodities."[37]

In one of his few discussions of slavery, Nabudere insists that Europe's industrial revolution would not have been possible without "the plunder, enslavement, and entombment of the native peoples of Africa, Asia and Latin America". He goes on to argue that the "triangular trade" together with colonialism constituted the two "external" factors that combined with "national debt, the mode of taxation, the protectionist system and the overall system of warfare that enhanced and protected

---

36   Ibid., vii.

37   M. Mamdani and H. Bhagat, "Comments on the Political Economy of Imperialism", 47.

it" to "hasten the process of transformation of the feudal mode of production into the capitalist one, and, as in England, shortened the transition".[38] Beyond this analysis though, there is little probing of the history and material legacies of slavery. Such elision recalls the important critique of Marxism by scholars writing from within what Cedric Robinson described as the "Black Radical Tradition", including W.E.B. Du Bois, C.L.R. James, Eric Williams and Oliver Cox. Nabudere shared a normative aim with these scholars, to produce scholarship not just for the purpose of knowledge production, as Peter Hudson asserts, but as "an integral part of the modern project of emancipation."[39] Yet his conclusions conflict with those of Cox, for example, who chastised Marx for "[relegating]" slavery "as subsidiary" rather than centring it in his study.[40] Also notable for its absence is any discussion of the role of racism, which another renowned insurgent scholar from Nabudere's Dar El Salaam cohort, Water Rodney, noted was not merely part of the superstructure at the time of Europe's enslavement and colonization of much of the world, but "an integral part of the capitalist mode of production."[41]

---

38   Nabudere, *The Political Economy of Imperialism*, 38.

39   Peter James Hudson, "The Racist Dawn of Capitalism", *Boston Review*, 1 March 2016.

40   As referenced in Stephanie Smallwood, "What Slavery Tells us About Marx", *Boston Review*, 21 February 2018. Robinson reserved similarly harsh words for what he regarded as Marx's treatment of slavery as "embarrassing residue of a precapitalist, ancient mode of production." Cedric Robinson, *Black Marxism* (Zed Publications, 1983).

41   Walter Rodney, *How Europe Underdeveloped Africa* (Bo-

Nabudere spends considerably more time analysing the primitive accumulation of colonial rule, explaining how Amsterdam became the financial centre of Europe as a result of its "seafarings earnings and the plunder by the Dutch East India company of Java and Malacca." By the seventeenth century, Holland was the leading country in Europe and "the guilder was the international currency before the pound was sovereign".[42] The slave trade and colonialism also enabled the deposit resources of the Bank of England to grow 'by leaps and bounds' during the closing decades of the eighteenth century and to "wrestle" European and colonial trade away from the Dutch.[43]

Nabudere fails to centre the history of slavery and its central role not only in jumpstarting capitalism but in fundamentally shaping the racialised stratifications that capitals; here, he was unable to draw parallels between the "robbery and plunder" of primitive accumulation and the super-exploitation of racialised communities today in both the centre and periphery. In particular, as Charisse Burden-Stelly explains, of "African descendants" with "Blackness... a capacious category of surplus value extraction essential to an array of political-economic

---

gle-L'Ouverture Publications, 1972), 88.

42 Nabudere, *The Political Economy of Imperialism*, 36.

43 Yet Nadudere's perspective diverges significantly from much of the recent writing on the history of capitalism, especially those authors (e.g., Jairus Banaji) who focus on "commercial capitalism", whereas Nabudere argues that (pre)colonial trade "cannot be compared with capitalist accumulation under the capitalist mode of production...where the aim of production is the extraction of surplus- value." Ibid., 145.

functions, including accumulation, disaccumulation, debt, planned obsolescence, and absorption of the burdens of economic crises."[44] This gap in Nabudere's analysis also leads to a lack of attention to the racialised discursive landscape, or what Jemima Pierre labels the "racial lexicon of development", through which Global South wealth drain has been justified and normalised even after the formal independence of peripheral states.[45]

*Concluding Remarks*

Despite these gaps and tensions, Nabudere's work stands out and must be appreciated for its foresight and its uncompromising Marxist-Leninist analysis. His book entails the study of the development of human societies in their essentially contradictory movement. It also involves a study of dialectical materialism, which gives us the "scientific tools for analysing these contradictory forces." He argues this approach is necessary to develop a better understanding of the different modes of production throughout history. He explains that the aim of his work is to "form both an ideology for the proletariat, and a scientific exposition of capitalist production at a specific stage of development."[46]

Although the more controversial aspects of his book require critical engagement, that Nabudere sought global

---

44 Charisse Burden-Stelly, "Modern US Racial Capitalism, Some Theoretical Insights", *Monthly Review*, 1 July 2020.

45 Jemima Pierre, "The Racial Vernaculars of Development: A View from West Africa", *American Anthropologist*, 122:1 (March 2020).

46 Nabudere, *The Political Economy of Imperialism*, ii.

revolution and centred an unapologetic anti-imperialism in his thought and action at a time when imperialist forces were ascendant, and resistance to them—in particular in the imperialist centre—was declining, is reason enough to revisit and celebrate his work. His insurgent knowledge production can provide much needed inspiration, in particular as we face down the latest episode of imperialist-induced crisis.

*The author would like to thank Ujju Aggarwal, Louis Allday, Audrey Bomse, Zeyad el Nabolsy and Zhun Xu for taking the time to closely read and provide extremely insightful and helpful feedback and edits to various versions of this article.*

# Reflections on Workers' Organization: Makhan Singh's *History of Kenya's Trade Union Movement to 1952*

Noosim Naimasiah

By September 2020, it was reported that 1.7 million Kenyans had lost their jobs due to the impact of COVID 19. In the context of an economy where 83.6% of total employment is in the informal sector, the greatest likelihood is that this account of job losses is a vast underestimate. The justification that this situation prevails the world over abdicates historical responsibility from a government that has eroded public resources (despite the low wages it pays and the high taxes it collects) and could have insulated its citizens from the shocks of the pandemic. Instead, the conditions that Makhan Singh wrote about in such painstaking detail in his *History Of Kenya's Trade Union Movement To 1952* continue to plague the country's so-called independent condition more than half a century later.

Makhan Singh remains a paramount figure in Kenya's history for laying the foundations of radical trade unionism and participating actively in the independence struggle. His activism began after his family moved to Kenya when he was 13 years old in 1927. He worked in the printing press founded by his father, as he could not afford to continue with his studies. Singh distinguished himself in his work by unifying the Indian and Kenyan trade unions; thereby undermining the colonial divide and rule racism. His calls in mass meetings for complete national liberation led to his detainment in India between 1940–1945, and later his confinement in colonial Kenya without any charges or trial for over a decade until 1961. In the book, Singh exhaustively relays the historical trajectory of the workers movement from its 19th century inception up to 1952. He contrasts the slave revolts that characterised the coast to the communal labour that was organised around family and kinship units in the hinterland. The fortified villages of Fuladayo, Makongoni and Mwaiba, formed by revolting slaves, were, as Singh explains, the first organised political alternatives to forced labour in Kenya.

Singh's work remains one of the few writings that discusses the history of slave revolts in Kenya, which were mentioned only in passing by the British colonial diplomat and administrator, Arthur Henry Hardinge, in his book *A Diplomat in the East* (1928). Singh shows how the transition to the colonial capitalist economy not only presents a shift in the mechanics of oppression but also in the strategies of resistance. On the back of a racial classification that dehumanised black people as biologically inferior, and thereby enabled their commodification in the context of slavery, "voluntary" wage labour under colonial capitalism was enforced through: direct statutory compulsion, imposition of hut and poll tax, dispossession of African lands, creation and use of chiefs to recruit their people as labourers, forcibly preventing labourers from leaving jobs they did not like, making ordinary disputes between employer and employee criminal offences, using famine-induced starvation to subdue people and legislating punitive laws (like the *kipande* registration system) for controlling the movement of African labourers. Resistance to this violence included spontaneous strike action, and later organised trade union strikes and boycotts.

Singh gives a comprehensive narrative of the context that animated the formation of the first strikes, associations and finally trade unions. One of the earliest strike actions was recorded in 1902 when fifty African police constables went on strike following the removal of their grievance allowances. This, along with many other isolated actions, were followed in 1921 by the formation of the Kavirondo Association and the Young Kikuyu Association. These associations were formed in wake of the death of hundreds of thousands of Africans in the First World War, (mainly as carrier corps) and the formal institutionalization of Kenya as a colony. It was the European soldiers who were compensated with African land, whilst taxes were increased and wages reduced for the Africans. These formations culminated in the General Strike of 1922 that sought the release of Harry Thuku, the chairman of what became the East African Association, one of the first multi-ethnic political organizations. The strike ended in a bloodbath where Muthoni Nyanjiru—one of the few women leaders in the strike—was amongst 150 Africans who were murdered along with scores of others injured by the colonial police force.

The response was to detain without trial political figures like Harry Thuku, and later, Fred Kubai, Chege Kibachia, and Singh himself. As divide and rule was a refined colonial strategy that sought to entrench division through race, gender and ethnicity, the incipient associations were only allowed to form if ethnically constituted. Chiefs, even where none previously existed, were appointed to undermine the authority of the local political systems. They also undermined locally constituted associations. For instance, the Kavirondo Taxpayers Welfare Association was created in opposition to the Kavirondo Association. It de-radicalised the demands for freedom and land with depoliticised demands for "better housing" and "better food". Racial divisions were sewn through preferential wages and the institutionalization of a hierarchy of education that ranked Europeans first, followed by Asians and Black Africans last. Conscious of how racially constituted organizing undermined working-class solidarity, Singh called for the unification of the Indian and African trade unions under the Labour Trade Union of East Africa.

The hiring of mostly male workers undermined the division of domestic labour. The women were left not only to care for the homes and the farms, but also to take up men's labour so as to substitute the meager incomes the men received. This labour, because it was not waged began to be seen as non-labour. This phenomenon is captured in a report written by the Committee on African Labour in 1942, a body which was appointed by the colonial government, did not have a single African member, and whose main recommendation was that the conscription of African Labour for essential services should be introduced. The colonial government stated in an addendum that:

> Taking 9/- per 30 day ticket as a basis this worked out at -/30 (cents) a day of six hours diligent work and if 50 percent was added for the cost of food and another 50 percent for housing it still only came to -/60 (cents) a day or 7d. for a day's work.

> He recognised that from the point of view of the employer the wage was determined by economic conditions outside their control, but no African could support a wife and family in the reserve on 30 cents a day and could only take such a small wage because his wife and family in the reserve grew their own food and also food for him when he was out of employment. Thus, the industry employing the native labourer on these conditions was really subsidised by the labour of women and children in the reserve.[1]

This data tangibly presents how the imperial revenue-making (and later, the profit-making basis for a neo-colonial regime) was predicated on forced labour after land dispossessions on a massive scale had fostered the conditions needed in order for proletarianization and

---

1 Makhan Singh, *History of Kenya's Trade Union Movement to 1952* (East African Publishing House, 1969), 110.

forced labour to be enforced. It also fundamentally underscores how women's free domestic labour was exploited in the reproduction of the worker—then and now.

But resistance persisted. Canteens, local dances and clubs were used to mobilise workers even after Harry Thuku was detained. These efforts resulted in the formation of the Labour Trade Union of Kenya in 1935 (later registered as "the Labour Trade Union of East Africa" in Tanganyika and Uganda). By 1940, strikes became a common feature, leading to the banning of the Kikuyu Central Association, Ukamba Members Association and Taita Hills Association and the detaining of their political leaders like Singh, who was detained without trial in India for a number of years. However, this only served to embolden trade unions. Crucially, Singh also provides evidence of how women slowly joined the labour market, and how they organised against exploitative work in the squatter camps, taxes, low wages, and poor conditions in the farms. He gives an example of the Thika Coffee pickers protest, where "in November, 1941, the African women in Thika area ... employed as coffee-pickers, were able to win an increase in coffee-picking rates through their united action".[2]

The Mombasa General Strike in 1947 organised more than 15,000 workers and paralyzed the railways, the docks, hotels, offices, banks and private offices. It led to an increase in wages and ushered in a new era of mass workers mobilization. Chege Kibachia, the President of the African Workers Federation, was arrested as one of

---

2   Ibid., 109.

the leaders of this strike. The Cost of Living and Wages Conference was held in Nairobi in September 1948 to herald the formation of the centralised organization of trade unions in the East Africa Trade Union Congress (EATUC), with Fred Kubai as President and Singh as General Secretary. By this time, domestic workers, night watchmen, shop messengers, stone and quarry workers, shoe-makers and wood workers had self-organised into associations that joined the union. By 1950, one of the biggest workers meetings was held in Kaloleni Social Hall by the EATUC to agitate against the newly enforced Ordinance for Employment of Voluntarily Unemployed Persons, a piece of forced labour legislation. They also agitated for the release of Kibachia. A massive boycott ensued against the government celebrations promulgating Nairobi as the capital city, in the clearest sign that had yet emerged of the collaboration between trade unions and national movements for liberation. The union was banned, along with publications from the World Federation of Trade Unions, which gave solidarity to liberation efforts by workers in the anti-colonial struggle. By this time, what Singh terms the Uhuru Oath Organization, better known as Mau Mau, was fully entrenched in various parts of the country to fight against oppression, leading to the state of emergency that was declared by the British colonial government in 1952.

By this time, Singh had already been held for two years without charges in India in 1940 for his participation in strikes and other anti-colonial activities. After his release, he was restricted to his native village in Gujranwala for a further two and a half years. On his return to Kenya in 1947, there was an unsuccessful attempt to deport him back to India for his radical communist views. Undeterred, the colonial government arrested him once more, this time for being an "undesirable person" as stipulated in the Deportation Ordinance of 1949. Despite his court defense presenting no legal cause for his arrest, he was detained for 11 years at a political prison in Lodwar and other facilities, and was not permitted to have any visitors, including his family. He was released unconditionally in October 1961 and immediately resumed his trade union and political activities up to and beyond 1963, when Kenya gained its independence. This book was therefore authored as a historical narrative that placed trade unionism at the center of the anti-colonial struggle by a man who paid a great price for Kenya's independence. Singh places trade unionism as a product of revolutionary agency against imperialist domination and for the freedom of the worker from capitalist exploitation. This is contrary to the current trade unions in Kenya that seek leadership as an admission ticket into the elite political class.

Singh's detailed research, published in 1969, includes memorandums, demand letters, minutes of union and associations, newspapers, colonial government policy papers, pamphlets as well as his own experience, and presents an exemplary record of the history of the labour movement in Kenya. The author however, in the tradition of political writings of the time, did not give his personal account of the movement, but only mentions his workings in a formal capacity.

That Singh was already sidelined at the time of the publication of this book shows the contradictions that corrupted trade unions, and a more personal history would have provided young union activists now with a living example of the problems that afflict such movements. However, it is pertinent to keep in mind the fate of other trade unionists and political leaders who decried the continued oppression and dispossession of land by the Jomo Kenyatta government—Pio Gama Pinto was assassinated in 1965, and when Singh's book was published in 1969, Achieng Oneko one of the freedom fighters who had been detained with Kenyatta before independence, was arrested by the president because he critiqued his government. Tom Mboya was assassinated in 1969 and the socialist Kenya People's Union, led by Oginga Odinga and Bildad Kaggia was outlawed in the same year. Fred Kubai's foreword to the book cited Kenyatta's great influence and the people's confidence in him, which given the political happenings of the time, seems to have either been borne out of ambition, as he was then the assistant minister for labour, or fear.

Singh's *History of Kenya's Trade Union Movement to 1952* provides the possibility for making historical analytical comparisons and studying the evolution in the conditions of labour. It shows how women's crucial position in the home was relegated to the private sphere, and was deemed unwaged and inferior, whilst men's labour, positioned in the public sphere, was waged and therefore superior; thereby installing new structures of patriarchy. It also contextualises the Kenyan labour movement in the colonial era within regional movements like the Tanganyika and Uganda Unions, its membership in the World Trade Union Conference and participation in the Pan African Congress held in Manchester. It demonstrates that lowly waged shoe-shiners, farm labourers and domestic workers in both urban and rural areas in Kenya have not only forged collective efforts locally, but also sought collaboration and solidarity regionally and internationally.

The fragmentation of labour movements by neo-colonial governments reinforced the colonial strategies of divide and rule. Exploitation that calcifies the oppression of the working class is undermined by the distinctions of ethnicity and gender. Labour movement leaders now form part of the bourgeoisie and a chasm has formed between them and the working people. Structural Adjustment Programs and the casualization of labour have rendered most unions ineffective in the workers' struggles. The days when labour unions demanded their land back, along with political freedom, social security and government services such as water, sanitation and health care, seem to be locked in history.

Singh's *History of Kenya's Trade Union Movement* therefore provides an important historical source for inspiration and organization for workers against capitalism and imperialism, and a critical source of reflection for those engaged in the pursuit for social justice in Kenya and beyond.

# Entrenching Inequality: The European Dependency School's *Underdeveloped Europe*

Sam Parry

> Despite the relevance of dependency theories to European problems, they have made little headway in our universities. There are other reasons, apart from our parochialism and linguistic weaknesses. First, an explicitly interdisciplinary school does not fit readily into the typical unidisciplinary syllabi and research programmes... An economist who picks up a book by a dependency theorist is likely to notice the lack of algebra. It would be very convenient if only social problems could be reduced to algebraic functions: the solutions would then be straightforward. Many of the propositions of dependency theory cannot easily be cast in mathematical terms, still less are they readily quantifiable. The theory is in large part about hierarchies, institutions, and attitudes.
>
> Dudley Seers[1]

---

1   Dudley Seers, *Dependency Theory: A Critical Reassessment* (Pinter Publishers, 1981), 15.

The Eurozone, Refugee, and Brexit crises left many liberal commentators scratching their heads. The creation myth of the European Union (EU) holds that the institution helped create a continent of peace and prosperity from the ruins of the Second World War. Furthermore, the EU as a political and intellectual project was meant to have created a "cosmopolitan Europe" whereby diverse countries would rally around a common cause and common interests. The EU, according to its official website, holds values such as human dignity, democracy, equality, and human rights while freedom, justice, sustainable development, and combatting discrimination are stated goals. Why then would a state decide to leave? Why would member states fall into economic turmoil and why would an institution that proclaims it supports human rights allow refugees and migrants to die at sea?

To begin, there are implicitly insular definitions of "peace", "prosperity", "diversity" and "interests" within the EU's intellectual and political project. Globally, the European Union does not bring peace and prosperity. One need only look at the sanctions it imposes against countries such as Nicaragua, Venezuela, Syria, Libya, Belarus, the DPRK and Iran amongst others. A full account of the European Union's exploitative relationship with regards to external actors is beyond the scope of this article, however, it is equally important to understand the contradictions within the European Union itself.[2] The EU does not bring prosperity equally to all member states; those nations and regions that were

---

2   Sam Parry, "The European Union: A New Era in European Imperialism", *Peace, Land & Bread*, 2020.

poor 40 years ago are still poor today. This leads us to ask important questions: in whose interests does the EU work? Was the EU institutionally designed this way or has it veered from its supposedly lofty ideals? To answer these questions, I find myself looking backwards in time and finding explanations for the foundations of today's crises in *Underdeveloped Europe: Studies in Core-Periphery Relations.*

This book, published in 1979 and edited by Dudley Seers, Bernard Schaffer and Marja-Liisa Kiljunen synthesises the arguments of a group of academics that became loosely known as the European Dependency School (EDS).[3] In 1975, the European Association of Development Institutes was created, with Seers being elected as President of the group. Their work was markedly different from the orthodox view prevalent in most European institutes where theory and practice were dominated by modernisation and liberal economic theory in its neo-classical and Keynesian variants. Seers argued in *Underdeveloped Europe* that these theories were "developed in the interest of dominant countries and for dominant countries, taking for granted their structural characteristics and interest in free trade".[4] What made the EDS different is that they broke away from a western exceptionalism so ingrained in academia.

*Underdeveloped Europe* marked "a new departure by

---

3   Rudy Weissenbacher, *The Core-Periphery Divide in the European Union: A Dependency Perspective* (Springer Nature, 2020), 5.

4   Dudley Seers, Bernard Schaffer, and Marja-Liisa Kiljunen, eds., *Underdeveloped Europe: studies in core-periphery relations. No. 1.* (Harvester Press, 1979), 25.

inquiring whether one can apply in Europe some of the theoretical insights obtained from work in the field conventionally called 'development studies'";[5] a school of thought derived from experiences in Latin America and typified by the work of scholars such as Raúl Prebisch, Paul Baran, Paul Sweezy and Andre Gunder Frank. At the heart of development studies and the work of the EDS was an analysis of the relationship between a dominant "core" of countries and a dependent "periphery". It is this dialectic that is central to understanding the world economy, and *Underdeveloped Europe* was the first book to use such an analysis within Europe.

Beforehand, "the influence of core countries, governments, and companies... largely remained absent from discussions as if there was a periphery without a core"[6] yet, one must be peripheral *to* something and one is peripheral *due* to something. For the first time, the core and periphery in Europe were not analysed independently of one another, there was an understanding that it was the relationship *between* such regions that was important. As *Underdeveloped Europe* states, "the economics taught in Western Europe, even in its periphery, ignores hierarchical relationships between countries, or within them. Further, the experience of the "Third World" could well be relevant in some respects to some problems of the European periphery—for example in dealing with governments and corporations of the core—if we are prepared to study them".[7] This qualitatively different way

---

5 Ibid., xiii.

6 Weissenbacher, *The Core-Periphery Divide*, 3.

7 Seers, Schaffer, and Kiljunen, eds., *Underdeveloped Europe*, xix.

of thinking was the starting point from which Seers and his peers analysed the European Union (or the European Communities as it was then known).

## *The Integration of Unequal Partners*

This book shared fundamental insights into the structure of the European Union that are still pertinent to us today. Seers—and members of the European Dependency School generally—were sceptical of future integration prospects. At the time of writing in 1979, the European Communities had grown from an organisation of six members (Belgium, France, Italy, Luxembourg, the Netherlands, and West Germany) to nine members, with the UK, the Republic of Ireland and Denmark joining. Others were to follow soon with Greece joining in 1981 and Spain and Portugal following in 1986. The structure of the institution was therefore changing from a "rich club" with one peripheral region (the *Mezzogiorno* or Southern Italy) to one of unequal partners, with Ireland, Greece, Spain, and Portugal clearly peripheral to the core.[8]

Seers argued that "if there are no major reforms in the

---

8  Peripheral countries/regions share some characteristics which make them structurally dependent on the core. These include: the primacy of exporting raw materials, the importation of value-added products, new products, technologies and innovations, the lack of local oversight in decision-making process, specifically around what and where to invest, this is due to both Foreign Direct Investment and needing core markets to buy their products, and migration flows whereby people move from the periphery to the core for work while retirees and holiday makers flow from the core to the periphery.

Community, there will be, after the enlargement, serious dualism, indeed a sort of colonial system. In the poorer group which already suffers whenever a government of the core adopts financially restrictive policies, the effects could be more severe if they give up the possibility of adopting measures to protect their national economy".[9] These major reforms were never forthcoming, nor were they ever truly part of the Community's aims. A laissez-faire economic approach was considered the "appropriate doctrine" by the Community, which "would make it difficult for any really left-wing government of the future to exercise controls and carry out far-reaching social changes".[10] This "would ensure that its industrial structures were made more efficient by exposure to competition, and contribute to the re-establishment of international free trade, which was an essential element in this neo-colonial scenario".[11] The policy of competition was enshrined in the Community; its codification in the Treaty of Rome meant that it would be a fundamental ideology of the European project. Fundamentally, the Treaty could therefore be used as an argument against regional or national industrial policy in the periphery which would "distort" competition; the European core's position of strength qua the periphery became codified.

This inherently unequal position between partners at the onset of enlargement helped sow the seeds for the

---

9   Seers, Schaffer, and Kiljunen, eds., *Underdeveloped Europe*, 27.

10   Dudley Seers, and Constantine Vaitsos, eds., *The Second Enlargement of the EEC: the integration of unequal partners* (Springer, 1982), 1-4.

11   Ibid., 4.

Eurozone Crisis in 2008 by deforming the way in which peripheral societies grew. The European Dependency School described this phenomenon in the periphery as "growth without development". Pollis, writing in 1985 stated that integration meant "the strengthening of those very sectors that would preclude the future autonomous industrialisation of Greece. Emphasis is placed on the expansion of the fishing industry … expansion of agriculture by increasing productivity … and last, the expansion of the tourist industry. The question of the development of Greece's industrial sector was largely ignored, undoubtedly premised on the doctrine of comparative advantage, since it is widely accepted that Community membership is destructive to Greece's non-competitive industries, albeit potentially beneficial to Europe's multinationals".[12]

Greece is an instructive example of how Community membership did not create peripherality but did help to entrench it. However, the dialectical relationship between core and periphery was obscured from view during the Eurozone crisis. "A paradigmatic picture suggested Germany as a role model, personified as the saving Swabian housewife, and proposed mechanisms of private households for national accounts. In that way, everybody could become export champions with a positive trade balance. In reality, somebody has to import these exports, and somebody has to pay for them. In the case of the EU, the Southern periphery very much belonged to both of these somebodies until

---

12  Adamantia Pollis, *International and Domestic Constraints on Socialist Transformation in Greece* (Praeger, 1985), 209.

their debt situation slowed this process".[13] Although the debt situation in peripheral European countries has slowed their ability to import goods from Germany and France, European "progressives" such as DiEM25 have found a new purpose for these "somebodies". David Adler, their Policy Coordinator stated that a "Green New Deal [would allow] German pensioners [to] gain from environmental investments in communities that have been hit by austerity in Southern Europe. ... We can deliver a healthy return on investments for, let's say, pensioners in France and Germany and, at the same time, provide meaningful jobs to workers in Greece".[14] DiEM25's official position during the Brexit referendum was to "remain and reform", however, their proposed reformation which only amounts to a continued process of value extraction from impoverished states illuminates the political dishonesty of this position and highlights the continued underdevelopment of peripheral countries which the EDS espoused.

Although Greece is an especially extreme case, it is no exception to the vulnerability of peripheral countries in an EU constructed by and for core countries. Seers, writing in 1980 almost prophetically deduced what would happen to peripheral European countries after enlargement and how this would be further exacerbated in a monetary union:

> Those [countries] in deficit ... have to adopt

---

13   Weissenbacher, *The Core-Periphery Divide*, 60.

14   "Transnational politics is damn hard: David Adler on DiEM25's experience", *Café Babel*, 2020.

deflationary policies. The more complete the degree of integration, the more serious this asymmetry is likely to be. If governments in an economic community have given up trade restrictions, foreign exchange control and even freedom to vary the exchange rate, then the only short-term weapons left to deal with a recession in exports (or rise in import prices) are fiscal and monetary policies that lower the level of employment—and wage controls to reduce costs and purchasing power. The effect is to make the governments of peripheral economies in an integrated system highly dependent on those of its core; if the latter give greater priority to curbing price inflation than to reducing unemployment, there is little the former can do but resign themselves to accepting the priority and shaping their own policies accordingly.[15]

*Reasserting the Importance of Space*

An equally important contribution made by *Underdeveloped Europe* was its geographical analysis. The core of Europe was described as an "incomplete egg" with the centre in western Germany. The "yolk" was defined as "Denmark, western Germany, the Benelux countries, Paris, the Lyon area, Switzerland and Lombardy".[16] The core in its entirety stretches as far as England (not including Cornwall) and Edinburgh to the west; the more heavily populated areas of Norway, Sweden, and Finland to the

---

15   Seers and Vaitsos, eds., *Integration and unequal development*, 19.

16   Seers, Schaffer, and Kiljunen, eds., *Underdeveloped Europe*, 19.

north; northern Italy to the south and *Catalunya* and the Basque Country to the south-west. The periphery could therefore be described not only as a group of countries but as a geographical space, stretching across frontiers, creating a "periphery in a much more literal sense".[17]

These findings are relevant to the present day in two ways. Firstly, Edward Soja argued that "the production of space has indeed been socially obfuscated and mystified in the development of capitalism, and this has allowed it to be used against class struggle".[18] This book helps to demystify the importance of space and how it is socially produced, illuminating how the unequal development between regions and nations is the very essence of capitalism, and is, as Mandel suggests, "on the same level as the exploitation of labour by capital".[19] It concurrently explains why those that suffered most during the Eurozone crisis were peripheral and why decisions made in Germany (and to an extent France) were just as important as those taken in Brussels due to the structural foundations of the EU. *Underdeveloped Europe* breathes life into "the notion that backward regions, such as those in southern Europe, are not formed autonomously, having, as it were, their own independent existence. Neither are they created incidentally, as a kind of accidental, haphazard by- product of growth elsewhere. Rather, they are part and parcel of the growth process in the

---

17   Ibid., xiv.

18   Edward W. Soja, "The socio-spatial dialectic." *Annals of the Association of American Geographers* 70:2 (1980), 224.

19   Ernest Mandel, "Revolutionary Strategy in Europe-a political interview." *New Left Review* 100 (1976), 46.

core, and essential to it".[20]

Secondly, *Underdeveloped Europe's* geographic perspective helps us understand the European Union's relationship with external nations. It is no coincidence that those countries that are peripheral within Europe are also those countries closest to the continents of Africa and Asia. Their geographical position has a dual role; firstly, the core uses these countries as a buffer against migrants. The Dublin Accord which enshrined in law that the country of arrival is responsible for migrants placed additional pressures on countries of the periphery like Spain, Portugal, Italy, and Greece. Secondly, it helps to explain why these peripheral countries would decide to join the European Union: inclusion in such a club may stop those countries from falling into the global periphery (which is different to the European periphery) though "at the cost of structural dependence".[21] Peripheral European countries can still attract migrants from poorer countries, ensuring there is enough cheap labour, while they themselves lose migrants to the core. *Underdeveloped Europe* helps us understand the contradictory process whereby there are internal contradictions inside the European Union, though externally the institution works as a unified whole to defend its shared interests.

*Conclusion*

Dudley Seers unfortunately passed away in 1983 and was

---

20 R. L. King, "Southern Europe: dependency or development?" *Geography* (1982), 224.

21 Seers, Schaffer, and Kiljunen, eds., *Underdeveloped Europe*, xviii.

therefore unable to develop and expand on his work as it relates to more contemporary conditions. This I think has added to his work being underappreciated today. The second-hand copy of the book used for the purposes of writing this review was withdrawn from Oxford University after not having been issued in over 30 years; a fact that seems on one hand disquieting, yet somehow instructive of why we are in the malaise in which we find ourselves.

This book has many important insights for us today and helps us truly understand the role of the European Union as an institution, both internally and externally. However, perhaps the most important contribution this book made was its understanding that the answer to many of our problems can be found outside of Europe, exemplified by it taking the theories of Latin American Dependency Theorists as its starting point. This book is truly special because it breaks away from a western and Anglo-centric worldview which is rife in many of our universities, in our politicians and in our society. It is a book that I suggest all those interested in understanding the European system more fully to read.

# A Pedagogy of the Collective—From the Soviet Union to Latin America: *Makarenko, His Life and Work*

Alex Turrall

> For twelve years you have laboured, and the results of those labours are priceless. Your revolutionary and astonishingly successful pedagogical experiment is, in my opinion, of world-wide significance.

Maxim Gorky to A.S. Makarenko, January 30, 1933[1]

> I was drawn to Makarenko because of the population he was working with, the unwanted, the kids who were rejected from society. It was like the *sem terrinha* [little landless children].

Marli Zimmerman, educational leader of Brazil's Landless Workers' Movement (MST)[2]

---

1 Y.N. Medinsky, "The Dzerzhinsky Commune". In *Makarenko, His Life and Work: Articles, Talks and Reminiscences* (University Press of the Pacific, 2004), 31.

2 Rebecca Tarlau, *Occupying Schools, Occupying Land: How the Landless Workers' Movement Transformed Brazilian Education* (Ox-

Generally, when we think about revolutionary pedagogical philosophies, one name and one book eclipses all. Testament to its compelling critique of capitalist and colonial education and revolutionary call to combat dehumanisation, Paulo Freire's *Pedagogy of the Oppressed* (1968) is one of the most cited works in the social sciences,[3] with Freire himself being a spiritual and intellectual guide for many aspiring educators.

Outside Freire, two other giants of pedagogy feature highly in the social sciences: the Soviet psychologist Lev Vygotsky and the American philosopher John Dewey. Important as they are, in the field of pedagogy they tend to overshadow work from equally significant people and theories that generally sit outside the Western canon. Soviet educator Anton Semyonovich Makarenko, whose revolutionary work is recorded so succinctly in the seemingly forgotten compendium, *Makarenko, His Life and Work* (1963), is one such figure.

The book, like this review, is split broadly in two parts. The first contextualises Makarenko's life and work through a collection of narratives and memoirs from academics, colleagues, and former students. The second contains a selection of lectures and works by Makarenko himself. What follows is an attempt to capture the essence of Makarenko and his extraordinary intervention in revolutionary education, as well as an exploration of its continued significance.

---

ford University Press, 2019), 55.

3   Elliot Green, "What are the most-cited publications in the social sciences (according to Google Scholar)?", *LSE Impact Blog*, 2016.

## The Gorky Colony

Part one opens with four short biographical sketches from Professor Y.N. Medinsky (author of *Public Education in the USSR*[4]). Among these is the remarkable story of the "Colony for Juvenile Delinquents". Founded by Makarenko in 1919 and situated six kilometres from Poltava, Ukraine, the colony was a 100-acre plot of land with dilapidated and ransacked buildings, whose "fruit trees had even been dug up and removed".[5] The first cohort was a group of 15 to 18-year-old boys:

> These boys loafed about, stayed out at nights, and openly defied the teachers. Acts of robbery were committed in the evenings… Food and money were stolen even from the colony. At times knife fights broke out.[6]

Unperturbed by the formidable challenge, Makarenko, instead of expelling these boys, formed a core of activists from the group and gave them the job of guarding the forest from illegal felling. This early intervention was an important first step in forming the collective. As Makarenko wrote, "[t]he guarding of the state forest raised us considerably in our own estimation, [and] provided us with extremely entertaining work."[7] The

---

[4] Y.N. Medinsky, *Public Education in the USSR* (Foreign Language Publishing House, 1954).

[5] Y.N. Medinsky, "The Gorky Labour Colony". In *Makarenko, His Life and Work*, 13.

[6] Ibid., 14.

[7] Ibid.

renaming of the colony to "The Gorky Colony" in 1920 (after Makarenko's personal hero Maxim Gorky) was symbolic of the transformation that had taken place. In just one year, the colony had restored a half-ruined ex-landowner estate into a fully self-sufficient farm. These opening manoeuvres, carefully planned and executed by Makarenko, were central to the consolidation of the collective, and built a solid foundation for further pedagogical work.

Due to these early successes, more young offenders were sent to Makarenko, but this brought new challenges. After a spate of robberies on the commune's food supplies and anti-Semitic attacks on Jewish communards, several new colonists had to be removed. While Makarenko and his colleagues considered these expulsions a failing in his pedagogical methods, the immaturity of the colony was also a major factor. However, "fighting the doubts that assailed him from time to time, he displayed supreme self-control and encouraged the weary teachers."[8] Indeed, only two years after its founding:

> … the colony had one hundred and twenty-four inmates. The farm, too, had grown, now having sixteen cows, about fifty pigs, eight horses, a large kitchen-garden, and a considerable area (up to seventy hectares) under grain crops. An agronomist was employed to run the farm, and he organised proper crop rotation and field work.[9]

This short introduction barely scratches the surface of

---

8   Ibid., 16.
9   Ibid.

Medinsky's provocative opening vignettes. From the Gorkyites takeover of the nearby Kuryazh Colony to the formation of the Dzerzhinsky Commune in 1927 and Gorky's eventual visit in 1928, what emerges is the story of a revolution within a revolution. This constant development, so characteristic of Makarenko's broader vision, was driven by Gorky's philosophy of the human, in which every person had "a vast range of possibilities". As such, Makarenko was always conscious of the potential for arrested development. "Material well-being could not be an end in itself", Medinsky writes, "it was simply one of the conditions necessary for the development of the human being, who strains towards the wide, light-filled spaces."[10]

Followers of Freire have much to gain from Makarenko. For while the two pedagogues depart in a number of ways, writing in 1985 Freire illustrates similar ideas regarding fundamental questions like revolution and the human:

> Because men are historical beings, incomplete and conscious of being incomplete, revolution is as natural and permanent a human dimension as education. Only a mechanistic mentality holds that education can cease at a certain point, or that revolution can be halted when it attains power. To be authentic, revolution must be a continuous event. Otherwise it will cease to be revolution, and will become sclerotic bureaucracy.[11]

---

10  Ibid., 21.

11  Paulo Freire, *The Politics of Education: Culture, Power, and*

The second section of part one extends Medinsky's fascinating introduction through a series of short biographies by former students and colleagues. "My Teacher" by the commune's farming specialist, Nikolai Ferre, offers an amusing tale of an "inventive thief" and a prized melon called "The Commissar". In "Who is Alyosha Ziryansky", a former student tells the story of a controversial trip to Sochi. And Kladvia Boriskina recounts a touching story about the Dzerzhinsky Commune's amateur theatrical group and her dreams of becoming an actress.

What becomes clear throughout these vignettes is Makarenko's flexible and always evolving approach to justice and discipline. His approach never rested on a one-size-fits-all policy. Instead—and representative of a profoundly dialogical program—he guided and was guided by the collective majority. Again, this hinged on his conception of the human, as Nikolai Ferre summarises:

> Thus, in the practice of everyday life, did Makarenko evolve his system of education. Its most important feature was consideration for "the human being in the child", its flexibility and the absence of a stereotyped approach to the children.[12]

So striking in these first-hand testimonies is how *Makarenko, His Life and Work* is not only an important document for educators, but also holds lessons about how a pedagogy of collectiveness and work can be used in

---

*Liberation* (Greenwood Publishing Group, 1985), 89.

12   Nikolai Ferre, "My Teacher". In *Makarenko, His Life and Work*, 104.

alternative models of transformative justice. Indeed, the colony's name change reflected a deeper transformative experience. Makarenko's pedagogy of the collective is summed up most succinctly in Gorky's first letter to the colony in 1925, in which he wrote, "This is really a system of re-education, and that is what it always can and should be, especially in our day. Away with yesterday and all its dirt and spiritual squalor."[13]

*In His Own Words*

Makarenko's lectures in the second part of the book deal with parental discipline, sex education, and play in relation to an overarching pedagogy of work. Although these are all worth revisiting for parents and educators alike, his philosophy of the collective is arguably his most significant legacy and documented most clearly in his lecture "My Experience".

"The first characteristic of a collective", writes Makarenko, "is that it is not a crowd, but a rationally organised and effective body."[14] Expounding his theory of the collective, Makarenko argues that the first step in organising any collective is founding "the primary collective" that cannot be further split into smaller units. In other words, a commune would be made up of several of these collectives, or "detachments". In his experience, the primary collective worked best with seven or less people (any more than this and it tended to split into

---

13  Y.N. Medinsky, "The Gorky Labour Colony". In *Makarenko, His Life and Work*, 20.

14  Anton Makarenko, "My Experience". In *Makarenko, His Life and Work*, 246.

smaller groups). With older communards leaving and new ones joining fairly regularly, Makarenko continues by outlining some thoughts on how to preserve a collective over time, the problems they face (e.g., do you separate them by age? Who is the leader? etc), as well as some success stories from his own pedagogical program. Overall, he suggests that an ideal collective is:

> ... one that feels itself to be united, closely-knit, and strong, while at the same time realising that this is not a group of friends who have come to some arrangement, but a phenomenon of a social type, a community, a body having certain obligations, a certain duty, a certain responsibility.[15]

The purpose of Makarenko's pedagogy of the collective was to instil a sense of community and duty to each other, of humility and mutual respect, of interdependence and communal self-governance. In short, it was itself a revolution against the arrogance and individualism that so characterises capitalist ideology. From this perspective it becomes clearer why Makarenko's counter-hegemonic methods have gone largely unacknowledged in the Western world. His legacy, however, has survived in different forms across two major communist movements in Latin America: Revolutionary Cuba and Brazil's Landless Workers' Movement (MST).

*Revolutionary Pedagogy in Cuba*

In the years immediately following the revolution, one

---

15   Ibid.

of Cuba's most remarkable achievements was its mass literacy program, which saw the eradication of basic illiteracy in just one year (1960-1961).[16] This campaign was driven by José Martí's maxim that "to be educated is the only way to be free", alongside Cuba's philosophy of the New Man. As Che Guevara wrote:

> Education is increasingly integral and we do not neglect the incorporation of the students into work from the very beginning. Our scholarship students do physical work during vacation or together with their studies. In some cases work is a prize, while in others it is an educational tool; it is never a punishment. A new generation is born.[17]

The emphasis on the integration of study and work twinned with the reconceptualisation of Man echoes the central tenets of Makarenko's pedagogy. In fact, Cuba appears to be one of the first countries outside the Soviet Union to integrate a Makarenkian pedagogy into its educational vision.

In 1962, after the mass literacy campaign had been completed, a network of teacher training schools known as Minas-Topes-Tarará was established across the island. This "chain" of schools offered its trainee teachers a versatile educational program that encompassed not just the Cuban landscape but the national class contradictions that still existed. In other words, it was an extension

---

16   Helen Yaffe, *Che Guevara: The Economics of Revolution* (Palgrave Macmillan, 2009), 77.

17   Che Guevara, *Man and Socialism in Cuba* (Guairas Book Institute: 1967).

of the pedagogy enshrined in the literacy campaign as outlined so powerfully by Fidel Castro in his talk to the teacher's brigade about teaching the *campesinos* in rural Cuba in May, 1961:

> you are going to teach, but as you teach, you will also learn. You are going to learn much more than you can possibly teach... Because while you teach them what you have learned in school, they will be teaching you what they have learned from the hard life that they have led. They will teach you the "why" of the revolution better than any speech, better than any book.[18]

It was the final school in this chain, located in Tarará, Havana that *Las Maestras Makarenko* (The Makarenko Teachers) were based. Run by central committee member Elena Gil Izquierdo as part of the Plan for the Advancement of Women, the Makarenko Pedagogical Institute was the final, most challenging step for trainee teachers and was designed, as its namesake suggests, to integrate study and work through a Makarenkian pedagogy.[19]

Due to a rapidly evolving revolutionary process, the Minas-Topes-Tarará was replaced with a new educational program towards the end of the 1980s. Although the Makarenko Institute closed along with the rest of these

---

18   Fidel Castro, "Speech to the Literacy Brigades at Varadero", 1961.

19   Alexis Lorenzo Ruiz and Xochil Virginia Taylor-Flores, "La experiencia pedagógica cubana, ¿una influencia heredada de Makarenko?", *Revista de Educación y Desarrollo*, 2013.

schools, it appears to have achieved significant success. Speaking at the graduation ceremony of the Makarenko Institute in 1966, Fidel Castro concluded that, "the revolutionary desire, the socialist desire, the communist desire as an educational ideal which combines study with work has been happily achieved with optimum results"[20]. While explicit references to Makarenko waned in Cuba from around 1990[21], it was around this time he was picked up elsewhere, in one of the largest workers' movements in Latin America.

*Makarenko in Brazil*

Much like the Gorky Colony's focus on young street waifs, the first schools of Brazil's Landless Workers' Movement (MST) arose out of a necessity to deal with "hundreds of children running wild", the *sem terrinha* (little landless children), in the first land encampments of the MST in the 1970s and 80s.[22]

In the proceeding decade, significant national coordination culminated in a unified 1997 manifesto on education. However, the MST's 1996 document "Principles of Education" demonstrates the clearest example of their shared vision with Makarenko's pedagogy of the collective as a counter to bourgeois

---

20   Fidel Castro, "Castro Speaks to Teachers and Girl Graduates", 1966.

21   Ruiz and Taylor-Flores, "La experiencia pedagógica cubana, ¿una influencia heredada de Makarenko?", 2013.

22   Rebecca Tarlau, "The Social(ist) Pedagogies of the MST: Towards New Relations of Production in the Brazilian Countryside", *Education Policy Analysis Archives*, 21:41 (2013), 10.

individualism:

> Most of the time students learn the culture of individualism... it is necessary to have education intentionally based on the culture of cooperation and the creative incorporation of lessons about the history of the collective organization of work.[23]

This consistency is likely more than coincidence. Ever since the Gorky Colony, workers movements outside the West have been interested in the work of Makarenko. Medinsky highlights such interest from a Latin American delegation (Brazil, Mexico, Argentina, and Peru) who visited the Dzerzhinsky Commune in 1929, writing in the visitors' book: "The delegation of Latin America is amazed at the achievements to be found in the first proletarian country... where the new man is being created and where a new psychology of the children is being moulded."[24]

While Makarenko's pedagogy is implied in the MST's founding educational documents, their education seminars make this more explicit. Educational leader Rubneuza Leandro outlines the importance of Makarenko's vision and practice for young people in Brazil:

> For Makarenko the collective is a living social organism, and because of this, it possesses organs, attributes,

---

23 Rubia Valente and Brian Berry, "Countering Inequality: Brazil's Movimento Sem-Terra", *Geographical Review*, 105:3 (2015), 12.

24 Y.N. Medinsky, "The Dzerzhinsky Commune". In *Makarenko, His Life and Work*, 32.

responsibilities, correlations, and interdependencies between its parts. If this collectivity does not exist, then it is a crowd, a group of individuals.[25]

To be sure, a closer look at the organisational structure of the more autonomous MST schools, such as the Educar Institute, reveals a strong Makarenkian influence. These schools are organised into small student collectives called *núcleos de base* or base nucleuses (NBs) formed of five or six students. These collectives are used in collaboration with Pistrak's pedagogy of manual labour and Freire's classroom pedagogy in order to transform the relationships within the school. Issues of discipline, discussions on curriculum and class schedule, and extra-curricular activities are first taken up in NBs, which in turn present the issues to the wider school community.[26] Consequently, MST schools practice student self-governance and a type of democratic centralism akin to the detachments or primary collectives elaborated by Makarenko.

One MST militant, Vanderlúcia Simplicio, sums up the importance of Makarenko's pedagogy of the collective, specifically in combatting alienation. After spending her entire education in a collective, in studying for her masters she had some revealing words about the culture of individualism so prevalent in academia: "classes are just battles of ideas between individuals, and there is less

---

25   Rebecca Tarlau, *Occupying Schools, Occupying Land*, 55.

26   Rebecca Tarlau, "Soviets in the Countryside: The MST's Remaking of Socialist Educational Pedagogies in Brazil", in *Logics of Socialist Education: Engaging with Crisis, Insecurity and Uncertainty* (Springer Publishing, 2012), 14.

learning than there would be if people were collectively discussing and developing these ideas together."[27]

*Fighting Alienation*

More than a century after the founding of the Gorky Colony, *Makarenko, His Life and Work* remains profoundly important. This name and work, either forgotten, ignored, or repressed not only in Western academia but radicalism as well, marks an important foundation for all educators concerned with forwarding a liberatory pedagogy. Furthermore, as Brazil's MST demonstrate so clearly, the many followers of Paulo Freire have much to learn from Makarenko. A combination of these approaches appears to be a powerful mixture.

As Che Guevara reminds us, we fight poverty but we also fight alienation. In our current era of acutely parasitic capitalism, Makarenko's pedagogy of the collective is an antidote to the rampant individualism and alienation that poisons every facet of the social body.

---

27   Ibid., 17-18.

# Reading Ivan Illich's *Deschooling Society in the Neoliberal University*

Justin Podur

A Catholic priest who eventually left the church, Ivan Illich wrote to issue warnings—some prescient, others less so. His 1971 book *Deschooling Society* seeks to speak to the "schooled", to convince them that the idea of "schooling" our way to a better society will never work. Writing at the time he did, Illich's work fits into a broader rethinking of education that occurred in the 1960s and 1970s. In the UK, AS Neale wrote about a school with no rules in the eponymously named book *Summerhill*, published in 1960. The Sudbury Valley School in Massachusetts was founded on similar principles in 1968 by Daniel Greenberg. John Holt's works, *How Children Fail* (1964) and *How Children Learn* (1967) argued passionately against any type of coercion in learning and strongly influenced the "unschooling" movement in the US.

The core idea—that the US school system kills freedom and ultimately learning—has been picked up many times since then, by writers like John Taylor Gatto, Jonathan Kozol, Nikhil Goyal, and Alfie Kohn. Illich's development of the idea forms a comprehensive critique and an original one. As a critic of all institutions, Illich's thinking has been identified with anarchism, and remains a useful perspective for thinking about the total institutional environment we are in today. Half a century after the book's publication, the educational apocalypse Illich predicted has arrived. In some—though not all— of its details, it looks just like he feared it would.

If we do not challenge the assumption that valuable knowledge is a commodity which under certain circumstances may be forced into the consumer, society will be increasingly dominated by sinister pseudo schools and totalitarian managers of information... Pedagogical therapists will drug their pupils more in order to teach them better, and students will drug themselves more to gain relief from the pressures of teachers and the race for certificates. Increasingly larger numbers of bureaucrats will presume to pose as teachers.[1]

Illich predicted an educational dystopia of commodity capitalism: "School sells curriculum--a bundle of goods made according to the same process and having the same structure as other merchandise." The result is education that "looks like any other modern staple. It is a bundle of planned meanings, a package of values, a commodity whose "balanced appeal" makes it marketable to a sufficiently large number to justify the cost of production." He wrote before the takeover of education by neoliberalism, and some of Illich's

---

1  Ivan Illich, *Deschooling Society* (Harper & Row, 1971).

libertarian prescriptions have actually come into effect in ways that would have repelled his anti-authoritarian instincts.

*The Crisis of the Neoliberal University*

In his book *Science Mart: Privatizing American Science*, historian Philip Mirowski traces three regimes of science organization—and therefore of universities—in the US. The first regime began around 1890 and persisted until World War II. In this period, corporations did much of their scientific research in-house: the famous Bell Labs and Dupont Labs were exemplars. There was no centralised government science policy. While technical and engineering education were growing, as documented by David Noble in *America by Design*, higher education was an elite affair teaching liberal arts and creating interconnections among the ruling class. Davarian Baldwin traces some of the history of this early period in his book *In the Shadow of the Ivory Tower: How Universities are Plundering Our Cities*. Baldwin notes that in this period, "higher education was a sort of 'finishing school,' meant to develop the character and enhance the networks of male students already well-positioned in families of power and influence." Built on slave trade profits and seized Indigenous land, "these lush, green campuses were further ensconced in at least quasi-rural environments, where the fresh air and open space were meant to serve as a balm from the foul smell and so-called dangerous ethnic amalgams found in cities."

During World War II, when the US replaced Britain as

the world imperialist leader, universities took a new form, one for which many faculty are still nostalgic. Scientific research was brought into the universities. Unlimited military funding anchored science and industrial policy. A nationalist ethos was shared between research and teaching: the idea was that the mandate would turn out democratic citizens who would both defend the nation and create a nation worth defending. The academic ethos of peer review, academic freedom and tenure, and a mix of pure research driven by curiosity and research in the national and public interest—these elements of the university are identified by Mirowski as belonging to this second, World War II-Cold War regime.

That regime gave way to what we are living through today: what Mirowski calls the "globalised privatization regime". In the new scheme, research has been brought back into corporations—Facebook, Google, Microsoft do their own proprietary research with no mandate or expectation to make their results public. Social science research is done in think-tanks, which tell their patrons what they want to hear. Scientific research and development can be also outsourced. Meanwhile university research is "published" in a closed system of more or less predatory journals,[2] while researchers are encouraged to find private sector partners and develop spinoff enterprises with their intellectual property.

Teaching is also being spun off using online teaching methods and contract faculty to deliver most of the education to a student class that collectively has

---

2   A system whose corruption is documented by scientist Bjoern Brembs among others.

borrowed trillions of dollars to pay for these educations and pays the loans back to banks for decades after leaving university. Full time staff at the universities is increasingly administrative. The patriotic mandate is gone: education is offered as a way for an individual to advance, a neoliberal investment in a credential which is an investment in oneself. People who work or study in these institutions are ideologically lost. The sincerity of the public mandate of the Cold War University was always questionable, but neoliberal universities don't even try to claim such a mandate. And as Baldwin points out, as business propositions, neoliberal universities try to trade on what's left over from their public mandate—notably their tax-exempt status and the free land they were given to advance that mandate—to make lucrative real estate deals based on "creative class" and "smart cities" hype.

With the removal of educational patriotism, government funding for universities is also being cut. In a dynamic labeled by professor and university critic Chris Newfield the "tuition trap", universities make up for the shortfall in government funding by raising tuition, which shows governments that universities can indeed use tuition to make up for such a shortfall, which spurs governments to impose further cuts, which lead to further tuition raises. The result is ever more indebted students in deeper financial obligations to banks, while universities keep raising tuition trying to find students' (and their parents') financial breaking point.

Universities also turn to foreign students, who can be charged higher than domestic tuition rates. "To maintain graduate enrollments, many departments in the sciences began to admit rising proportions of foreign students. While this had a salutary effect on the rather parochial atmospheres of many American university towns, it also had the deleterious effect of revealing the essential bankruptcy of the Cold War justification of education as serving the objectives of state building. Many of the students in scientific/technical areas were not US citizens, and periodically some politician would demand to know what the universities were doing by training the workforce of potential competitors at American expense."[3] One such politician was Tom Cotton who recently said "If Chinese students want to come here and study Shakespeare and the Federalist Papers, that's what they need to learn from America. They don't need to learn quantum computing and artificial intelligence from America." Cotton worried that students would "go back to China to compete for our jobs, to take our business, and ultimately to steal our property and design weapons and other devices that can be used against the American people." Significantly, the US is becoming a more hostile place to Chinese students and researchers, with hundreds of scientists under investigation, unsolved murders of Chinese researchers , and anti-Asian racist violence. As China's universities advance, Chinese students' tuition may end up staying at home. This will only deepen the university's crisis.

Today the right-wing attacks universities as bastions of left-wing thought. This is nonsense. There are no such bastions. Universities serve the elite and their right-wing,

---

3   Philip Mirowski, *Science Mart: Privatizing American Science* (Harvard University Press, 2011), 116.

not some imaginary left-wing university conspiracy. They serve their corporate masters better to the degree that students are saddled with immense debt levels and that curricula are constrained and oriented towards narrow corporate priorities.

Today's debate about academic freedom and the importance of the university (which Mirowski argues were freedoms concomitant with the Cold War university model) is anticipated by Illich, who concludes that on balance, the dissent and free thought coming out of universities is probably not worth it: "There is no question that at present the university offers a unique combination of circumstances which allows some of its members to criticise the whole of society. It provides time, mobility, access to peers and information, and a certain impunity... but... only to those who have already been deeply initiated into the consumer society." Like Jeff Schmidt's important book *Disciplined Minds*, which reveals hidden elitist assumptions in the curricula and entrance exams for graduate and professional schools, Illich is arguing here that the university creates people who dependably exercise their creativity in the service of elites, not in the service of the downtrodden.

Aaron Swartz tried to make MIT's journal articles available openly on the Internet. He was arrested, threatened with a 35-year jail sentence, and was ultimately hounded to suicide by a US prosecutor. Alexandra Elbakyan has managed to fulfill Swartz's dream on Sci-Hub. Before the rise of predatory monopoly journal companies and the struggle against them, Illich worried that institutionalised science was already undermining the possibilities of massive scientific learning and advance by locking science away in institutions: "Until recently science was the one forum which functioned like an anarchist's dream. Each man capable of doing research had more or less the same opportunity of access to its tools and to a hearing by the community of peers. Now bureaucratization and organization have placed much of science beyond public reach... the members as well as the artifacts of the scientific community have been locked into national and corporate programs oriented toward practical achievement, to the radical impoverishment of the men who support these nations and corporations."

The school system, like the university system, has been transformed since Illich's writing. In the US, public education has been mostly destroyed and teacher's unions mostly broken. Programs like Teach For America have turned a profession that should provide a good livelihood into a volunteer, charity-like program—a humanitarian intervention into exoticised urban neighbourhoods. For profit-testing and the utterly irrational goal of trying continually to raise a school's average test scores relative to other schools dominates all discussion of schools, teaching, and education. Both US political parties, Democrats and Republicans, see nothing but political benefits from attacking public education. The elite send their children to private schools, while public schoolchildren, their parents, their teachers and teachers unions are a relatively powerless constituency, easily scapegoated for social ills.

A libertarian streak and the 1970s context led Illich to the belief that certain aspects of the market could act as a check against totalizing state institutions. He was wrong. Half a century later, it is the market that is totalizing, with the state's bureaucracy and politicians serving private profit. Students' time, teachers' labour power, credentials, and professional associations have all been cannibalised for the sake of private profit, and the school itself is increasingly irrelevant in a post-pandemic world where children are confined to their homes and computer screens, through which they are controlled for the benefit of private educational corporations and tech companies. A further revolution, layered on top of previous changes unforeseen by Illich, has occurred: private philanthro-capitalists, notably Bill Gates and Mark Zuckerberg, who accumulated fortunes through government-sponsored monopolies, have now taken over the shaping of public school curricula and testing. Tanner Mirlees writes about this in *Edtech, Inc.* As Edtech promises innovation just around the corner—just over the horizon—never in the present—the present moment is full of austerity for most, and great liberal education for the wealthy.

## *A Deeper Critique: Illich Identifies Schooling as the Contradiction*

Mirowski may have exaggerated the differences between the three university regimes. In *America by Design*, historian David Noble quotes the president of Stevens Institute Alumni Association in 1896: "The financial side of engineering is always the most important... the young engineer... must always be subservient to those who represent the money invested in the enterprise." Noble continues: "From the outset, therefore, the engineer was at the service of capital, and, not surprisingly, its laws were to him as natural as the laws of science... his design of machinery, for example, was guided as much by the capitalist need to minimise both the cost and the autonomy of skilled labour as by the desire to harness most efficiently the potentials of matter and energy." If Illich is right, the Cold War university was no model for education and trying to return to it is as undesirable as it would be futile.

Fifty years into the neoliberal regime, what can we gain from Illich's libertarian critique? In the 2020s, the statement that *school should not exist* sounds preposterous, even reactionary. But Illich's critique is profound enough that paying attention to it could help us avoid past mistakes as we try to envision something beyond the current neoliberal model.

Illich separates schooling (unnecessary) from learning (necessary) and teaching (whose usefulness is debatable): "Teaching, it is true, may contribute to certain kinds of learning under certain circumstances. But most people acquire most of their knowledge outside school, and in school only insofar as school, in a few rich countries, has become their place of confinement during an increasing part of their lives." In other words, people learn wherever they are. If they happen to learn in school, that is merely because that is where they were stuck. And teachers are as often obstructions to learning as they are enablers of it. Illich elaborates on his only concession about the value of teaching, that it "may contribute to certain kinds of learning under certain circumstances":

"The strongly motivated student who is faced with the task of acquiring a new and complex skill may benefit greatly from the discipline now associated with the old-fashioned schoolmaster who taught reading, Hebrew, catechism, or multiplication by rote."

When teachers stick to what they are actually good at—drilling skills with motivated students—they provide something of value. In 1956, for example, a group of teenage native speakers of Spanish taught several hundred teachers the language in six months using the US Foreign Service Institute Spanish manual. "No school program", Illich comments, "could have matched these results." Unfortunately, when they claim a more exalted social role for what they do, teachers eschew useful drill teaching in favour of an ever-growing list of fad methods for education. Worse, they contribute to a mystique of schooling and the creation of schooled minds. "Schools are designed on the assumption that there is a secret to everything in life; that the quality of life depends on knowing that secret; that secrets can be known only in orderly successions; and that only teachers can properly reveal these secrets. An individual with a schooled mind conceives of the world as a pyramid of classified packages accessible only to those who carry the proper tags."

Like any commodity, schooling rises in value with scarcity. The scarcity itself is created because people try to protect their jobs from competition, "making skills scarce and on keeping them scarce, either by proscribing their unauthorised use and transmission or by making things which can be operated and repaired only by those who have access to tools or information which are kept scarce. Schools thus produce shortages of skilled persons."

Certification is another problem, for Illich: "[i]nsisting on the certification of teachers is another way of keeping skills scarce. If nurses were encouraged to train nurses, and if nurses were employed on the basis of their proven skill at giving injections, filling out charts, and giving medicine, there would soon be no lack of trained nurses." Sharing one's knowledge should be a right, but that right is taken away through certification, to be "conferred only on the employees of a school." In 2021, in the midst of the "microcredentials" fad—selling the credential without any guarantee of the knowledge—Illich's critique of certification is sobering.

An artificial division of society ensues: "education becomes unworldly and the world becomes noneducational." And because learning is such a ubiquitous, natural human activity, confining learning to schools requires extensive re-engineering of the whole society and not just the school. "In American society, children are excluded from most things and places on the grounds that they are private... Since the last generation the railroad yard has become as inaccessible as the fire station." In this passage you can see how different Illich's world is from our own. For people born after the 1970s or 1980s, the idea of accessing a railroad yard or a fire station on anything other than a controlled school trip sounds as unlikely as visiting a Roman Colosseum to watch a live chariot race. Many of the things Illich was trying to preserve in *Deschooling Society* have been decisively lost.

The critique of schooling leads to a devastating critique of the university, which is schooling taken to the extreme. Illich estimates that a US student's education costs 5x the "median life income of half of humanity", and a university student in Latin America has 350x the "public money spent on his education as on that of his fellow citizens of median income." The result is the creation of a global schooled elite: "the university graduate from a poor country feels more comfortable with his North American and European colleagues than with his nonschooled compatriots."

The education machine is also a cooptation machine: "Having a monopoly on both the resources for learning and the investiture of social roles, the university coopts the discoverer and the potential dissenter." And the hidden curriculum of university is an education in consumption, "imposing consumer standards at work and at home". Educating the elite (and increasingly the masses) in consumption at university is a relatively new phenomenon corresponding to the expansion of university education. Illich laments the current bureaucracy and anticipates the neoliberal university when he contrasts it with the medieval counterpart: "To be a scholar in the Middle Ages meant to be poor, even a beggar... The old university was a liberated zone for discovery and the discussion of ideas both new and old... The structural purpose of the modern university has little to do with the traditional quest... Students see their studies as the investment with the highest monetary return."

## Can Ilich Help Us Imagine Education Beyond Neoliberalism?

There appears to be no end in sight for the neoliberal university. The trends - rising tuition paid by indebted students, part-time contract teachers, a growing army of administrators, privatised research—all continue. Mass higher education will also probably continue to exist in some form, however neoliberalised. The Bernie Sanders movement proposed debt relief for students before it was scuttled by Biden; the Republicans are at present running a focused campaign against education using the slogan "critical race theory" as the enemy. Any good way out of the neoliberal system would have to address the financial domination of everything, criticised (including in its student dimensions) by Michael Hudson in the book *Killing the Host*. Free tuition would go some ways towards decommodified and definancialised education. Decommodifying housing in cities would also go a long way to getting universities out of the real estate game.

In 2004, I interviewed the rector of the Universidad Bolivariana de Venezuela.[4] She suggested I imagine the possibilities if everyone in society had a university education. Illich would probably object that this would be a waste of resources. But let's say we could, through a colossal struggle, achieve an education system that was neither neoliberal nor bound up with imperialist, Cold War agendas. What would such a system do, and what would it be for? To answer this question, we could do well to pick up Illich again.

How might we imagine getting out of our own

---

4    Justin Podur, "Venezuela's Revolutionary University", *Venezuela Analysis*, 22 September 2004.

educational dystopia? Need we become like the educational reformers mocked by Illich, those "who feel impelled to condemn almost everything which characterises modern schools-and at the same time propose new schools"?

Illich proposes a series of laws - that would presumably have to be duly passed by governments - to end schooling as we know it. To begin, "we need a law forbidding discrimination in hiring, voting, or admission to centers of learning based on previous attendance at some curriculum." In the future, asking someone where they went to school will be considered taboo, "like inquiries into his political affiliation, church attendance, lineage, sex habits, or racial background."

How could society be sure people had the skills needed, whether to fly a plane or to perform a surgery, without school? Illich would have us replace public universities with publically funded testing. Learn wherever you like: your credential will come from passing a test. This type of testing was the basis of entry into the Chinese bureaucracy for thousands of years, through the famous exam system. That exam system was brought to Europe by the Jesuits in the $17^{th}$ century and impressed the Prussians, who built their educational system around it. Others in Europe emulated the Prussians. After 1911, imperialist powers forced China to drop their "traditional" exam system and adopt the "European" education system—which had incorporated elements from China hundreds of years before, but had come to emphasise the student going through the curriculum over taking the test at the end. Illich suggests updating the Chinese system for the modern era: "For three millennia, China protected higher learning through a total divorce between the process of learning and the privilege conferred by Mandarin examinations."

In Illich's system, testing would have to be a public service and its integrity would have to be guaranteed. After some discussion, Illich ultimately concludes that testing is necessary, even if it should be restricted. But the testing Illich proposes is very different from our test-score driven schooling systems. In our system, the state conditions funding to teachers on how well students perform on privately produced, state-administered tests—students have to prove to the state that they did well without cheating. In the Chinese exam system, the state's legitimacy was based on a guarantee to the students of fairness in grading and scoring—the state had to prove to the students that their test score was based entirely on their performance.

The acquisition of skills, too, should be publicly funded. Illich presents three levels for how such a system could work.

*Free skill centers:* "One way would be to institutionalise the skill exchange by creating free skill centers open to the public. Such centers could and should be established in industrialised areas, at least for those skills which are fundamental prerequisites for entering certain apprenticeships--such skills as reading, typing, keeping accounts, foreign languages, computer programming and number manipulation, reading special languages such as that of electrical circuits, manipulation of certain machinery, etc."

*Educational currency:* "Another approach would be to give certain groups within the population educational currency good for attendance at skill centers where other clients would have to pay commercial rates."

*A skill exchange bank:* "Each citizen would be given a basic credit with which to acquire fundamental skills. Beyond that minimum, further credits would go to those who earned them by teaching... only those who had taught others for an equivalent amount of time would have a claim on the time of more advanced teachers. An entirely new elite would be promoted, an elite of those who earned their education by sharing it."

Beyond teaching and testing technical skills that keep a modern society running, does Illich provide for any role for education in a broader sense? The study of history, philosophy, mathematics, music, art, drama? To Illich, these highest forms of learning should be the least formal, the least associated with "schooling". That is because this type of learning "relies on the surprise of the unexpected question which opens new doors for the inquirer and his partner." There is a role for the teacher here, but as a guide: "The educational guide or master... matches individuals starting from their own, unresolved questions... helps the pupil to formulate his puzzlement since only a clear statement will give him the power to find his match, moved like him, at the moment, to explore the same issue in the same context." He envisioned something that the Internet easily provides today, "an educational network or web for the autonomous assembly of resources under the control of the learner."

This educational vision would require a series of social

changes. Planned obsolescence and industrial secrecy would have to give way to an economy of "durable, repairable, and reusable" goods. Institutions from railway yards and fire stations, legislatures and factories opened: "To deschool the artifacts of education will require making the artifacts and processes available--and recognizing their educational value."

Illich's libertarian streak might not appeal to those disillusioned with the 50 years of neoliberalism that has run amok through the world since he wrote the book. Nevertheless, the radical question about the abolition of schooling itself is a better starting point than looking to tinker with so deeply flawed a system. Universities and public schools probably do have a role in a good society, but Illich is right that mandatory attendance at school and a job market revolving around credentials from pretentious institutions do not. Finding a path from here to an education system that meets social needs while respecting the freedom of its members remains to be done. Illich challenges us to make sure our ideas pass the test of freedom.

# A Pedagogy of Nature: Vasily Sukhomlinsky's *My Heart I Give to Children*
Alex Turrall

> We headed along a path to the grapes. In a quiet corner hidden by trees, grape vines were growing. Spread over a metal frame, they formed a green shelter. Inside the shelter the ground was covered with soft, green grass. Peace reigned in there, and from the shelter's green twilight the whole world looked green. We spread out on the grass… "This is where our school begins. From here we will look out at the blue sky, the orchard, the village, and the sun".[1]

Born in 1918 to a peasant family in the small village of Vasilievka, Ukraine, Vasily Sukhomlinsky became a pioneer of holistic education in the Soviet Union[2] and "the most influential Soviet educator of the 1950s and

---

1 Vasily Sukhomlinksy, *My Heart I Give to Children*, trans. Alan Cockerill (EJR Publishing, 2016), 31.

2 The Russian term used for holistic education is "*vsestoronnee razvitie*", which refers to the "all-round development" of the student; see: Alan Cockerill, *Each One Must Shine* (EJR Publishing, 2009), 25.

1960s."[3] At this time, Sukhomlinsky "was at the forefront of public interest", his works were being translated across the world, and he was "awarded almost all the honours that can be paid to an outstanding educationist."[4] Overall, Sukhomlinsky wrote 30 books, 500 articles,[5] and around 1,200 children's short stories.[6]

Sukhomlinsky was seriously injured while fighting in the Second World War, and in 1942 was sent to a military hospital in the western Urals (where he spent much of his time as a principal of a secondary school in Uva). When he returned to Onufrievka (the district centre for his village of Vasilievka) he was appointed the district head of the Department of Education, overseeing the regeneration of education in a region that had been devastated by the Nazi occupation. And in 1948, he was appointed principal of a combined primary and secondary school in the nearby town of Pavlysh, a position he held until his untimely death in 1970 aged only 51. Since that time, Sukhomlinsky's important work slowly faded from the pedagogical canon, and his legacy underwent the subtle anti-Communist distortions so characteristic of the post-Soviet era.

*My Heart I Give to Children* (1968) is a relatively late work from this esteemed educator. Many of his earlier

---

3   Alan Cockerill, "Translators Introduction". In: *My Heart I Give to Children*, x.

4   Simon Soloveichik, "Sukhomlinsky's Paradox" In: *V. Sukhomlinsky On Education* (Moscow: 1977), 7.

5   Ibid.

6   Robin Duckett, "Empathy, Curiosity and Creativity: Education for the Antrhopocene", *Sightlines Initiative*, 2021.

works remain untranslated and other later works remain unpublished. As one of the only available English translations, the book offers a rare insight for English readers into Sukhomlinksy's extraordinary pedagogical program. Although it was originally published in the German Democratic Republic (or East Germany) in 1968, with the first Soviet edition appearing a year later in 1969, this review uses the most widely available English translation, published and translated by the Australian educator and linguist Alan Cockerill in 2016.

The book is split in two main parts. Part one explores the development of the Pavylsh School's first preschool class in 1951. The second part follows this class as they progress through their primary school years. Rather than interrogate the distinction between pre and primary education, this review seeks to capture the soul of Sukhomlinsky's pedagogical vision which combined nature and fairy-tales with academic and aesthetic education. Before we begin the journey into the fairy-tale landscape of rural Ukraine, however, it is important to first confront the ghosts that haunted this otherwise idyllic scene.

## *The Long Shadow of War*

> The war has left deep scars, wounds that have not yet healed. These children were born in 1945, some in 1944. Some of them became orphans while still in their mother's womb.[7]

The chapter *My Students' Parents* illustrates Sukhomlinsky's

---

7   Sukhomlinksy, *My Heart I Give to Children*, 19.

keen awareness of the devastating impact of the Second World War on communities, and especially children, across the Soviet Union. Here he documents the complex ways that families had been traumatised and how this was reflected in the souls of the children. "The greatest trauma for many of these children's hearts", he writes, "was that they had been exposed to evil too early in life… darkening their joys, hardening their souls, convincing them that people were bad and that there is no truth in the world".[8]

Sukhomlinsky himself was no stranger to such trauma. Immediately after graduating from the Poltava Pedagogical Institute at the age of 23, he joined the Red Army to fend off the advancing Nazi army. Sustaining a serious shrapnel wound near Rzhev in 1942, that would trouble him the rest of his life, Sukhomlinsky returned home to his own tragedy. While on a mission with partisans in Nazi occupied Ukraine, his wife Vera was captured and imprisoned. In prison she gave birth to the couple's first child but after refusing to give up the names of her detachment, Vera was tortured, her newly born son killed in front of her, and she was eventually hanged.[9] In a separate article, the book's translator, Alan Cockerill, writes: "For years he found it difficult to sleep at night, and woke early to lose himself in his work. His love for children was what kept him sane. Each morning he looked forward to the sound of their

---

8   Ibid.

9   "From the Publishers" In: Vasily Sukhomlinsky, *To Children I Give My Heart*, trans. Holly Smith (Progress Publishers: 1981), 2.

chatter as they arrived at school."[10] *My Heart I Give to Children* must be considered against this tragic backdrop. What emerges from its pages is a story of a community torn apart by the horrors of war, who then found a path to collective transformation through Sukhomlinsky's healing pedagogy of nature.

## *A Pedagogy of Nature*

> Man lives on nature—means that nature is his body, with which he must remain in continuous interchange if he is not to die. That man's physical and spiritual life is linked to nature means simply that nature is linked to itself, for man is a part of nature.[11]

In *Nature: The Source of Health*, Sukhomlinsky illustrates the impact of the environment both on children's health and cognitive development. There are several fascinating insights in this chapter, ranging from diet and bees to eyesight and solar radiation. But two themes that demonstrate Sukhomlinsky's attempt to reconcile man with nature are exhibited most clearly in his understanding of phytoncides and fairy-tales.

## *Phytoncides: An Elixir of Health*

"Air saturated with the phytoncides of grasses (wheat, rye, barley, buckwheat and meadow grasses)", Sukhomlinsky

---

[10] Alan Cockerill, "Pavlysh Secondary School", *In Search of Sukhomlinsky*, 2009.

[11] Karl Marx, "Estranged Labour", *Economic and Philosophical Manuscripts of 1844* (Progress Publishers, 1959).

writes, "is an Elixir of health."[12] As such, not only did he take his students on long walks through the fields and woods to breath in the air infused with these phytoncides, but he also advised parents to plant certain trees (usually nut trees) near their children's windows, to provide constant exposure to phytoncides in their early years.

"Phytoncide" is now used as "a generalised term for natural chemicals released by plants into the environment"[13], to defend themselves from attack by herbivores and decay.[14] However, literature on these natural phenomena was almost entirely absent during Sukhomlinsky's lifetime, which begs the question, where did he encounter this concept?

It seems likely that Sukhomlinsky was drawing on the work of pioneering Soviet biochemist Dr Boris Tokin. After coining the term "phytoncide" in 1928, Tokin went on to publish the book *Phytonzide* in 1956. Tokin demonstrates the "astonishing biological effects of herbal ingredients and fascinating possibilities of the practical use of these phenomena".[15] For example, Tokin found that a "drop of water infused with

---

12  Sukhomlinksy, *My Heart I Give to Children*, 58.

13  Craig et al. "Natural environments, nature relatedness and the ecological theater: connecting satellites and sequencing to shinrin-yoku", *Journal of Physiological Anthropology*, 35:1, 2016, 2.

14  Zhu, S-x.; Hu, F.-f.; He, S.-y.; Qiu, Q.; Su, Y.; He, Q.; Li, J.-y. "Comprehensive Evaluation of Healthcare Function of Different Forest Types: A Case Study in Shimen National Forest Park, China" *Forests*, 12:207, 2021, 2.

15  Christoph Richter, "Phytonzidforschung—ein Beitrag zur Ressourcenfrage" ("Phytoncide research - a contribution to resource questions"), *Hercynia N.F.* 24:1, 1987, 95.

spruce, fir or pine needles added to a drop of water containing protozoa (parasites) will kill them [the parasites] instantly"[16] [authors translation]. Put simply, in discovering phytoncides, Tokin's work unveiled a broad relationship between natural air and processes of decay.

These remarkable findings were largely ignored until a revival in the 1990s; a project fuelled by interest in the "hygiene hypothesis". Based on a 1989 British Medical Journal article,[17] the hygiene-hypothesis states that the industrialised world had seen a rise in allergic diseases (e.g., hay-fever) as a result of the "diminished opportunity for early-life exposure to pathogenic (and diverse commensal) microbe exposure via increased hygiene, antibiotic use, smaller family sizes and lower exposure to bacteria in foods, and the overall environment."[18]

This rise in allergic diseases, however, has not been observed to the same extent in the non-industrialised world,[19] leading analysts to conclude that urbanisation not only leads to the loss of macro-biodiversity (building industrial cities necessitates extinguishing plant life) but is also linked to the loss of microbial diversity previously symbiotic with the human body. Phytoncides are considered key constituents of this microbial

---

16 Ibid., 97.

17 David Strachan, "Hay fever, hygiene, and household size", *British Medical Journal*, 1989, Nov 18; 299 (6710): 1259–1260.

18 Craig et al. "Natural environments, nature relatedness and the ecological theatre", 3.

19 William Parker & Jeff Ollerton, "Evolutionary biology and anthropology suggest biome reconstitution as a necessary approach toward dealing with immune disorders" *Evol Med Public Health* (2013), 1, 90.

biodiversity,[20] and are said to have anti-inflammatory, antimicrobial, antifungal, analgesic, and anti-stress properties.[21] This growing body of research now represents "a cornerstone of immunology".[22] These recent studies demonstrate both Sukhomlinsky's sharp scientific mind and his understanding of the symbiotic relationship between man and nature or, as Marx would have it, man as nature. Indeed, when he wrote that phytoncides are an "Elixir of health", he had to some extent anticipated the next 50 years of western environmental anthropology and immunology.

The health benefits of nature could not, for Sukhomlinsky, be an end in themselves however. They were instead a component part of a more complex pedagogical program in which the health of the child was dialectically related to their cognitive development. The health benefits of nature filled children with a "life giving energy", that allowed them to develop their intellectual and creative endeavours to their full potential.[23]

But nature had another function. "Most importantly," writes Sukhomlinsky, "children must be taught to think in the midst of nature, at that life-giving wellspring of thought from which streams of living water constantly

---

20   Craig et al. "Natural environments, nature relatedness and the ecological theatre", 3.

21   Zhu, S-x.; Hu, F.-f.; He, S.-y.; Qiu, Q.; Su, Y.; He, Q.; Li, J.-y. "Comprehensive Evaluation of Healthcare Function of Different Forest Types", 2.

22   William Parker, "The 'hygiene hypothesis' for allergic disease is a Misnomer", *British Medical Journal* (2014).

23   Sukhomlinksy, *My Heart I Give to Children*, 56.

flow".[24] Monsters and myths, suns and moons, good vs evil, nature also held the key to the magical land of fairy-tales and dialogical education.

*Fairy-tales and Freire*

> "The Sun is scattering sparks", said Katya softly. The children could not tear their eyes away from the enchanting world, and I began to tell them a story about the sun.[25]

From here, Sukhomlinsky drew upon his student Katya's spectacular image of the sun scattering its cosmic sparks by telling the children a tale of two giant blacksmiths and a golden anvil, all the while sketching a picture in his notebook, bringing the story to life. After a moment of silence there came a flurry of questions from the youngsters. "Dear children," came his reply, "I will tell you all that another time", leaving the curious minds yearning for their next lesson. Deeply moved by the spontaneity of this mutual dialogue, that night Sukhomlinsky went home and dreamt about the silver sparks of sunlight, and he was inspired: "I would introduce the little ones to the surrounding world in such a way that every day they discovered something new in it, so that every step led us on a journey to the wellsprings of thought and speech, to the wondrous beauty of nature".[26]

Sukhomlinsky's re-presentation of Katya's scattering sparks, not through the sanitised language of adults,

---

24 Ibid., 36.

25 Ibid., 32.

26 Ibid., 34.

but through the children's own language of fairy-tales is an example of Paulo Freire's dialogical method par excellence. For Freire, "liberating education consists in acts of cognition, not transferrals of information."[27] Thus, a liberatory educator should follow a "dialogical" and "problem-posing" pedagogy. This is:

> ... constituted and organised by the students' view of the world, where their own generative themes are found. The content thus constantly expands and renews itself. The task of the dialogical teacher in an interdisciplinary team working on the thematic universe revealed by their investigation is to "re-present" that universe to the people from whom she or he first received it—and "re-present" it not as a lecture, but as a problem.[28]

For Sukhomlinsky, although nature was important, it had to be animated by stories, for "without stories the surrounding world is just a beautiful picture painted on a canvas. Stories bring that picture to life."[29] However, when combined with fairy-tales, nature offers the optimum environment for the realisation of a dialogical pedagogy. During the day, the children had made up and heard several stories. Some about the blacksmiths, and others about the sun's mystical garland. As the sun was setting, one child, Lida, asked, "The blacksmiths have brought the sun its silver garland... Where does it put

---

27 Paulo Freire, *Pedagogy of the Oppressed*, trans. Myra Bergman Ramos (Continuum, 2005), 79.

28 Ibid., 109.

29 Sukhomlinksy, *My Heart I Give to Children*, 35.

yesterday's garland?" After a moment of silence, a quiet child, Fedya, offers the teacher a helping hand: "The garland has melted across the sky." Sukhomlinsky builds his final story of the day around this image, finishing his narrative: "Soon the sun will enter its magic garden, and the stars will come out."

"What are stars? Why do they come out? Where do they come from?", another colourful avalanche of problem-posing curiosity from "those little researchers and explorers of the word."[30] Nature, fairy-tales, and cognitive development are dialectically related; nature both inspires and requires the story, but for Sukhomlinsky the fairy-tale has its own unique purpose too:

> Children see living images and then imaginatively recreate those images in their own representations. The viewing of real objects and the creation of imaginative representations of those objects: there is no contradiction in these two stages of the cognitive process. The fantasy image in a story is interpreted by a child, and created by that same child as a vivid reality. The creation of fantasy images provides fertile ground for the vigorous development of thought processes.[31]

Combined with a dialogical pedagogy, sharing in children's fantastical world of fairy-tales is an important practice for progressive educators. Again, although primarily concerned with adult literacy, Freire shared this view of child education. Drawing on the work of his

30   Ibid., 20-37.

31   Ibid., 50.

daughter Madalena Freire in her book on child education, *A Paixão De Conhecer O Mundo* [The Passion to Know the World] (1994), Freire asserts: "Teachers must be able to play with children, to dream with them. They must wet their bodies in the waters of children's culture first. Then they will see how to teach reading and writing."[32]

Twelve years after musing that "the sun is scattering sparks", Katya wrote an essay about her homeland and repeated this phrase to describe her love of nature.[33] Stories, therefore, leave an indelible mark on the consciousness of the child, conjuring up permanent fantasies that they too can pass on like Sukhomlinksy taught them. As he concludes: "In my view the main aim of our whole system of education was to teach people to live in the world of the beautiful, so that they could not live without beauty, so that the beauty of the world created an inner beauty.[34]

Although they capture some of the essence of Sukhomlinksy's pedagogy, a focus on phytoncides and fairy-tales hardly scratches the surface. Art, music, caring for animals, collective farming, these are no less important elements that constituted daily life in the Secondary School of Pavlysh and offer important lessons in prefiguring a revolutionary educational system.

Sukhomlinsky's compelling analysis of the dialectical relationship between nature, fairy-tales, and education is illustrative of a specifically communist pedagogy. It

---

32  Paulo Freire, "Reading the World and Reading the Word: An Interview with Paulo Freire." *Language Arts,* 62:1 (1985), 18.

33  Sukhomlinksy, *My Heart I Give to Children,* 35.

34  Ibid., 72.

is interesting, therefore, that the book's translator, Alan Cockerill, attempts to distance Sukhomlinsky from the Soviet system which allowed such a vision to flourish. Such a revision of Sukhomlinsky's ground-breaking work in communist education requires some attention.

*Ideological Distortion*

Editing documents to increase popularity and readership is of course nothing new. The process of publishing any book or article anywhere in the world will go through an editorial process of some kind. While much of this can be innocent (sharpening arguments, checking for errors, etc,), there have been major exceptions. The erasure of Islam from the poetry of Rumi is a particularly notable example of ideological and cultural distortion, a sanitised version used to soothe the Western liberal gaze and reproduce orientalist tropes of Islam.[35] But what is the case for *My Heart I Give to Children*?

In the introduction to the 2016 edition the translator, Alan Cockerill, outlines various aspects of his translation which are worth considering in detail. Cockerill's translation is based on the 2012 re-publication of the book by Sukhomlinsky's daughter, Professor Olga Sukhomlinskaia. Cockerill argues this edition, based on an unpublished 1966 manuscript, contains "less material of an ideological nature (which was included in the first edition in response to editorial pressure)". The 2012 edition also contained material from the 1969 Soviet version but as revisions in footnotes (as a

---

35 Rozina Ali, "The Erasure of Islam from the Poetry of Rumi", *The New Yorker*, 2017.

commentary to identify the editorial changes between the 1966 manuscript and 1969 publication).[36] Cockerill's translation does not contain a commentary on these missing elements leaving the reader to question what "material of an ideological nature" has been removed and, importantly, why? This section starts to illuminate the problem.

Cockerill gives us some indication of his own ideological standpoint in his 1999 biography of Sukhomlinksy, *Each One Must Shine*. For Cockerill, Sukhomlinksy's life and educational work are split across three main eras: Stalinism, the Khrushchev "thaw", and post-Khrushchev authoritarianism. It is during the thaw years that Cockerill suggests that Sukhomlinsky's views were "maturing and becoming more liberal" which "brought him into conflict with party ideologues."[37] This period is juxtaposed most significantly against those of the so-called Stalinist era, with Cockerill branding Stalinist education as "authoritarian in the extreme", following a "uniform syllabus" with a strong focus on standardised lessons and textbooks.[38] It is true that the educational reforms of the 1930s took a sharp turn away from the pedagogical experiments that characterised the 1920s.

---

36   Cockerill, *My Heart I Give to Children*, xiii.

37   Alan Cockerill, "Sukhomlinsky's German Connections: The Publication of My Heart I Give to Children in 1968 Berlin" in *Cossacks in Jamaica, Ukraine at the Antipodes: Essays in Honour of Marko Pavlyshyn*, edited by Alessandro Achilli, Serhy Yekelchyk and Dmytro Yesypenko (Academic Studies Press: 2020), 530.

38   Cockerill, *Each One Must Shine* (EJR Publishing: 2009), 197.

Due to generations of Tsarist underdevelopment and the looming threat of Nazi invasion, the Soviet Union was under intense pressure to industrialise and thus required a steep uptick in specialists across the country. Perhaps Cockerill would disagree with this view, but what does Sukhomlinsky have to say on the subject? After reading educational reforms planned for 1958, Sukhomlinsky wrote this letter to Khrushchev that same year:

> The decisions taken by the Party's Central Committee during the 'thirties concerning work in schools, were essential at the time. They played an important role in the development not only of our country's culture, but of its whole national economy. They were directed at strengthening knowledge of the foundations of science and scholarship, they put an end to all sorts of hair-brained schemes to replace a systematic course in secondary education with "complexes" and "projects". Thanks to the implementation of these decisions a cultural revolution was effected in our country. There is more good than bad in the fact that there are 2.5 million people in our country at the present time, who have completed secondary school but not embarked on tertiary studies.[39]

Consequently, it appears that one of the main "party ideologues" that Sukhomlinsky was coming into conflict with was the same one that Cockerill has praised as being most closely aligned to Sukhomlinsky's humanistic values. Given Sukhomlinsky's vast body of work, one could perhaps be forgiven for missing this crucial insight. But

---

39   Ibid., 158.

this letter is pulled directly from Cockerill's biography itself.

Cockerill further argues that Stalinism was a "return to Tsarist goals and methods" and "bore closer resemblance in its political culture to the Church States of medieval Christendom or to the Russia of the tsars, than to modern pluralistic societies in the West."[40] His analysis of Stalinism is drawn almost exclusively from Robert Tucker's account, which is not so much concerned with numbers and data but is rather a wholly rhetorical critique of the Soviet Union from 1921-1953. Sticking to educational developments alone, it might surprise Cockerill that literacy rates in the Soviet Union jumped from 57.6% to 99.3% from 1920 to 1959 (with a rapid increase specifically from 1926 to 1939, where it grew from 71.5% to 93.5%). More relevant to his point about the supremacy of Western democracies, by 1959 the Soviet Union had a higher average literacy rate for men and women (98.3%) than Britain (98%), the United States (98%), and France (96%).[41] Perhaps the people of medieval Christendom were more literate than we realise?

Ultimately, however, the most revealing accusation is made in relation to the purges, in which Cockerill concludes: "The purges also served to eliminate many liberally-minded intellectuals from the leadership echelons, replacing leaders of middle-class origin with

---

40   Ibid., 139-40.

41   Boris Mironov. "The Development of Literacy in Russia and the USSR from the Tenth to the Twentieth Centuries." *History of Education Quarterly* 31:2 (1991), 229-52.

ones of peasant stock."[42] An interesting claim from a defender of "modern pluralistic societies." For Cockerill, 1966 saw the end of the thaw and a return to Stalinist dogma. It's here that Cockerill suggests that a state campaign was launched against Sukhomlinsky in 1967 for his essay *"Idti vpered! [Let us go forwards!]"*. The attack against Sukhomlinsky came from an article in *Uchitel'skaia gazeta [The Teacher's Newspaper]* entitled "We need a campaign not a sermon" by B. Likhachev, a lecturer at the Vologda Pedagogical Institute. Likhachev accused Sukhomlinsky of "abstract humanism" and of departing from the pedagogy of Anton Makarenko. As the first educator to elucidate the theoretical underpinnings of collective pedagogy, Makarenko was considered a Soviet hero, thus departing from him was tantamount to anti-Communist betrayal. However, after Makarenko's death a certain orthodoxy took hold of his teachings, which were sometimes used to promote student discord. Rather than being a critique of Makarenko, who Sukhomlinsky's lists as his major inspiration, it was instead a critique of this orthodoxy.

Two responses in favour of Sukhomlinksy and against the baseless claims of Likhachev were published by A. Levshin in *Literaturnaia gazeta [The Literary Newspaper]* and F. Kuznetsov in *Literatura v shkole [Literature in the School]* that same year, with Sukhomlinksy penning his own response in *Literaturnaia gazeta*. Indeed, even following the attacks in *Uchitel'skaia gazeta*: "Sukhomlinsky himself was given space to present his views on the pages of Komsomol'skaia Pravda, Izvestiia, and Pravda, official

---

42   Cockerill, *Each One Must Shine* (EJR Publishing: 2009), 140.

newspapers of the Communist Youth League, the Soviet government, and the Communist Party of the Soviet Union respectively".[43] Any sober analysis indicates that there was significant support both from individual academics and major news outlets of the Soviet state, a state which by this point had ostensibly shifted back into Stalinism. As such, it is curious that the above evidence is presented by Cockerill himself.

Finally, what did Cockerill remove from the 1966 manuscript, supposedly the truest illustration of Sukhomlinsky's views, untouched by communist authorities? In fairness to him, Cockerill does identify the sections he removed with three asterisks, thus leaving the reader to fill in the gaps. To illustrate one of these omissions I rely on Holly Smith's 1981 translation, *To Children I Give My Heart*.

In the chapter entitled *On the Threshold of an Ideal Life*, Sukhomlinsky discusses the importance of moral role models for children. Here, Cockerill includes the brave story of the Polish educator of the Warsaw Ghetto, Janusz Korczak, who refused his own freedom, choosing instead to accompany the children to Treblinka, to calm them and mitigate the horror they were about to face. What is left out, however, are the numerous mentions of Lenin and other Soviet heroes who inspired the children and were, in Sukhomlinsky's view, just as important as the sacrifices made by Janusz Korczak. For example:

---

43  Cockerill, "Sukhomlinsky's German Connections: The Publication of My Heart I Give to Children in 1968 Berlin" in *Cossacks in Jamaica, Ukraine at the Antipodes: Essays in Honour of Marko Pavlyshyn*, edited by Alessandro Achilli, Serhy Yekelchyk and Dmytro Yesypenko (Academic Studies Press: 2020), 534.

> The children were seized by joyful excitement when they heard the story of how, during the difficult years of the Civil War and the years of devastation, Lenin showed great concern for orphans. I wanted Leninist humanity to enter the lives of the children as a great moral value...[44]

Cockerill is of course correct, Lenin's concern for orphans (and children more broadly) *is* an overtly ideological position. Not all societies give due attention to the care of their children. But why must it be wiped from the record? Surely anyone concerned with the rights of children should be aware of the ideological currents that seek to establish such rights and made great strides in doing so?

The effect of such redactions paint Sukhomlinsky's communist views as essentially circumstantial. For Cockerill, he was largely misinformed or confused, a product of his Stalinist upbringing, navigating his trauma of the Second World War, trying to reconcile his humanist values within the limits of an otherwise oppressive communist state. In other words, Sukhomlinsky's pedagogical intervention owed everything to his personal vision of humanistic education rather than resulting from the influence and guiding ethos of Soviet pedagogy. Cockerill consummates this view by suggesting that Soloveichik, the primary Soviet journalist who popularised Sukhomlinsky's work after his death, "considered that Sukhomlinsky was a genius who owed his best ideas not to Soviet pedagogical science, but

---

44  Sukhomlinsky, *To Children I Give My Heart*, trans. Holly Smith (Progress Publishers: 1981), 125.

to his love for children and his own natural talent as a teacher, working as he did in relative isolation."[45] On the one hand, it is revealing that such an authoritative claim comes with no accompanying citation. On the other, it appears to be in direct contradiction to Cockerill's own understanding of Soviet pedagogy. Cockerill admits that "Soviet views of education through the collective (and Western interpretations of Soviet practice) have been formed principally under the influence of [Anton] Makarenko's ideas."[46] It is interesting then that Soloveichik quotes Sukhomlinsky as saying:

> There is no other teacher whose work I have admired and respected as much as Makarenko's. It was in his works that I sought true wisdom of which I was so desperately in need. All my modest experimentation in teaching has been a result of that search.[47]

Clearly Sukhomlinsky was driven by a profound love for children, but that does not negate his training in the Soviet pedagogical sciences, which were formed, as Cockerill himself suggests, around the principles of Sukhomlinsky's primary inspiration, Makarenko. Sukhomlinsky is then, in fact, wholly illustrative of the Soviet educational system, which he dedicated his life to upholding and developing.

---

45   Cockerill, *Each One Must Shine* (EJR Publishing: 2009), 75.

46   Ibid., 92.

47   Simon Soloveichik, "Sukhomlinsky's Paradox" In: *V. Sukhomlinsky On Education* (Moscow: 1977), 32.

## Guided By Love

> The ideas of the Great October Socialist Revolution are the source of one of the New Man's most important and valuable qualities—his orientation towards the future.[48]

Although his life was cut short by shrapnel fragments from his wartime injury entering his heart at the age of 51, Sukhomlinsky left behind several lifetimes of wisdom, stretching far beyond the field of education as we know it. Grounded in a revolutionary ecological pedagogy, *My Heart I Give to Children* offers a radical alternative for prefiguring communist education. With a number of his works remaining either unpublished or untranslated, *My Heart I Give to Children* contains only a snapshot of the pedagogical vision of this extraordinary educator and a guide to navigating the enduring legacy of 1917. Given Cockerill's spurious analysis of this Bolshevik educator, and at a time of mounting ecological and political crises, a more accurate appraisal of Sukhomlinsky's life and work is a project of great importance.

"At the risk of seeming ridiculous," Che Guevara suggested, "the true revolutionary is guided by a great feeling of love." Vasily Sukhomlinsky stands out as a fearless defender of this maxim.

*The author wants to thank Martin Jensen for helping them think through the approach to analysing Stalinism. Editing is a pedagogical process, and for this they been very fortunate to have Louis Allday's kind and patient guidance through writing this review.*

---

48   Ibid., 51.

# Index

## A

Africa  12, 21-22, 108, 124, 126, 166-167, 171, 184, 186, 188, 208-209, 211, 213, 218, 226-227, 229-230, 235-239, 242-245, 247-250, 261-262, 264, 269, 271-272, 286

Agriculture  99, 158, 171, 282

Algeria  22, 214

America  20, 28-29, 31, 33-34, 38, 42, 52, 70-71, 73, 80-82, 84, 86, 106, 109-110, 133, 185, 261, 279, 288, 295, 298-299, 304, 307, 309-310, 314

Authoritarian  25, 159, 183, 188, 238, 304, 333

## B

Berlin  25, 214, 333, 337

Bolsheviks,  340, 342

Bourgeois  20-21, 24, 32, 93, 99, 183, 214, 218, 236-238, 245, 252, 298

Brazil's Landless Workers' Movement  288, 295, 298

Britain  18-25, 73, 75, 106-107, 118, 120-123, 128, 150-152, 163, 165, 168-173, 177-178, 196-197, 201-202, 206, 211, 228, 254, 260, 267, 272, 326, 327, 335

Bush, George W.  29-31, 37, 41-43, 50, 88

## C

Cabral, Amílcar  28, 50, 199

Canada 182-186, 190-191, 193-194

Capitalism 23, 258, 262, 264

Catholic 169, 173, 175-177, 302

China 14-15, 74-77, 81-83, 101-104, 107-112, 230, 307, 316-317, 325

Church Committee 13, 15, 35

CIA 11-15, 32-33, 35, 37-39, 57, 83, 109, 177

Colonialism 11-12, 17, 21, 114, 116-118, 120-122, 125-126, 128, 138, 147, 162, 165, 175

Comintern 19, 23, 25, 109, 110

Communism 35, 74, 102, 112, 115

COVID-19 162, 258, 266

Cuba 42, 112, 295-297, 298

D

Democracy 8, 97, 172

Dependency theory 186, 276

E

Economy 23, 27, 73, 80, 155, 158, 163, 174, 176, 212-213, 216-217, 220, 222, 232, 246, 253-254, 256, 266-267, 279, 281, 319, 334

Education 116, 165, 185, 218, 224, 288, 290, 292, 296, 298, 300, 315, 321, 335, 339

Empire 19-21, 29, 31, 33, 70-71, 121, 165-166, 168, 170-172, 203, 251

England 14, 16, 18, 20, 27, 31, 89, 106-107, 111, 115, 117, 139, 149, 166, 169, 170-171, 184, 260, 262-263, 284, 322

Environment 303, 324-326, 329

Europe 19-23, 26, 28, 32, 106, 108, 118-119, 121, 124, 163, 166, 168, 174, 182, 185, 187-188, 208, 214, 217, 227, 237, 239, 259-263, 276-287, 314, 316

## F

Fanon, Frantz 153, 206-207, 214

Fascism 18-28

First World War 27, 118, 121, 268

France 20, 23, 121, 166, 280, 283, 285, 335

Freedom 196-199, 203-204, 207, 242, 246, 257, 269, 273-275, 277, 284, 302, 305, 308, 319, 337

Freire, Paulo 186, 197, 202, 206, 289, 292, 300-301, 328-331

France 22, 36-37, 67, 115, 165, 177-178, 182, 184, 214, 254

## G

Germany 20, 22-23, 27, 39, 73, 120, 152, 208, 252, 280, 282-285, 322

Guevara, Che 112, 296, 301, 340

## H

Hirji, Karim 215, 218, 223-233

Hitler, Adolf 21-22, 24

Human Rights 88-89, 235-245, 277

## I

Ideology 20, 94, 125, 223, 237-238, 240, 243-244, 247, 252, 259, 264, 281, 295

Inernational Monetary Fund (IMF) 232, 255

Imperialism 11-12, 16, 18, 22, 24, 27-29, 43, 82, 118, 121-122, 244, 246, 249, 251-253, 256-257, 259-264, 277

India 18, 21-22, 27, 109, 121, 123, 166, 230, 263, 267, 271-273

Iraq 40-41, 46, 84

Ireland 21, 162-165, 167, 169-173, 175, 178, 180, 280

Israel 114, 116-118, 124, 126-129, 144, 146-147, 156-157, 159, 177

Italy 20, 23, 27, 252, 280, 285-286

## J

Japan 22-23, 73, 86, 91-92, 108-109

## K

Kenya 39, 209, 225, 266-268, 270-271, 273-275

Korea 65, 74-78, 81-83, 85, 88-97, 99-100

Korean War 72-73, 75-77, 79-82, 89, 98-99

## L

Law 24, 30, 42, 48, 94-95, 138, 153, 183, 240-241, 253, 255, 286, 316

Lenin, V.I. 18, 24, 101-102, 166, 337-338

Leninism 112, 224, 246, 249-250, 253, 259, 264, 338

Liberation 90, 114-116, 118, 128, 138, 140, 142, 248, 251, 293

Literacy 78, 93-95, 296, 297, 330, 335

Literature 101, 112, 115-116, 139, 153-154, 158, 225, 325

London 11, 86, 164, 172, 247-248

## M

Mao, Tse-Tung 101-102, 106-107, 109-111, 158, 246-247, 257

Marx, Karl 173, 241, 253, 262, 324, 327

Marxism 222, 224, 262

Media 13, 16-17, 45, 47-48, 54, 58-59, 72-73, 86, 88, 90, 147, 159, 164, 183, 190-192

## N

Nakba 125, 133, 137, 143-145, 147-148, 153, 155, 157

Nationalism 27, 119, 138, 161, 177, 193-194, 201, 211

Nature 35, 47, 74, 120, 127, 178, 185, 190, 238, 322, 324-333

Nazi 21, 152, 165, 321, 323-334

Neoliberal 154-155, 235, 306, 311, 314-315

Nixon, Richard  33, 54, 60, 66-67, 70, 83

Nkrumah, Kwame  11-13, 223

Nyerere, Julius K.  215, 217-219, 221, 223-229, 232

O

October Revolution  101, 254

P

Palestine  114-125, 127, 129, 133-140, 145-146, 148, 150-152, 160

Peace  20, 24, 57-58, 70, 74, 76-79, 83-84, 277

Peasants  90, 92-95, 98-99, 103-105, 107, 110, 132, 137, 219, 240

Pedagogy  250-251, 289, 293-301, 324, 329-331, 336, 338-340

Prison  58, 67, 69, 145, 273, 323

Protestant  169-170, 172, 175-176

R

Racism  20, 67, 85, 114, 125, 129, 183-185, 187, 194, 201, 262, 267

Rebellion  62, 169, 178, 201

Republic  51, 88-89, 93, 103, 163, 167-169, 172, 177-179, 211, 280, 322

Resistance  59, 63, 85, 91-92, 119, 128-129, 135-138, 142, 146, 148-153, 156-157, 159, 169-170, 172, 175, 177, 183, 191-193, 200, 202, 213, 265, 267, 271

Revolution  15, 18-22, 25-26, 28, 41, 67, 78, 83, 88-90, 93, 96-97, 99, 101-103, 108, 149, 153, 162, 165, 175, 178, 192, 200, 226, 254, 296, 340

Rodney, Walter  50, 208-223, 226-227, 249, 262

S

Second World War  82, 123, 196, 277, 321, 323, 338

Shivji, Issa  218-219, 226, 235-236, 243, 245

Socialism  26-27, 99, 215-217, 221, 223-225, 229, 249

Soviet  22-23, 35-37, 40, 73-77, 81, 90, 105, 114-115, 231, 288-289, 296, 320-323, 325, 332, 334-339

Stalin, Josef  16, 19, 23, 25

Stalinism  18, 333, 335, 337, 340

Syria  16, 39, 85, 127, 150, 277

T

Tanzania  39, 209, 215-221, 223-225, 229-234, 247-248, 256

Terror  36, 40, 49

Trade Unions  266, 268, 273

U

Ujamaa  217-218, 224, 229

Ukraine  290, 320, 322-323, 333, 337

Underdevelopment  18, 167, 186, 189, 216, 243, 249, 283, 334

Uprising  18, 33, 36, 64, 67, 90, 106, 111, 116-117, 132, 146, 184-186, 203, 209-210, 212, 218, 219, 221, 223-227, 231, 233, 235, 244, 247, 249-250, 287-289, 302, 304, 306-307, 315

V

Vietnam  34-36, 41, 47, 51-54, 56-58, 61, 64-66, 68-70, 72, 82, 84, 159, 248

Vietnam War  36, 72, 82

W

Workers  98-99, 126, 219, 266, 271, 288, 295, 298

Z

Zionism  114-117, 119-120, 123, 125, 128, 137

www.ingramcontent.com/pod-product-compliance
Lightning Source LLC
Chambersburg PA
CBHW020900080526
44589CB00011B/381